GREAT TRAIN
JOURNEYS
OF THE WORLD

Time Out Guides Ltd
Universal House
251 Tottenham Court Road
London W1T 7AB
United Kingdom
Tel: +44 (0)20 7813 3000
Fax:+44 (0)20 7813 6001
Email:guides@timeout.com
www.timeout.com

Published by Time Out Guides Ltd, a wholly owned subsidiary of Time Out Group Ltd.
Time Out and the Time Out logo are trademarks of Time Out Group Ltd.

© **Time Out Group Ltd 2009**

10 9 8 7 6 5 4 3 2 1

This edition first published in Great Britain in 2009 by Ebury Publishing.
A Random House Group Company
20 Vauxhall Bridge Road, London SW1V 2SA

Random House Australia Pty Ltd 20 Alfred Street, Milsons Point, Sydney, New South Wales 2061, Australia
Random House New Zealand Ltd 18 Poland Road, Glenfield, Auckland 10, New Zealand
Random House South Africa (Pty) Ltd Isle of Houghton, Corner Boundary Road & Carse O'Gowrie,
Houghton 2198, South Africa

Random House UK Limited Reg. No. 954009

For further distribution details, see www.timeout.com.

ISBN: 9781846701511

A CIP catalogue record for this book is available from the British Library.

Printed and bound by Firmengruppe APPL, aprinta druck, Wemding, Germany.

The Random House Group Limited supports The Forest Stewardship Council (FSC), the leading
international forest certification organisation. All our titles that are printed on Greenpeace approved
FSC certified paper carry the FSC logo. Our paper procurement policy can be found at
http://www.rbooks.co.uk/environment.

Time Out carbon-offsets its flights with Trees for Cities (www.treesforcities.org).

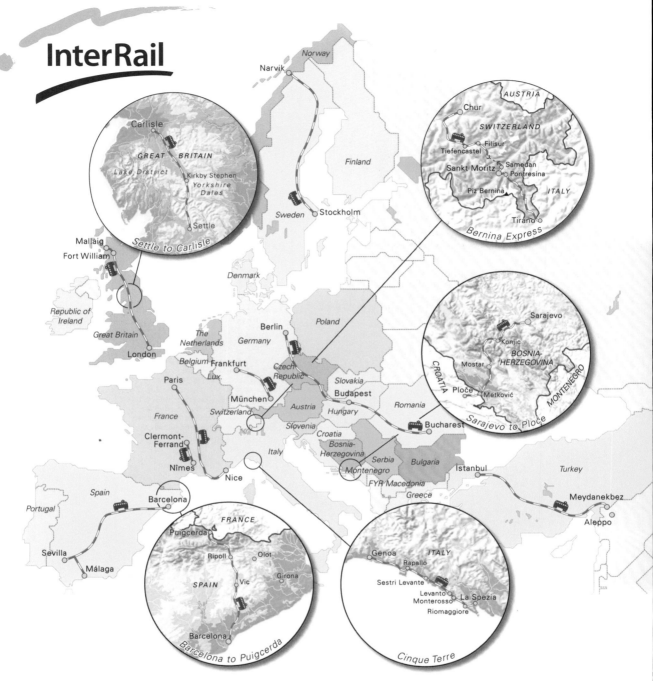

InterRail

Experience Europe's Great Rail Journeys with an InterRail Pass

The InterRail Global Pass lets you discover Europe at your own pace and gives you access to a vast rail network spanning thirty countries.

Many of the European train journeys in this book are available to InterRail Pass holders, such as the inspirational routes shown here.

Who we are

EDITORIAL
Editor Andrew Eames
Deputy Editor Hugh Graham
Proofreader Patrick Mulkern

Managing Director Peter Fiennes
Editorial Director Ruth Jarvis
Business Manager Dan Allen
Editorial Manager Holly Pick
Assistant Management Accountant Ija Krasnikova

DESIGN
Art Director Scott Moore
Art Editor Pinelope Kourmouzoglou
Senior Designer Henry Elphick
Graphic Designers Kei Ishimaru, Nicola Wilson
Advertising Designer Jodi Sher

PICTURE DESK
Picture Editor Jael Marschner
Deputy Picture Editor Lynn Chambers
Picture Researcher Gemma Walters
Picture Desk Assistant Marzena Zoladz
Picture Librarian Christina Theisen

ADVERTISING
Commercial Director Mark Phillips
International Advertising Manager Kasimir Berger
International Sales Executive Charlie Sokol

MARKETING
Marketing Manager Yvonne Poon
Sales & Marketing Director, North America & Latin America Lisa Levinson
Senior Publishing Brand Manager Luthfa Begum
Art Director Anthony Huggins

PRODUCTION
Group Production Director Mark Lamond
Production Manager Brendan McKeown
Production Controller Damian Bennett
Production Coordinator Kelly Fenlon

TIME OUT GROUP
Chairman Tony Elliott
Chief Executive Officer David King
Group General Manager/Director Nichola Coulthard
Time Out Communications Ltd MD David Pepper
Time Out International Ltd MD Cathy Runciman
Time Out Magazine Ltd Publisher/ Managing Director Mark Elliott
Group IT Director Simon Chappell
Marketing & Circulation Director Catherine Demajo

MAPS
Kei Ishimaru, Pinelope Kourmouzoglou.

PHOTOGRAPHY
Front cover Shinkansen Bullet Train and Mount Fuji, Japan © DAJ/Getty Images.
Back cover Top to bottom: The Ghan, Australia, Tourism NT; Indian Pacific, Great Southern Rail; Caledonian Sleeper, Andrew Eames.
Introduction & openers page 3 The Bernina Express, swiss-image.ch/Peter Donatsch; page 6 The Ghan, Tourism NT; page 7 (left) Meeting Place Sculpture, St Pancras International, Rob Greig; page 7 (right) North Yorkshire Moors Railway; page 11 Union Station, Toronto, Lynn Chambers; page 8 (left) Urdata Menike train, Sri Lanka © Yadid Levy/Alamy; page 8 (right) Qingzang railway, Tibet © Sergiu Turcanu/Alamy; page 9 Durango & Silverton railroad, © Images Etc Ltd/Alamy; page 13 AVE high speed train, Spain, courtesy of Renfe; pages 14-15 Crossing Continents, Amtrak passenger train, California, courtesy of Amtrak; pages 60-61 State of the Art, UK Channel Tunnel portal, Folkestone © qaphotos.com/Alamy; pages 88-89 Border Buster, the Bernina Express, Swiss Alps near St Moritz © Brenda Kean/Alamy; pages 124-125 Cultural Experience, Deccan Odyssey, Maharashtra, India © Suzy Bennett/Alamy; pages 180-181 Scenic Spectaculars, Railway viaduct, Ribblesdale, Yorkshire Dales © david martyn hughes/Alamy; pages 232-233 Heritage Railways, Durango and Silverton Steam train, Colorado © Gavin Hellier/Alamy.
All photography by Alamy Images, except page 20, 173 (middle right), 173 (bottom), Jeremy Head; page 43 © VIA RAIL/Matthew G Wheeler; page 29, 30 (right), 33, 188 courtesy of Orient Express; pages 45 (right) Lynn Chambers; page 45 (top left) Melanie Fordham; page 48, 67 (right) Heloise Bergman; page 48 (bottom right) Perth Tourism; pages 48 (bottom left), 51 Great Southern Rail; pages 53, 54 (top right), 54 (bottom right), 140, 143 (right), 144 (top right), 144 (bottom), 185, 176 (top left), 176 (top right), 230 Suzy Bennett; pages 54 (left), 57 Tourism NT; pages 58, 59 Miniatur Wunderland; pages 62, 63, 64 (top left) Rob Greig; page 67 (left) Olivia Rutherford; page 64 (right), 64 (bottom left) courtesy of Eurostar; pages 68, 71, 113 courtesy of Renfe; page 71 (right) Turespaña; pages 72 (bottom right), 74, 201 Tomasetti Rutherford; pages 72 (middle right), 160 (middle right), 160 (bottom right), 163, 220 (bottom) Andrew Eames; pages 72 (bottom left), 75 Tyson Williams; pages 77, 78 (top right), 78 (bottom right) www.bahn.co.uk; page 78 (left) Jochen_Keute/Deutsche Zentrale für Tourismus; page 81 www.bahn.co.uk; pages 82 (top right), 82 (bottom right) 87 Japan National Tourism Organization; page 82 (bottom left) Danielle Demetriou; pages 91, 93 (bottom) swiss-image.ch/Peter Donatsch; page 95 swiss-image.ch; pages 97 (bottom), 99 (top left), 99 (bottom left), 102, 103, 104, 106 (top), 217 (bottom), 218 Susanne Kries; pages 97, 100 Fumie Suzuki; pages 108, 109 Vanda Vucicevic; page 115 Miles Adrian Reilly; page 117 Andreea Anca; page 118 (bottom) Laura Hirst; page 111, 210 Peterjon Cresswell; page 118 (top), 118 (middle left), 123 Andreas H Lunde; pages 127, 128, 129, 131, 132 (bottom) Philip Cornwel-Smith; page 149 Amar Grover; page 150 Rohit Markande; pages 164, 231 Ethos Marketing; pages 166, 169 Emma Levine; page 167 Gardel Bertrand_Hemis.fr; page 173 (top right), Royston Ellis; page 183 Michael Sayles; page 184 www.yorkshiredales.org.uk; page 195 Edward Reeves; page 204 Archive Agenzia in Ligur; page 222 courtesy of First Group; page 225 (top right) Rudy Vandecapelle; page 225 (top left) Neil MacLeod; pages 227, 228, 229 Rovos Rail; page 243, 244 North Yorkshire Moors Railway.

Contents

53

62

243

170

140

239

Get the local experience

Over 50 of the world's top destinations available.

ENTRANCE TO TRAINS

About this book

Trains no longer belong only to trainspotters. In an age when it can seem as if the romance has leached out of travel, they call out to a new generation that cherishes the individual, the ethical and the authentic. The travel and tourism statistics all tell the same story: people are rediscovering railways in a big way. Time Out's *Great Train Journeys* collects together the world's best train trips, selected not for their anorak value but for the sheer pleasures they offer. If you thirst for a way to travel that will take you straight to the heart of the local experience, as well as being safe, environmentally friendly, inexpensive and scenic, then this book is for you.

The trips that we have chosen will suit travellers with a weekend to spare or a fortnight to fill; people happy to spend 24 hours a day on board and those who prefer to stop off at interesting places en route (our 'Sidings' boxes tell you where). They are designed as holidays in their own right, rather than just a means of getting from A to B.

All are all in some way exceptional, whether it be for the cross-section of local life they carry, the scenery they pass through or the distances they travel, and those criteria are reflected in the sections of the book. Crossing Continents, for example, features the giants of long-haul. State of the Art offers cutting-edge trains, the new generation of high speed. Border Busters moves effortlessly between nations, while Cultural Experiences reflects a slice of local life. Scenic Spectaculars does just what is says on the tin, and Heritage Railways portrays rail gems that we nearly lost.

We've made a point of selecting scheduled services, but for the less adventurous we've also included a few private luxury trains. We couldn't cover everything, and our choice is inevitably subjective. Nevertheless, these are the journeys that we hope you'll enjoy. We certainly did.

Union Station, Toronto

Discover the city from your back pocket

Essential for your weekend break, 25 top cities available.

Introduction

I have a confession to make: I like trains. There, now I've got it off my chest, and I feel a great deal better for it. Actually, it wasn't too hard, not as hard as it would have been a dozen years ago, when publicly confessing to enthusiasm for rail travel would have been tantamount to social suicide. But trains have moved on, and so has the travelling public, and now it's OK to unzip the anorak, blow the whistle and wave the flag.

In an increasingly homogenised, globalised world, the distinctiveness and the individuality of world trains are to be celebrated: you never know what you're going to get. While car brands are tediously universal, and aircraft all look the same, trains are different the moment you cross a frontier. Different style, different technology, different clientele, different cultural experience. They come in all shapes, sizes and speeds.

But they do have certain things in common. Firstly, they allow travellers great insight into a destination, running unfettered through country and city, crossing gorges, bisecting plains and peering into a nation's backyards; on a plane you see nothing, and on a motorway you see the back end of the lorry in front. Secondly, they take the pulse of a place, transporting a cross-section of locals and travellers, some of whom will have the time, and the interest, to talk. Thirdly, there's a metaphysical quality to trains: because they stick to the route, and spring no unwelcome surprises, your mind is allowed to wander. On a train you're an individual, not a row of battery hens, and a long journey is a suspension of reality and a time for reflection, as you are left unbothered by trolley dollies or traffic lights.

And finally, there is the spectacle of the big beast. I can't help but admire a gleaming – or grimy – piece of heavy machinery that is about to haul me up a hill or across a country, sometimes travelling at speeds of up to 200mph. I don't think that makes me weird, just a bit of a boy, with childhood wonder intact.

Andrew Eames, Editor

AVE from Barcelona to Málaga

There are times when quicker, and cheaper, is not necessarily right. Times when you don't want to cross from one ocean to another in an air-conditioned tube at 35,000 feet. Times when you want to know what it is that lies in between.

Fortunately, there are still long-distance railways that do this continent-crossing job. Some are adventurous, others are luxurious. But whatever the style, and wherever the destination, you'll arrive at the other side having joined the dots and felt the bumps, having seen a few views and made a few friends. Such journeys will deepen your understanding of the lands you're passing through – and allow your mind to travel, too. For at its best, a long train journey is a contemplative experience, one where you can assess where you've been, where you are and where you want to go.

Crossing
Continents

Start
MOSCOW
Finish
BEIJING
Via
IRKUTSK
ULAN BATOR
Service
THE TRANS-
MONGOLIAN
EXPRESS
Journey time
7 DAYS

Steppe it up

Banish yourself to Siberia and discover the delights of Mongolia on this incredible journey. By **Jeremy Head**

Tsar Alexander III fully understood the importance of uniting the huge Russian continent when he ordered work on the Trans-Siberian to commence in 1891. The new railway would open up vast tracts of mineral-rich land beyond the Urals, provide a convenient way to ship convicts off to Siberia and enable the swift movement of troops to the Amur region, which was under increasing threat from the Chinese. The first commission he set up to assess the line's construction declared that it would bankrupt the country. So he disbanded it, and formed a new one, which conveniently reached a more positive conclusion. Today,

The Mongolian steppe

Russia's iron arteries cross multiple timezones, linking smoky metropolises and muddy hamlets, facilitating trade, offering (relatively) comfortable transit across inhospitable terrain, and providing the tourist with vibrant, gritty, unforgettable insights into new worlds.

For many, the ultimate Russian train journey remains the Trans-Siberian, rattling across the continent for eight days and nights from Moscow to Vladivostok. But for decades Vladivostok was a closed city shrouded in Cold War secrecy. For the tourist, there's not a much to do when you reach this eastern outpost of the old Soviet empire. However, the Trans-Mongolian, which

follows the route of the Trans-Siberian for four and a half days into central Siberia, and then forks south, through Mongolia and on to Beijing, offers a far more exciting final destination, and fascinating stop-offs en route if you have time. This newer section of track from Russia to China wasn't completed until 1956, but the route it traces is far older, following the tortuous old tea caravan trails that linked Peking with Moscow; a journey of 40 days' hardcore discomfort.

Today, the Trans-Mongolian offers a more comfortable journey, but the austere Soviet-era influence remains: this is no Orient Express. Yet the romance and sense of adventure is undeniable. As 'Train Number 4' rolls out of Moscow's Yaroslavsky Station at 9.35pm, ahead of it lies a seven-day journey and nearly 5,000 miles of track – a distance so monumental it seems hardly possible.

The vodka express

The train is huge and finding the correct carriage can be confusing, particularly in the dimly lit darkness of a long Russian night. So passengers should arrive at Yaroslavsky armed with tickets, visas and plenty of time. It's also a smart idea to pack some provisions. There's a restaurant car on the train and opportunities to buy food on station platforms, but Cup a Soups, Pot Noodles, an apple or two, coffee and tea (with a mug to boot) are particularly handy. They're easy to buy from kiosks and mini-markets in the vicinity of the station. And this is Russia, so stick a couple of bottles of vodka in your bag as well.

And while you journey in greater comfort than those tea merchants of old, conditions on board are basic. I shared a four-berth compartment in second class, which was comfortable but cramped. Toilet facilities are not dissimilar to what you'd find on a train in Europe, but if you're thinking of showering, forget it. At best, there's just one shower for the whole train, and that's only available on certain services.

Once you've located your compartment and said hello to your companions, dump your bags and step back on to the platform. Here the tension of imminent departure is palpable. Couples hug goodbye, people knock on the windows and wave to each other, carriage attendants chivvy passengers on to the train. But don't stray too far. Despite its size, this leviathan starts to move so gently that it's almost imperceptible; the huge loco up in the dim distance is hardly heard. The start of this colossal voyage is almost an anti-climax.

It's an odd feeling getting to know three strangers with whom you could be spending a whole week in close confines. If, like most tourists, you've booked your tickets through a tour operator, it's not uncommon to be sharing with compatriots. Along with a Russian girl and her five-year-old lad, who shared her bunk, my companions were a couple from the UK called Christine and Duncan, who became friends. But the Trans-Mongolian is certainly no tourist train. It mainly provides a vital service for Russians, Mongolians and Chinese who can't afford the plane, or need to transport lots of luggage; so be prepared to make new acquaintances.

This is where that vodka can come in handy. Even the most basic of introductions become warmer with a couple of shared shots out of plastic cups. The compartments are Tardis-like. It seems impossible that the accumulated kit of four passengers can be stowed in such a tight

BELLS & WHISTLES

BEST BITS
Leaving Moscow at night. Small station stops in Siberia. Pre-border mayhem between Russia and Mongolia. When the train changes bogies at the Chinese border.

TOP TIP
Take plenty of memory cards for your camera. You'll need them.

PHOTO OP
Station stops, Ulan Ude in particular. Lake Baikal after Slyudyanka, though taking decent shots from the train is difficult.

PACK THIS
Wet wipes for keeping fresh and cleaning up picnic gear. A universal plug for the basin. Low-denomination US dollars. A torch for finding stuff at night in the compartment. A Russian phrasebook.

ANORAK INFO
In Russia, all trains run to Moscow time. Station clocks become increasingly and bizarrely out-of-synch the further you are from Moscow. Thus you reach Ulan Ude at 1.30pm local time, but clocks on the platform read 8.30am.

USEFUL PHRASE
Ha-ra-shaw means 'good' in Russian. Use to show appreciation of shared food or vodka and to show you've understood (even if you haven't).

TRAVELLERS' FARE
Sovietskio champanski is drinkable and cheap.

OVERHEARD
'Your friends paid for it.' So says the waitress in the restaurant car, when bottles of vodka you didn't order arrive at your table. Prepare for a drunken encounter with the inquisitive Russians at the next table.

space, but it disappears under the lower berths and in space above the upper bunks.

Babushkas, blinis and beer

After its stately departure, the train picks up speed rattling into the dark night. The windows are smeary, and their grime mutes the brief flashes of orange light from smoky factories and giant blocks of flats on the outskirts of the Russian capital.

The next morning, it's the heat that wakes you. Despite the ferocious cold in winter, Russian sleeper trains are often muggy, particularly in the upper bunks. And if you started that bottle of vodka, you'll almost certainly have finished it. Stumble blinking out into the corridor, tongue furry in your mouth, and the bright sunlight is violent. But the train is rattling along, the corridor windows are open and the cooling breeze blissful. Outside the windows, the smokescapes of Moscow have given way to pine-fringed hills dotted with tiny wooden huts and criss-crossed

by mud tracks. The Russia of storybooks. Many of the huts have wisps of smoke curling from their chimneys. Each has a garden packed with carefully spaced vegetables. Little old ladies in headscarves stagger along with bags full of stuff, old men and kids peer out of windows as this huge monster thunders by.

The first station stop in daylight (Kirov or Balezino, depending on how early you've woken) is always a revelation. Stops on these trains aren't two-minute halts, they're 25-minute sojourns, where the train community steps into another world. In an instant, the platform becomes a market place. Food is hawked by all and sundry: huge, khaki-coloured smoked fish the size of your thigh, plastic bags of blini (Russian pancakes, which taste surprisingly good), dusty fruit and vegetables, cheap biscuits, bottles of beer. Regular travellers seem to know which station has the best fish and which the best blini, so follow the crowd. Or else just snap pictures. It's all immensely photogenic.

Chinese attendants hanging out, left; the Chinese restaurant car, top; Russian women selling blinis on a station platform, bottom

Station stops also provide a chance to meet other tourists. They're easy to spot, ungainly with their bulky cameras and fumbling attempts to make purchases. It's very sociable: a sequence of 'where are you froms', 'how far are you goings' and promises to drop by their carriage to say hello. And then there's a blast on the train's hooter and it's time to hurry aboard. Back in the embrace of the train, the sensation of being cocooned from the outside world returns. For the past 25 minutes, you have bumped up against local life in the middle of nowhere in Siberia – then in an instant, it's left behind.

A taste of Russia

Seven days on a train might seem like a lifetime, but the hours drift by surprisingly easy, to the rattle of wheels across tracks. That's partly because everything takes longer to do in the cramped compartment: getting up, finding a book, making some lunch. Typical utterances:

'Could I just put my foot here so I can get my bag?'; 'Could I borrow your bottle opener?'

And the scenery outside changes all of the time too. Clumps of houses and forest give way to rolling hills, which are followed in turn by endless plains. Fold-down seats in the corridor allow you to perch and idle away hours just watching it all clickety-clack by; this is also a good way to get out of your compartment and meet fellow passengers.

Corridor friendships are struck up swiftly, accompanied by a shared beer or cups of tea made with hot water from the samovar boiler, which the friendly carriage attendant (known as the provodnitsa and almost always female) keeps stoked at the end of the each carriage.

Restaurant cars are provided by the country you're travelling through. Generally the Chinese restaurant car is best, and once you cross the border into China, it's jammed at mealtimes. The Russian car is a different story. At the Paris Great

Into the great wide open: Siberia

Exhibition in 1900, soon after the opening of the track linking Moscow to Siberia, the Russian government put on a lavish display featuring a full-size restaurant car with mahogany panels and extravagant menus. But today, the Russian culinary experience is hit and miss. Inside the battered menu, dishes are listed in Russian, English and German; but the choice is limited to the few items that have a price scrawled beside them in pencil. It's worth persevering, however. If you become a regular for dinner during the four nights you're in Russia (otherwise it's picnics or food vendors at the stations), the meals get progressively better, particularly if you dig out your phrasebook, order a few beers and befriend the waitress (with her scary mauve perm). You might find the kitchen makes more of an effort.

SIDINGS

Most tourists break the journey in several places. Ideal for history buffs, Ekaterinburg is Russia's fifth-largest city and the site of the murder of the last Russian royal family, the Romanovs. Other claims to fame: it was also the setting of the U2 spy plane affair and the birthplace of Boris Yeltsin.

Lake Baikal, the world's largest freshwater lake, is 400 miles wide, and home to unique and diverse wildlife. It's spectacularly scenic, great for hiking, cruises on local ferries and even husky sledding in winter. Tour operators offer homestays in Listvyanka, an hour from Irkutsk.

The Mongolian capital, Ulan Bator, is a fascinating concoction of ex-Communist drabness and Asian dynamism. Visits to the main square (Sukhe Bator), the Gandan Monastery and the ghostly temples of the Bogd Khan Palace feature on most travellers' itineraries. Many tourists do overnight stays on the steppe in traditional Mongolian *ger* tents too.

The greatest lake

Irkutsk, the capital of Siberia is reached in the early hours of day five. Then, just as the sun begins to rise, the train skirts the mighty Baikal, the world's largest freshwater lake, giving some of the most spectacular views of the journey (so make sure you're awake, particularly after the Slyudyanka station stop at 08.10am).

The stunning views were made possible by hard labour. Most of the early sections of railway were constructed by gangs of convicts with picks and shovels, and this part around the lake was some of the most difficult terrain, requiring 30 tunnels and over 200 trestles and bridges. Prior to 1904, trains had to be loaded on to boats to cross the lake, a trip that was particularly unpredictable in winter, when thick ice often marooned ships in port for weeks.

Perhaps the most exciting station stop of all is Ulan Ude, reached later on the fifth day. It's the last major town before Mongolia. Out on the platform, deals are cut at a frantic pace. Women test the quality of pairs of Levis, stacks of washing machines are unloaded, and rugs, underwear, cigarettes and shoes are bought and sold. Little old ladies scuttle between the crowds, surreptitiously producing bottles of beer from the depths of their bags.

The pace of transactions goes into overdrive as carriage attendants call you back to the train. The commotion is crazy back on board too. Corridors are crammed with boxes. Everyone stashes booty behind bulkheads and in under-floor compartments to avoid paying customs duty. Some German friends even had a guy come into their carriage and, using a special key, open a compartment in the floor. Box after box of cigarettes were stashed beneath their feet.

Border posts always raise the levels of adrenaline (particularly if you have a stash of cigarettes hidden beneath your feet). But apart from the various officials coming into the compartment to check passports and dish out customs forms, the crossing into Mongolia is

Lake Baikal in Siberia, top, is the world's largest freshwater lake; Beijing Station, right

actually quite tedious. The toilets are locked, which can make the waiting uncomfortable. The train sits there for hours; outside it's dark, and guards with big guns and scary dogs prowl the platforms. By the time the train finally glides on, it's long after midnight.

Visions of China

The Mongolian capital, Ulan Bator, is reached at 7.30am on day six. In the corridors, chaos returns as stuff is reclaimed from hiding places and re-packaged, then passed through windows straight down to the platform and sold right there. For a big chunk of the trip out of Mongolia, and on towards China, it's a single track line.

Mongolia is one of the world's most sparsely populated countries and the greenness of the steppe extends for miles, broken only by the odd squat, rotund form of a traditional nomad *ger* tent and the occasional herd of wild gazelle bucking away from the trackside. The steppe slowly becomes brown, then yellow, as it gives way to the vast Gobi desert. Here, quite suddenly, is the heat of the Far East, unexpected and welcome after chilly Russia. Keep your eyes peeled and you'll see a wild camel or two if you're lucky.

Another night of interrupted sleep follows as the train crosses the border into China. To make things more laborious, the track gauge in China is different. The carriage doors are locked and the train is shunted into a huge shed. With the passengers still on board, the coaches are uncoupled and massive hydraulic lifting bars inserted under them. In unison, the carriages are all lifted several metres clear of the bogies, which are then pushed out from underneath. New, narrower-gauge bogies are then rolled into place and the carriages slowly winched back down. The whole process is fascinating to watch, but it takes several hours.

Most of the time, though, this train makes you feel as if you're caught in a time warp, destined to rattle along these tracks for eternity. But the next day is the last on the train. Outside, it's Asia-proper now. Every inch of land is cultivated. People toil in conical straw hats in the hot sun, irrigating and planting. The time seems to speed up as the final destination approaches and the train hurtles across the plains towards Beijing. The sudden realisation that new friends made on board will go their separate ways in a couple of hours spurs more conversation and the exchange of email addresses.

And finally, suddenly, the train has arrived. After a week on board, it takes a while to repack and sort through all the junk accumulated en route. Now that the train has come to a halt, the stillness of final standstill feels strange, despite the hubbub on the platform. After thousands of miles and seven timezones, your body is tuned to the constant swaying of the train. The journey may be over, but its memory remains. For days after you get off the Trans-Mongolian, you still feel the rhythm of the rails under your feet.

TRAVEL INFORMATION

Organising the trip yourself is feasible, but it's not straightforward coordinating visas and train schedules. It's easiest to get a tour operator to do it for you. There are on-line timetables at www.poezda.net/en/web. Search for train '4'.

Tour operators such as the Russia Experience (www.trans-siberian.co.uk) offer all sorts of train options and trip durations with excursions and homestays too. You can do the Trans-Siberian (but not the Trans-Mongolian) in complete comfort with GW Travel (www.gwtravel.co.uk). GW's *Golden Eagle Express* is a full-service, luxury train often pulled by steam engine.

Bryn Thomas' excellent *Trans-Siberian Handbook* (www.trailblazer-guides.com) is packed with maps and descriptions of all routes. Indispensable.

Size matters

Back in the 1820s, when British engineer George Stephenson was starting to experiment with Puffing Billys and Rockets and other dinosaurs of steam locomotion, he had his beasts run along parallel tracks, spaced 4ft 8ins apart. Legend has it that this width dates back to a Roman stipulation about chariot axles, but whatever the backstory, it has since become the standard gauge for the world's railways.

However, some people are never satisfied when it comes to size. There are plenty of wider and narrower gauges, varied by topography, nationality and even state security, and some nations (Australia, for example) still have a variety of widths that stem from the sheer bloody-mindedness of individual states.

In general, a narrow gauge is better suited to mountainous terrain, as it can accommodate tighter bends and lighter carriages. But narrowness means less stability, so speeds have to be slower. Broad gauge, on the other hand, is all about going full steam ahead across big countries such as the USA or India.

Most of the time, most passengers will be blissfully unaware of these issues of size, but some journeys can be rudely interrupted for the sake of an unpleasant-sounding bogie change. The most obvious examples are around Russian-speaking territories and on the Trans-Siberian and Trans-Mongolian. Imperial Russia, fearing that the railways could become their Achilles heel, deliberately adopted a broader gauge than the rest of Europe to deter invasion, and passengers still find themselves jacked indelicately into the air at key border crossings while engineers fiddle around in their undercarriage.

Bogie-fiddling is a feature of railways from mainland Europe – standard gauge – into the (broad gauge) Iberian peninsula, too, although the Spanish now have both systems on adjustable axles, and border-crossing trains make a discreet visit to a special shed to have the operation.

These discrepancies do give rise to some curious anomalies, like at Latour de Carol, in the Catalan Pyrenees, a small station where three different rail gauges (broad, standard and narrow) terminate. Some people get excited about this kind of thing, but for this book's purposes, that's enough already.

Andrew Eames

Changing the bogies on the border of China and Mongolia

Start
LONDON
Finish
VENICE
Via
PARIS
Journey time
31 HOURS

In search of Poirot

Made famous by Agatha Christie, the Orient Express retains its old mystique and blue-blooded luxury. By **Andrew Eames**

The Venice Simplon-Orient-Express (VSOE) is arguably the world's most famous train, and it is certainly Europe's longest, but it nearly didn't make it into these pages. The reason is simple: it is not actually a 'real' train, inasmuch as it doesn't appear on national timetables, and this book's main focus is proper working trains that reflect something of their host nation. But unlike most tourist trains, it has unquestionable pedigree, including a legacy of films and novels and a history that spans two world wars. Furthermore, it unzips Europe from top to bottom in a substantial journey of 1,071 miles that lasts a full 31 hours. And finally, also unlike other tourist trains, it has not compromised its integrity with on-board jacuzzis or gymnasiums, nor even – shock for some customers – installed toilet facilities in its sleeper cabins. So while some people may still contend that the only true remaining Orient Express is a Turkish kebab shop outside Paris' Gare du Nord, it is impossible to ignore.

The reason for the VSOE's success as a (very costly) way of travelling between London and Venice is simple: it has style and integrity. It is a throwback to the golden era of the railways, when emperors and presidents were regular train travellers. Moreover, its carriages are the real deal, most of them dating back to the 1920s and 1930s, a romantic and magical period to which they have been lovingly restored.

In reality, the first Orient Express, subtitled the Magic Carpet to the East, dates back to 1883. That year, a certain Georges Nagelmackers, a Belgian engineer, announced in the pages of the London Times his intention to run a new generation of long-distance luxury train with proper sleeping cars (he called them Wagons-Lits), all the way from London to Istanbul. Expected journey times, he declared, would be a mere 75 hours, which would make the service hugely attractive to civil servants and merchants making long journeys to colonial properties in Asia and the Middle East.

Unfortunately, Nagelmackers' announcement was a tad premature, given that not all the rail networks supposedly involved were actually completed, and his train couldn't run on rails that weren't there, however well upholstered it was. But the alternative sea journey was so much slower that, after a shaky initial period involving horse-drawn carriages and boat transfers, the new train rapidly became a major success. Between 1890 and 1914, every royal, aristocrat and adventurer wanted to experience the route. Many of the crowned heads of Europe would travel on the train incognito with their mistresses – Leopold II of Belgium with a famous dancer called Cleo de Merode, Carol II of Romania with Madame Magda Lupescu – just to experience the mystery and magic of luxury trains. And if the mistress wasn't available, then they'd sometimes ask the cabin staff to procure a companion somewhere along the way.

By the 1920s, the Orient Express was so popular it was running four times weekly in each direction. But the service was interrupted, and re-routed, by war, in which it also played a walk-on part: it was in a Wagons-Lits car at Compiègne that the Allies accepted Germany's surrender at the end of World War I. Two decades later, in June 1940, Hitler ordered the same car back to the very same spot, and forced the French to surrender to Germany there.

Today, however, the train no longer registers on any timetables. It officially ceased to exist in the late 1970s after a long decline, unable to compete any more with the increasing convenience of air travel. It ended its days ignominiously as little more than a sleeping car attached to a succession of local expresses, and passengers had to complete the 1,872-mile journey from Paris to Istanbul carrying their own supplies of food and drink. No cabin attendants – or mistresses – in sight.

Restored to glory

But that wasn't to be the end of the story. In 1977, a shipping millionaire called James Sherwood attended a Sotheby's auction in Monte Carlo,

---

SIDINGS

The route described in these pages is a shortened version of the original *Orient Express*, which used to run all the way through from Paris to Istanbul. That route itself varied from one decade to the next, depending on the friendliness of the countries it crossed. Now that Europe is one harmonious whole again, the restored train makes the complete journey through to Istanbul once more, but only once a year, on a journey that takes five nights and six days.

The routing on that special trip is via Budapest and Bucharest and through Bulgaria to Istanbul's Sirkeci station. Adding to the feeling of old-world authenticity, the journey is taken at a leisurely pace, with overnight stops in hotels in Budapest and Bucharest, so that passengers don't have to endure the whole route without en suite facilities. One night without a bathroom is just about acceptable on the *VSOE*, but five nights would be deeply unpleasant for all concerned.

In the Hungarian capital, passengers have a guided tour of the city, with dinner (and lunch the following day) in local restaurants. In Romania, passengers disembark in the Transylvanian mountain town of Sinaia to visit Peles Castle, which was also visited by the very first *Orient Express* passengers in 1883. They have a sightseeing tour of Bucharest before overnighting in a city hotel that was infamous as the gathering place of spies and crooked politicians during the communist era. Next day, once across the border and into Bulgaria, they have an off-train excursion to the town of Varna, on the banks of the Danube, before crossing the country to enter Turkey via the Thracian Plain. This last part of the journey is along a section of track that inspired the controversial film *Midnight Express*. Westerners awaiting trial on drug-trafficking charges in Turkey would have their passports confiscated, but wouldn't be held in custody. So the accused would board this stretch of railway that veered briefly into Greek territory, and jump off the late-night train and disappear into the darkness, thus avoiding a jail term.

Besides the once-yearly adventure to Istanbul, the Orient Express company also operate shorter journeys within Europe, journeys that include ultra-popular tourism destinations like Prague, Rome, Krakow and Vienna. In the UK, the *British Pullman* and sister train the *Northern Belle* have their own circuits, mostly steam-hauled. These are often themed, and include a murder-mystery staged on the *British Pullman* (and in the Brighton Pavilion); the events are modelled on Agatha Christie's stories.

A vintage Swiss vista near Lucerne

where he bought two original coaches that had been restored for use in the classic 1974 film *Murder on the Orient Express*. The cinematic adaptation of Agatha Christie's book of the same name had been a box-office hit, starring Albert Finney, Lauren Bacall and Sean Connery, and the auction therefore attracted a lot of media attention. Impressed by the interest generated, Sherwood set about finding more coaches, and hatched a plan to resurrect the Orient Express as a privately run train, on a truncated route.

Which is why today's journey begins at London's Victoria Station, where the umber-and-cream coaches of the British Pullman are dripping gently from a last-minute hose-down. The Pullman is charged with the task that was once performed at precisely 11am every day by the famous *Golden Arrow*: getting passengers as far as the English Channel in suitable style to link up with the Orient Express. In its 1930s heyday, the passengers would then have boarded their very own boat, the *Canterbury*, at Dover, for the crossing to Calais Maritime. Today's passengers, however, have to go through the Channel Tunnel by bus, because the original British Pullman coaches are wood-framed and therefore don't meet the modern safety requirements for crossing under the sea.

Top brass

For passengers, the first sign of movement out of Victoria is the gentle tinkling of touching glassware, and as the train broaches the Thames, the first pouring of chilled Saumur is already frosting the glasses. As the train passes through Brixton, one of the most run-down inner-city areas of London, the talk on board is all about whether to plump for the smoked haddock timbale or the roast breast of Kentish guineafowl wrapped in mature Cumbrian ham with a tarragon and riesling reduction.

The Pullman's coaches are unique, with brass window frames that must be a Sisyphean task to polish, and marquetry floral motifs delicately crafted from polished veneers of boxwood, sycamore, walnut and a sort of Burmese rosewood called padouk. Many of these coaches were originally used with the actual *Golden Arrow*, and it took some sleuthing

by Sir James and his team to track them down and have them restored to their former glory.

The same goes for the rake of 17 navy-blue *Wagons-Lits* that wait for passengers alongside the platform at Calais, each with its own crest and polished metal lettering. Many of these, too, first saw service in the 1920s and 30s, and have had to be dug out of final resting places in forgotten sidings all over Europe.

Inside, their wood-panelled cabins have luggage racks of polished brass, and a shiny lever that raises and lowers the window. Each cabin has a padded banquette sofa that transforms into bunk beds with crisp sheets, under the skilful manipulation of the cabin stewards. There's a sink in the corner covered with a lid which, when lifted, allows the sound of train wheels to invade the room. A levered ventilation panel in the door means that passengers can watch the slippered feet of

Riding high: the Swiss Alps, fine dining and first-class service

As the day draws on, passengers begin to assemble in the bar car, dressed for dinner, and some have plainly made more effort than others. It used to be said that 'you could never be overdressed on the *Orient Express*', a maxim that Noël Coward plainly took to heart: when he set off to travel to Asia in 1929, he took 27 pieces of luggage and a gramophone.

These days, there are very few single travellers taking an aperitif in the bar. Much of the *VSOE*'s business comes from anniversaries, honeymoons and courting couples, with a smattering of aristocrats and minor celebrities. All are here, under the watchful eye of the sallow-faced pianist, who never misses a beat, either on the keyboard or in the room. And there'll probably be a discordant couple or two, either deliberately scruffy or overly décolleté, ordering champagne and caviar in the company of a bouffant old bullfrog with the granular complexion of someone who has lived too well, and is unlikely to do so for much longer.

There's a brief stop for more passengers at Paris Gare de l'Est, then the summons for dinner comes as the train bumps around the Ceinture, a lurching, pothole-prone belt of track that links the Gare du Nord with Gare de l'Est and all stations south. The restaurant car is looking fabulous; the walls are decorated with opalescent Lalique glass panels of sculpted, small-breasted nymphs tra-la-la-ing with bunches of grapes, the chairs are upholstered in cut moquette velvet and the tables are glittering with Limoges china and heavy wine glasses by Cristallerie. Outside it is dusk, drawing on to darkness, and a full, harvest moon rises above the Parisian rooftops, puffy, swollen, the colour of mature cheddar and covered in lunar acne. Inside, the pan-fried scallops have arrived.

Afterwards, in the bar car, there's been a noticeable loosening of cummerbunds and social boundaries. The scruffy and the brassy are ordering champagne together and the bouffant old bullfrog is signing the bill, while the braying

others pad by on the carpeted corridor outside, just as Hercule Poirot might have done. And down at the end of the corridor is a small boiler for the carriage heating, still coal-fired.

Dress for success

The first mainland leg of the journey, to Paris, runs across unfenced fields, bisecting rows of willows planted in straight lines as if they were part of a grand plan for something that never quite materialised. If the British landscape is a mosaic of homes and farms, fields and gardens, the French equivalent comes in great, sweeping swathes, painted with a far thicker brush. Giant carpets of colour are broken only by the speck of a tractor, the smear of a war cemetery and the smudge of a red brick town. It is a landscape that draws clear lines between agriculture and domesticity; this is where we live, it seems to say, and beyond that line is farming.

BEST BIT

The people-watching, quickly followed by the landscape-watching.

TOP TIP

You'll need some kind of dressing-gown to sashay down the corridor at night, because there's no toilet in your cabin.

PHOTO OP

You (and your cabin steward) on the platform, with the train behind.

PACK THIS

Formal dinner wear, and Agatha Christie's *Murder on the Orient Express*.

ANORAK INFO

In the Sotheby's sale at Monte Carlo, two more original Orient Express coaches were bought by the King of Morocco for his private train.

USEFUL PHRASE

Excusez-moi, êtes-vous Monsieur Poirot?

SOUVENIR

An on-board boutique sells art nouveau brass table lamps, so you can re-create the whole dining car effect back home.

DESIGN DETAIL

Admire the marquetry – inlays of different coloured wood – that creates floral patterns across the walls. Very hard to do, very expensive to restore.

OVERHEARD

'I always sleep on deck when we're on our boat in the Virgin Islands.'

voices of the British middle classes become ever louder. The pianist is playing on, unruffled, and unsurprised by anything he sees.

Slumber on the Orient Express

Settling down for the night in a sleeper train is one of life's greatest pleasures, particularly when the train in question is a touch aged and arthritic. At first, there's breathless silence while the train is held up at a signal, broken only by the distant cough of a passenger somewhere down the corridor. Then comes the click of a spoon on a tea-glass, like the conductor calling his orchestra to attention, followed by a timorous creak, a metallic scrape, and then an answering chorus of scrapes, creaks and groans, which eventually sorts itself out into a rhythmic clippety-clop as the train gets under way. Sleep is not far behind.

The next morning, breakfast is served in the cabin, and it lives up to its genteel setting, comprising a silver teapot, croissants and pastries wrapped in napkins, a purple orchid in a vase and Sir Nigel's Vintage Marmalade from Fortnum & Mason. Outside, France has become Switzerland, then Austria. The train moves between sheets of light and dark, ploughing across valley bottoms like a slicer, drawing its handsome blue blade across rivers, orchards, sports grounds, and whipping its tail across the backsides of generous, well-organised villages with generous, well-organised houses.

Inside the coaches, nobody really moves from their cabins until lunchtime. It is a strange, unaccustomed luxury to lie back in starched sheets in a rhythmically rocking bed to watch some of Europe's finest scenery put on a matinee performance outside the window. In the foreground, a rushing stream; in the middle-ground, a house with floral window boxes in meadows surrounded by woodland; in the background, a mountain with a snow-capped peak against a deep blue sky.

Gradually, though, as the *VSOE* climbs, the streams become more violent, and the land they

The lie of the land at Gothard, Switzerland

tumble through becomes more brutal, jagged and raw. Houses, where they exist, are parked on ledges out of harm's way. Outcrops of rock appear out of nowhere, throwing punches that fall just short of the window. Concrete roofs protect the track at vulnerable spots and metal barriers are strung across the mountainsides like rusty suspender belts, preventing the trees from sliding embarrassingly downward and revealing naked bumps of rock. Even the train sounds alarmed, and the tracks slap it this way and that, so that it screams and squeals like a stuck pig.

Lunch is served as the *VSOE* punches through the last of the long Alpine tunnels and

hits the daylight on the other side, with the relief of a swimmer who hits the surface after holding their breath for too long under water. Then it starts to descend through the vineyards and fruit orchards of Italy's Trento Valley.

Finally, shortly before 6pm on the second day, having exchanged the Alps and the Dolomites for mountains of scrap metal in Italy's industrial lowlands, the train rolls along the causeway across the Venetian lagoon and into Santa Lucia station. With the last hiss of the brakes, the VSOE magic evaporates, and as passengers disembark from the train, they are brought back to reality with a bump.

TRAVEL INFORMATION

The Venice Simplon-Orient-Express has around 25 departures a year, each way (Thursdays and Sundays from London, and Wednesdays and Saturdays from Venice) and the company can arrange air travel for the return leg. It is very rare for passengers to travel both ways on the train. Orient Express has agencies all over the world, details on the website www.orient-express.com.

Start
NEW ORLEANS
Finish
LOS ANGELES
Via
HOUSTON
TUCSON
PALM SPRINGS
Journey time
52 HOURS

California dreaming

From the deep south to Los Angeles via desert skies, the Sunset Limited is one hot ticket. By **Paul Mansfield**

At Union Station in New Orleans, the smell of magnolia mingles with the whiff of swampland. And as the Sunset Limited rolls out of the city at noon, at the start of its 2,000-mile journey west, there's another faint aura – one of uncertainty. North America's last remaining transcontinental train has been running between Florida and Los Angeles, and the Atlantic and the Pacific, since 1894, but the track east of New Orleans has not been repaired since Hurricane Katrina in 2005. So, for the moment, the train starts its journey at New Orleans, on the Gulf of Mexico, and some fear

the original route might never run again. Adding to that uncertainty are President Obama's new plans for high-speed routes that may overlap with the Sunset route. While such investment is good news for train travellers in the US, it might render the Sunset Limited obsolete.

This would be a sad fate for the oldest, continuously operated, named train in America. The Sunset Limited has its roots on the west coast, where in 1894, a group of entrepreneurs, including legendary hotelier Mark Hopkins, launched a service from San Francisco to New Orleans. In its first manifestation, it was an all-

Los Angeles, above; the Amtrak train, right

Pullman train, a lavish affair with silver finger bowls and onward steamship connections from New Orleans to New York. The train itself continued as far as Jacksonville, Florida, with connections to the then largely unknown backwater of Orlando. The inaugural, 2,764-mile trip from Los Angeles to Florida took three days; the current, shortened version takes just over two, and runs three times a week.

On board, the double-decker 'Superliner' carriages have old-fashioned decor and clunky fittings. Larger cabins have two fold-down bunks, plate-glass windows and a lavatory with shower. You can also choose to travel coach class, and sit upright the whole way.

As the train rocks across the points outside New Orleans, it lurches and sways precariously, but the view from 20 feet up is unbeatable, and in the lounge car, the windows arch above your head. The Sunset makes a dramatic farewell to New Orleans, tracing a graceful arc around the bay and exiting stage left across the Mississippi, over the four-mile Huey P Long bridge, grand project of the former state governor after whom it is named. Long, a champion of the left, was assassinated the year the bridge opened – 1935.

Across the river lies a dark, jungly landscape of abandoned factories, cypress swamps and bayous. Not the prettiest country, but, like New Orleans itself, possessed of its own appeal.

As the Sunset Limited crosses the border into Texas in a blaze of yellow and crimson, you're reminded of the sheer scale of the USA, and of this journey in particular. Twenty-four hours (and a great deal of points-rattling) hence, the train will still be travelling through the Lone Star state.

The cast of characters

Eating alone is not an option for the Sunset's passengers: tables in the brightly lit dining car are laid for four, and are quickly occupied when the time comes. For the most part, the food is standard diner fare: solid breakfasts cooked to order, served with unlimited coffee; lunches of soup, burgers and turkey sandwiches. There are also more ambitious dinners of steak and fresh fish. These are cooked on stoves in the two-tier diner car, but rumours abound about reduced services and increased use of microwaves, as the Sunset Limited's future remains uncertain.

The diners who fill the tables are a diverse bunch: senior citizens and students, mothers with young kids; tourists; ex-military personnel (they travel at a discount); groups of friends; solo drifters criss-crossing the country in search of work... Black and white, rich and poor, all of America, it seems, is dining here, and everyone is talking to everyone else. Even in a country in which conversations between strangers happen easily, this is unusual and exhilarating.

The Sunset is a community on the move, and it becomes closer and friendlier at every stop. Where else would you find white college boys from Los Angeles engaged in long conversations with elderly black tourists from small-town Louisiana? Or an oil man from Houston helping a single mother feed her two babies lunch? Or a sprawling Mexican family treating themselves to a big Sunday lunch? It's a real cross-section of America, and after a day everyone seems to know everyone else. No topics – not even politics – are banned, and there are enough mysterious strangers to satisfy anyone's curiosity, from the fierce-looking fitness instructor who claims to be in 'counter-intelligence', to the suave character who gets on in Houston having 'lost' his luggage in some mysterious way at the border. But then on the Sunset Limited, everyone has a story to tell and – crucially – the time to tell it.

There's Betsy from California, who is visiting her daughter at Military College in Texas, and proudly produces the girl's picture. 'She was the daughter from hell, but the military seems to have knocked some discipline into her. Lord knows, how they did that. I tried for years and didn't get nowheres, but they sure did. Hell, I even like seeing her these days. Another beer?'

Then there's the mysterious man who claims to be in the 'motion picture business' and tries hard to impress two pretty teenage girls. 'It's an unpredictable business, of course, but I will do my darndest to get you a photo shoot when we

The train leaves New Orleans via the four-mile Huey P. Long Bridge

get to Palm Springs. [To one girl] You could be a commercial model, and you [to the other] will be the make-up artist.' Incredibly, they volunteer their contact details.

In the corridor, a middle-aged man is talking wearily into his mobile phone. 'She said *what*? Kirsty, I really can't do anything about that. She's not allowed near the house. It's in the terms of her parole. She knows that. I don't care if she is your friend. Will you please just wait until your mother and I get there? Honey? Please don't do anything stupid. Honey?'

The wild west

Late evening on day one, the Sunset Limited reaches Houston, the Texan capital, whose glittering downtown office blocks loom overhead as we wait at a dingy little station below. One passenger recalls missing a train here because nobody could tell him where the station was. It's a sad fact that all across America, especially in

its most opulent cities, there are people who have no idea they live near a train line, even though it was probably the railway that brought their ancestors here in the first place.

Next to the dining car, in the glass-sided lounge car, there's a bar downstairs and things are livening up. A card game is on; some students are tipping back beer. A rangy drifter called Bob is drinking whiskey, telling anyone who'll listen about the mosquitoes back in Louisiana; big enough, he says, to 'stand flat-footed and rape a turkey'. Outside the countryside is pitch black, unknowable.

But in the morning, you wake to the Technicolor glory of the Texas plains: a landscape of scrub and sagebrush; a sky of flinty blue. Every so often the flatlands part to reveal a deep chasm in the earth. At Pecos Canyon, the train rolls at walking pace across an iron bridge that is 91 metres high. Below, a cowboy on horseback stands at the river's edge. This country is rich

American dreams: children in the Mexican border town of Juarez, above, look towards El Paso, Texas, bottom

BELLS & WHISTLES

BEST BIT
The scenery is fantastic, the train comfortable and the food excellent, but it's the other travellers that make the Sunset Limited.

TOP TIP
Before you book your cabin, think carefully about the options. Although the top cabins have their own toilets, sharing a cosy room right next to a loo is not everyone's idea of luxury.

PHOTO OP
The Huey P Long bridge over the Mississippi, the longest railway bridge in the USA. It was built with enough clearance for navy destroyers to pass underneath.

PACK THIS
Pictures of your children to pass round.

ANORAK INFO
In September 1993, the eastbound Sunset Limited derailed and fell off a bridge into water near Mobile, Alabama, in Amtrak's worst rail disaster. Forty-seven people were killed.

TRAVELLERS' FARE
There's a small bar below the observation car that sells snacks. Many non-sleeper car passengers bring along their own supplies.

OVERHEARD
'Last call for dinner, ladies and gennelmen!'

---

with stories of the Old West. Just down the line is the town of Langtry, where 'Judge' Roy Bean once dispensed idiosyncratic justice from the town saloon and held illegal boxing contests on a sand bank in the river. But the Sunset Limited pays little heed to history, heading straight as an arrow through the landscape, running head-to-head with the diesel trucks on Interstate 10, which are on their way to El Paso.

The second sunset of the journey is another multicoloured extravaganza over Alpine, west Texas, where the mountain silhouettes really do look like Alps-in-miniature. As darkness falls, the train reaches El Paso. No other border town better illustrates the great chasm between Mexico and the US. On the American side, a smart downtown of glaring neon lights looks across the Rio Grande to the Mexican city of Juárez, a humble place where dim streetlights reveal a jumble of adobe houses. The smell of cooking and woodsmoke drifts across the border on the warm, southern wind: Mexican kids peer through the chain-link fences, down by the tracks

that separate them from the promised land of the north. Here are two separate worlds standing side by side, watching each other.

High and dry
After dinner, the Sunset Limited rolls briefly into New Mexico, and in the Club Car there's an inspired video showing of the classic western *The Man Who Shot Liberty Valance*, with James Stewart and John Wayne. As these two struggle to bring law and order to the Wild West, the Sunset Limited is running through Lincoln County, where the same scenario happened for real in 1881. Sheriff Pat Garrett, having recently joined forces with the law, tracked down and killed his old friend Billy the Kid.

Then, in the early hours, the ghostly lights of a freight yard flicker outside, and the whistle gives a long, mournful moan. This is Tucson, Arizona, a major tourist destination – but not many people want to arrive at this ungodly hour.

The last morning brings the most spectacular sight yet: a sunrise of pink and cream skies, the

This journey connects two famous American cities with very different profiles. New Orleans, the capital of jazz, with its French Quarter, its Mardi Gras festival and recent history of disaster. And Los Angeles, the world's entertainment capital and fantasyland.

Houston, Texas – the other big name on the route – is more of a business centre than a tourist destination. But there are other interesting stops. El Paso is a dusty town of freeways and motels ringed by mountains and facing its poorer Mexican sister, Juárez, across the river. It's an easy walk or bus ride across the border (there's also a hop-on-and-off tourist tram). Bring your passport. Juárez is a buzzy town, with a few mission-style buildings and a scruffy collection of bars, shops and restaurants, and a colourful, bustling Sunday market in the plaza opposite the cathedral. Expect knock-off CDs and tatty souvenirs, along with hawkers, beggars and strolling musicians. You can also get good Mexican *comida*; wash it down with bottles of Don Esquis and margaritas.

For a more sanitised slice of the Old West, try Tucson, an American-Mexican blend, with a long history of settlement by Native American peoples, Spanish explorers and Anglo frontiersmen. Despite its large size (and its one million inhabitants), the city feels like a sleepy desert town, with encircling mountains and a glorious climate of cool nights and sunny days. Cultural offerings include historic sites, museums and good restaurants. It is eminently walkable, and intriguingly alternative, a mecca for healers and spiritualists. It also has a wonderful old-style resort: the Arizona Inn (www.arizonainn.com), a 1929 railroad hotel, is spread across 14 acres, and has pink adobe-style bungalows hung with bougainvillea, plus tennis courts, gardens and a swimming pool.

If you want to continue to explore California by train, the route north of Los Angeles heads up the coast to Seattle (Amtrak train the *Coast Starlight*). There are some particularly fine coastal stretches between Los Angeles and San Luis Obispo, with views over the Pacific.

red earth dotted with cacti and purple sage, a silver moon hanging high above. Now the landscape is changing from Arizona high desert to California plains. Two hours past Yuma – a scrappy town surrounded by dunes – lies a surreal sight: a body of blue water, glittering like a mirage and flanking the track for 30 miles. This is the little-known Salton Sea, a saline lake – and preview of the ocean ahead. Sensitive souls claim to be able to sense water in these parts (a dried-up creek here, a hidden spring there), but this is really an arid land. So the desert city of Palm Springs, the next stop, seems like an oasis, with groves of palms and vines ringed by the San Jacinto mountains; graceful, black and green, their upper slopes dusted with snow.

Now the crew is growing excited: 'Los Angeles, one hour!' LA is their home city. And then the train is entering a jungle of concrete freeways – the Golden State, the Pasadena – and running neck and neck with rush-hour traffic heading to the coast. It crosses the LA River and slows for the last time. After 52 hours, 2,000 miles, five states and three time zones, the Sunset Limited pulls into LA's sleekly restored Union Station, which dates from 1939 and looks from the outside like a giant Mission church. An hour later many passengers are on the beach.

Will the Sunset Limited survive? It would be nice to think so. But in the arrivals hall at LA a young Californian woman who'd come to pick up a friend was listening to her friend's enthusiastic account of the journey with barely contained boredom. 'You know,' she said airily, nudging the subject to a close, 'I don't think I've been on an American train in my life.'

Grand
designs
at Union
Station,
Los Angeles

TRAVEL INFORMATION

Full details of timetable, fares etc are on www.amtrak.com. The most inexpensive option is Coach Class seating, which will need to be reserved. Sleeping car passengers have a choice of Roomette, Bedroom or Bedroom Suite (two adjoining bedrooms) that can accommodate one to four people. In Superliner Roomette service, toilet and a shower are located nearby. Viewliner Roomettes feature in-room toilet and washbasin facilities. Bedrooms offer a sink, an enclosed toilet and shower facilities. Bed linen and soap are always included, as are meals, bottled water, morning coffee and juice, the daily newspaper and the assistance of a sleeping-car attendant.

Rocky mountain high

From great lakes to a peak performance, on the train that built Canada. By **York Membery**

Canada may be a young country, but it boasts many superlatives, including the most lakes of any country, and some of the world's least-explored wildernesses – this is, after all, a nation that's four-fifths uninhabited. More significantly for this book, it also has one of the longest train journeys in the world, along a track that played a formative role in the country's creation. A railway that practically stitched the nation together.

Canada was only granted 'dominion' (semi-independent) status within the British Empire back in 1867, but even in those days, it wasn't the Canada we know today. Back then, it was a loose confederation of semi-autonomous provinces, mostly on the Atlantic side, which decided to get together partly out of fear of American annexation, a real threat at the time. However, distant British Columbia, on the Pacific side, would only finally agree to join the resulting Canadian Confederation on the condition that the government of the day built a railway – 'an iron ribbon linking sea with shining sea' – to join the two sides together.

It was a huge undertaking. Work began in 1881, but the sheer scale of the project, not to mention the challenges posed by the country's geography and climate, made progress painfully slow. The newly formed Canadian Pacific Railway company (the CPR) was forced to call in William Cornelius van Horne, a larger-than-life,

cigar-chomping American railroad executive, to get the job done. On 7 November 1885, the last spike was hammered in at Craigellachie, British Columbia. It had taken 12,000 men (largely navvies and Chinese coolies), 5,000 horses, and 300 dogsled teams to complete, and a man a mile is reputed to have died blasting a route through the Rockies and traversing treacherous stretches of the fast-flowing River Fraser beyond.

For the next 75 years, the Canadian Pacific Railway made big money out of transporting migrants across Canada. In fact, the CPR itself played an active role in luring migrants from Britain and Europe, advertising land for sale for a mere $2.50 an acre on the prairies, and laying on special colonist carriages, which offered only basic sleeping facilities and a small kitchen at one end of the car.

One of those migrants was my father, who arrived in Canada back in 1928, with just £10 in his pocket. Having declared at immigration that he was not 'in any way mentally or physically defective or tubercular', he set off for a job in Victoria, British Columbia.

In those days, taking the train was the fastest option available to him, even though the journey took the best part of a week. And although he was only to stay a few years – the Wall Street crash of 1929 eventually sent him packing – it was this epic journey that started a lifelong love affair with a vast land.

Picture this: the Rockies are the visual highlight of the journey

Start
TORONTO
Finish
VANCOUVER
Via
PARRY SOUND
WINNIPEG
EDMONTON
JASPER
Journey time
3.5 DAYS

Into the wild

Retracing his steps these days doesn't take quite so long, at three-and-a-half days, but the Canadian still sets out three times a week from Toronto for Vancouver, across the wilderness that is the Canadian Shield, the prairies' vast wheatlands and the snow-capped Rockies. En route, it passes through four time zones – Eastern, Central, Mountain and Pacific – and covers a staggering 2,100 miles.

The journey begins at Toronto's Union Station, which was opened by Edward, Prince of Wales (using a pair of gold scissors), in 1927. This imposing building, with its colonnaded Front Street façade and magnificent ticket lobby, looks like a big-city station should. It is the busiest station in Canada, and for my money one of the grandest railway stations in North America, which makes it a fitting departure point for as historic a train service as the Canadian.

Today's passengers check in at the departure lounge of Via Rail (Canada's national train network), in the bowels of the station, before heading to the long platform above, where the massive, 26-carriage train awaits, sleek and retro in stainless steel. It is hard not to feel awestruck.

Facilities on board are grander than in my father's day. Smartly dressed attendants greet passengers and carry their bags to roomettes (single-berth cabins). These feature sliding doors that lock from the inside, and zip-shut curtain doors that you close behind you when you're out and about. The cabins are all of 6ft 5in long and 4ft 6in wide, but a lot has been packed within their walls – everything from a fold-down bed and a bench seat to a stainless steel washbasin and a toilet concealed under a moveable seat. By contrast, my father would have shared a bathroom with a couple of dozen or more other immigrants from all over Europe. He certainly wouldn't have had access to anything as magnificent as the Skyline dome car, down the corridor, a great place to watch Toronto's landmark CN Tower receding from view.

Within a couple of hours of departure, the patchwork quilt of farmers' fields has given way to 'cottage country', a summer refuge where Toronto-dwellers get their annual fix of the great outdoors. Thick woodland rears up on either side. 'On the left is Lake Muskoka.' The train's senior attendant, Bill, announces this over the PA as a sheet of wide open water appears to the left, before adding with a chuckle: 'It's one of 60,000 lakes in Ontario, so I won't be telling you the name of every single one.'

First stop is Parry Sound, a small town that marks the gateway to the Canadian Shield, the vast wooded wilderness studded by rocks and

BELLS & WHISTLES

BEST BIT
Dining in a room with the world's best view.

PHOTO OP
The moment the Rockies come into view – and everyone makes a paparazzi-style dash for the dome car.

PACK THIS
The Last Spike by Pierre Berton, about the building of Canada's transcontinental railway. Plus binoculars for seeing the wildlife.

ANORAK INFO
The General Electric locomotives pulling the *Canadian* are 4,250 horsepower, 12 times the average bus.

USEFUL PHRASE
'A Sleeman's honey brown beer please.' (The best beer in North America, IMHO)

OVERHEARD
'Winnipeg's got three seasons: winter, construction and mosquito.'

lakes that stretches all the way to the Manitoba border, hundreds of miles away. It's a primeval landscape, untouched by man, and we soon get our first taste of Canadian wildlife when a passenger spots a beaver. It will be the first of many such sightings on the trip.

Lunch is served in the art deco dining cars, of which there's one for every six sleeper cars. The Philadelphia-built rolling stock itself dates back to the 1950s, and while it has since been fully refurbished, it still conjures up the feel of Hitchcock's *Strangers on a Train*. The culinary experience is of high standard, and the food, be it Manitoba pickerel or British Columbian salmon,

flies the Canadian culinary flag and is designed to reflect the flavours of the provinces en route.

For my first dinner on the train (there are two sittings, 5pm and 7pm), I had a fish chowder starter followed by grilled trout topped with a butter white wine and caper sauce. And with a breakfast menu that included everything from eggs benedict to the 'chef's omelette special', plus a three-course lunch, I wasn't in danger of starving. One way of working off all that eating is to walk to the end of the train, a distance of a third of a mile. This is something only to be attempted once you have got your 'train legs', since navigating the narrow corridors of a

Retro fest: Toronto's grand Union Station and the classic deco-style train

swaying train, and squeezing past all the well-upholstered passengers, is quite a skill.

Happily, there are other opportunities to stretch one's legs. At around 9.30am on day two, the train pulls into the quaintly named Sioux Lookout, a one-street town in remote western Ontario, where it stops for 20 minutes to take on water, fuel and food. Frankly, though, a 20-minute stopover is enough.

Splendour in the grass

Soon afterwards, we cross the Manitoba border, where the Canadian Shield gives way to the grasslands, which stretch all the way to the Rockies. In the afternoon, we reach the first settlement of any real size since leaving Toronto – Winnipeg, once the hub of Canada's fur trade, and now Canada's seventh-biggest municipality. Some passengers disembark for a couple of nights, but I can't help wondering if a city that

boasts about having Canada's windiest street corner is really worth a two-day delay.

Train time passes surprisingly quickly. Admiring the scenery, looking out for wildlife (prairie dogs on this leg of the journey) and counting the number of container cars on the mile-long, juggernaut-like cargo trains that thunder by – it all eats into the hours.

And then there's the social life in the Skyline Dome Cars and the wraparound Park Car, at the rear of the train. The Canadian provides a great opportunity to meet people, not just the tourists travelling Cabin Class (who seem to be mostly Brits, Americans and Canadians of a certain age), but real people travelling Comfort Class – ie the modern equivalent of steerage.

Everyone has a story to tell. Take Jim, the retired signwriter from America's Midwest, who is making the trip of a lifetime with his wife, having beaten brain cancer. In the Comfort

Wild things: a bald eagle in British Columbia; an elk in Jasper, Alberta

Class bar, I meet a train-crazy punk from Ontario, with a mohican haircut and a nose ring, who is making his fifth journey across the country on the Canadian. Here, too, are the hockey-mad construction worker from Winnipeg heading to booming Vancouver in search of work, and the two girl students from the Maritimes heading out west in search of adventure.

On the third day, having crossed the pancake-flat Saskatchewan at night, the train pulls into Alberta's capital, Edmonton, the gateway to Canada's North. It's time to replenish supplies again; such is the length of the train that station staff have taken to wearing roller skates.

Soon after leaving Edmonton, the prairie flatlands give way to hillier, wooded terrain and there is a growing sense of anticipation, for we are approaching the Rockies, the wall-like slab of mountains that divides British Columbia from the rest of Canada, and the climax of the journey.

The Rocky picture show

Fifty miles west of Edmonton, we pass Wabamun Lake – so calm an expanse of water that it was christened with the Cree word for 'mirror' (the Cree are one of Canada's First Nation tribes). Suddenly, the Rockies come into view, and the calm gives way to chaos, as camera-wielding passengers charge to the front of the observation car like celebrity-chasing paparazzi.

Over the next few hours, the Canadian snakes its way past jagged, snow-capped peaks and crosses deep gorges, carved into the rock, as it is hauled ever higher by three giant diesel locomotives. Each of the latter is 'powerful enough to supply a small town's electricity needs', according to one of the drivers.

SIDINGS

Toronto is Canada's financial, economic and cultural hub – and one of the world's most multicultural cities, reflected in the diversity of its cuisine. If you can afford to, stay at the Fairmont Royal York (www.fairmont.com/royalyork) – built by the Canadian Pacific Railway across the street from Union Station. Vancouver, a feast of sea and mountains, is one of the world's most gorgeous cities. Stanley Park is one of the Americas' great green spaces.

But it's not just the scenery that is breathtaking: so is the wildlife. Passengers are likely to see everything from elk to eagle, beaver to deer. Indeed, it's not unusual to see elk and mule deer strolling down the high street in Jasper, the mountain resort that is the Canadian's last stop before Vancouver.

After the excitement and visual intensity of the Rockies, the last leg of the journey is something of a letdown. But that's life: you wouldn't have a high without a low.

Carpet-like coniferous forests line the last stretch of track, under steady drizzle falling from leaden skies. Vancouver may be one of the world's beautiful cities, sandwiched between the Pacific and BC's coastal mountains, but the Canadian approaches the city via its drab east side and sneaks, almost apologetically, into Via Rail's Pacific terminus.

Our journey was a few hours late. The reason? A mudslide in the Rockies. As train-delay excuses go, it's not bad.

TRAVEL INFORMATION

The Canadian departs from Toronto every Tuesday, Thursday and Saturday evening, and from Vancouver every Tuesday, Friday and Sunday evening. There's a choice of Silver & Blue or Comfort Class, and prices vary greatly according to time of year. Customers can book direct on the VIA website, www.viarail.ca. Many international tour operators also sell tickets.

Start
SYDNEY
Finish
PERTH
Via
ADELAIDE
BROKEN HILL
COOK
KALGOORLIE
Service
THE INDIAN
PACIFIC
Journey time
3 DAYS

All over down under

Coast to coast in the land of Oz. By **Peter Lynch**

A country, a continent and the world's largest island; whichever way you look at it, Australia is huge. Its formidable landscape means that crossing from one side of the nation to the other has always been a major undertaking. For the past 45,000 years, only the Australian aboriginal peoples have known its harsh secrets as they traversed the continent along a maze of 'songline' routes they'd inherited from their ancestors.

Edward John Eyre was the first European to make the 2,704-mile east–west crossing. Back in 1840, the English-born explorer travelled from Sydney to Adelaide and then Adelaide to Albany in Western Australia. Two centuries later, the Great Southern Railway's Indian Pacific follows Eyre's epic journey from ocean to ocean, in a twice-weekly service that still requires a whopping 65 hours to complete. En route, the train crosses some of Australia's most iconic landscapes, from mountains and desert to vineyards and pastures.

Although a transcontinental rail link has existed since 1917, bizarrely the track had different gauges, requiring several changes of train en route. It was not until 1969 that one unbroken track finally linked Sydney to Perth.

Kangaroo course

Pulling out of Sydney's Central Station in early afternoon, the train takes a few hours to escape the suburbs and reach the fertile farmland, where grazing cows and sheep dupe unwary travellers about what lies ahead. By the time we reach the Central Dividing Range of the Blue Mountains, it is already dark, and passengers were settling down for their first night on board.

The cheapest grade of travel is Red Service, where passengers – usually backpackers and locals – sleep in a 'day-nighter' seat. Its main advantage is that it offers a six-month unlimited travel pass, and the opportunity for tourists to mingle with the locals. Its disadvantage? The seats, although comfortable by day, do not make for a good night's sleep. That said, Red Service passengers can splash out extra on shared twin cabins with upper and lower berths, shared showers and complimentary towels.

Gold Service, by contrast, boasts a luxurious feel with better beds, en-suite facilities and more space – but you'll pay for the privilege. And gold and Red rarely meet: they each have separate lounges, and the former has its own dining car with complimentary meals (in Red, you must buy your meals from a buffet).

At dawn, kangaroos and emus pause from feeding to peer at the train as we speed past. We are still in New South Wales at 6.20am as the train makes its first stop: at the quintessential outback town of Broken Hill.

The two-hour stopover offers just enough time to stroll down Argent Street, which is as wide as the Champs-Elysées – except there's nothing much at either end. Broken Hill's covered

East meets west: the Indian-Pacific starts in Sydney, above, and ends in Perth, left, via one-horse towns like Rawlinna, Western Australia, far left

sidewalks provide welcome shade from the blazing sun, and there is just time to buy fresh cakes from the bakery. Despite the early hours, the town is already busy with shoppers hurrying about their business before the sun becomes too hot. Opal sellers on the platform do some last-minute trading with passengers, and we pull out on time at 8.20am.

The route to Adelaide passes through more arid bush country, but the South Australian capital is heralded by a new landscape of vineyards and orchards of olives and apples. At almost half a mile long, the train is too long for Adelaide's main station, so we pull into the unprepossessing Keswick station, two miles out of town, at mid afternoon.

During the 90-minute stopover, there is just enough time to squeeze in a taxi ride into the city, have a brief look around and drink an ice-cold beer. Back on the train, we notice a considerable influx of locals among the travellers; apart from its tourist appeal, the Indian Pacific is a vital link between southern Australian communities.

Some like it hot

Leaving Adelaide and backtracking north around the Spenser Gulf, we slow down, but don't stop, at Port Augusta, a truck stop for lorries about to set out across the Nullarbor plain, also known as the southern gateway to the Northern Territory. During the night, we pass Woomera, famous for its centre for rocket and missile testing.

At sunrise, the lush Adelaide countryside is replaced by red sandstone and endless bush; domes of grey-green spinifex (a spiny grass) are punctuated by just the occasional gum tree, which break up an apparently lifeless landscape.

The train enters the forbidding Nullarbor Plain around 9.30am. Ancient and featureless, this former sea floor is pancake-flat, dotted with limestone boulders and spinifex. Amid these bleak surroundings, the train reaches its top speed on an arrow-straight stretch of track that runs unbroken for a staggering 296 miles.

Arriving at Cook in the middle of the Nullarbor, we are 1,739 miles out of Sydney with another 1,100 miles to go until Perth. Cook was built as a railway town, but business changes have left it deserted; it's a strange place to stop. The train's air-conditioning is so effective that the desert heat comes as a shock, and disembarking passengers quickly don sunglasses and hats.

Only four residents now rattle around among Cook's hundred deserted houses; a shuttered school, hospital and a sand-filled swimming pool add to the poignant air of a ghost town. On the edge of town, all that can be seen are a series of shimmering mirages. This is a land where only Aboriginal people and desert-adapted creatures have any chance of survival.

The 20-minute stop to refuel is more than enough time; when the train whistles, most passengers are already back on board.

As the train continues across the featureless Nullarbor Plain, we see few signs of life, apart

A kangaroo on the Nullarbor Plain

SIDINGS

Broken Hill is ideal for getting a hands-on feel for the quintessential Australian Outback. Originally founded as a mining town, it has working and derelict mines to explore along with the famous Royal Flying Doctor Service and the School of the Air. The Royal Exchange (www.royalexchange hotel.com) is a recently refurbished hotel on Argent Street, the main drag.

While at Broken Hill, an Outback tour to Mutawintji National Park is a memorable experience, as is the Sculpture Symposium, a collection of sandstone art works on the edge of town. The classically harsh bush and desert landscape are intimidating and dangerous to the inexperienced, but full of unusual flora and fauna: desert-adapted acacia, cypress pine, falcons, wedge-tailed eagles, frogs, snakes, emus, kangaroos and lizards.

Adelaide, South Australia's capital, is the stopover of choice for those who crave culture and urban charm rather than raw nature. Its wide boulevards, city squares, greenery and classical architecture make it the most European of Australian cities.

From Adelaide, the best day trip is to the nearby Barossa valley vineyards, where you can paddle in the dribble of Jacob's Creek. A short ferry ride across the Southern Ocean to Kangaroo Island is a nature-lover's dream. It has great beaches and up-close encounters with New Zealand fur seals, penguins, wallabies, kangaroo, koala, echidna and the rare duck-billed platypus.

Adelaide is the place to branch off the Indian Pacific route, either south-east to Melbourne or north to Alice Springs in Australia's red centre, and on to Darwin in the tropical north.

BEST BIT

The deserted town of Cook on the bleak Nullarbor Plain. Don't let the train leave you behind in this burning hot limestone desert.

TOP TIP

You can only bring hand luggage on this trip.

PHOTO OP

The train during the stop at Cook, against the backdrop of the empty desert.

PACK THIS

Because the air-conditioning is so strong, nights can be cold, so bring warm clothes. Passengers who have to sleep in their seats should bring an inflatable neck pillow.

ANORAK INFO

The 296-mile stretch of track on the Nullarbor Plain is the longest straight section of railway track in the world.

USEFUL PHRASE

Get your beer parlance correct. A pint will get you a large beer in New South Wales and South Australia, and a middy will get you a 285ml glass. Elsewhere ask for a schooner (425ml). A pony is half a middy.

OVERHEARD

'Craig, have you seen my teeth? I think I left them in the dunny.'

from some huge wedge-tailed eagles and a herd of feral camels. Ambling through this inhospitable terrain, they have adapted well to the Australian Outback after being released by Afghan drovers during the last century.

Gold rush

By late afternoon, we have left the plain, and the landscape begins to come back to life, with greenery, trees and foraging emus. A surprising number of burnt-out cars are the first indication of human habitation. Then, at 8pm, we arrive at the macho gold-mining town of Kalgoorlie.

It is dark and the shops are shut – but the pubs are open. The Grand Hotel is heaving with bull-necked miners eating mountains of food off plates the size of tea trays. Meanwhile, behind the bar, scantily clad barmaids pull pints and heave crates of beer. For train passengers, the two-and-a-half-hour stopover is enough time for one of the organised trips to the 24-hour gold mine or to Kalgoorlie's other big attraction – the famous brothel museum.

Waking up on the final morning, we are greeted by the sight of rolling farmland dotted with sheep, cattle, freshly baled hay and the occasional vineyard. A team of West Australian quarantine officials board the train and check passengers for out-of-state food products that must be disposed of or destroyed.

The train finally pulls into East Perth Station at around 9am, more than two-and-a-half days (65 hours) after leaving Sydney. Passengers from seat-only class look a bit dishevelled and glad to have arrived, but those who travelled with cabins and beds look much perkier, as if they've just checked out of a luxury hotel.

TRAVEL INFORMATION

For more information and booking details, visit www.gsr.com.au. Whistle-stop coach tours are usually available at Broken Hill, Adelaide and Kalgoorlie and last approximately one hour. There is a modest extra cost, and pre-booking is not necessary. Trains usually depart Sydney on Wednesdays and Saturdays at 2.55pm and arrive in Perth on Saturdays and Tuesdays at 9.10am.

Queen of the desert

The heat is on, but you'll keep cool in this stylish train across the Australian Outback. By **Suzy Bennett**

Red hot: the Ghan journeys into the heart of the Outback

In 1846, Harry, the first camel to set hoof in Australia, shot its owner. John Horrocks brought the beast from the Canary Islands to help explore the Outback, but Harry was clearly unhappy in his new pioneering role. He regularly bit local Aborigines and animals, taking particular exception to goats, but, because he could carry large loads and clomp about for days in the desert without water, Horrocks kept him on. Then, one day, while Horrocks was out hunting, Harry lurched into the explorer, setting off his gun and blowing half his master's face off. Harry was swiftly put down.

The Ghan railway owes much to Harry and the hapless Horrocks, who died soon after the accident, from gangrene. Subsequent Victorian explorers, having learned from their bungling predecessor's mistake, drafted in a series of professional Afghan camel herders to handle the temperamental animals. These men enabled the exploration of Australia's Outback and the laying of foundations for a transcontinental, north–south railway. And it is after these Afghan herders that the Ghan is named.

Nowadays, passengers can travel top to bottom through Australia without coming into

contact with any dangerous dromedaries, or indeed any other of the country's murderous wildlife. Running 1,850 miles from the sweltering tropics of Darwin in the north, straight through the Never Never, into the searing Tanami desert and down into Adelaide where Antarctic waves roll in, the Ghan train whisks its passengers in hermetically sealed comfort through one of the most desolate and desiccated lands on earth.

The two-night, three-day journey actually begins at Palmerston, a desolate freight station a few miles south of Darwin – unless there are flash floods, in which case passengers are decanted into cars to skip the Darwin section and start at Katherine instead.

The wizard of Oz

With its steel-clad carriages, the Ghan is a sleek, shiny tube of retro chic, and glints so painfully in the morning sun that passengers are forced to don dark sunglasses when they arrive, making the platform look like a Blues Brothers' convention. It is astonishingly long: at over half a mile long, with 45 carriages, it is one of the

Seeing the sights: the forests of the Northern Territory, left, and a local in Never Never, right world's longest diesel trains. Onboard, it takes 35 minutes to walk its entire length.

Although the service is fairly new – the final section linking Alice Springs to Darwin opened in 2004 – the carriages actually date from the 1960s, and the interior has a deliciously old-world feel: all wood veneer, stainless steel and hand-cranked Venetian blinds. There are three classes, covering a range of budgets, from the new luxury Platinum service to 'sit-up' backpacker class. Cabins, though small, are an ergonomic marvel, squeezing the facilities of a first-class hotel into a space no bigger than a minibus, with twin berths, a wardrobe, table, armchairs and an ensuite bathroom.

It's been said that the Ghan is scenically boring, unless you value monumental emptiness and the colour red. But the first day's vistas through the fertile 'Top End' to Katherine are the stuff of tourist-office marketing dreams: lush emerald forests, ancient gorges and crocodile-strewn billabongs. If you want to see the Never Never, this is as close as it gets. Aborigines are a visible presence, ancient fossil sites abound and wildlife is as colourful and extraordinary as it gets, which is saying something in Australia.

For such a stylish train, the Ghan has a unique lack of pomp. As you'd expect with Australians, staff are relaxed, affable and unfailingly obliging, while small courtesies such as wake-up coffee and morning newsletter delivered by suited stewards evoke an earlier age. Almost all passengers are holidaymakers: retirees and backpackers heading for the red centre, plane phobics, train enthusiasts and the 'holiday-of-a-lifetime' set. The food is as delicious

BELLS & WHISTLES

BEST BIT
With the scenery so unrelievedly barren, there are no specific highlights on this journey. Pleasure comes from kicking back and enjoying the endlessly unfurling scenery and gentle routines of train life.

TOP TIP
Think twice before you pick anything up in the desert. It's nearly all deadly; even caterpillars can lay you out with a single nip.

PHOTO OP
Stick your camera out of the window to snap the silver train against a backdrop of red desert.

PACK THIS
The Ghan crosses three climate zones, from the tropics to the desert to temperate Adelaide, so pack for all weathers and take plenty of high-factor suncream, a hat and sunglasses.

Mosquito repellent is a must if staying overnight in Darwin, Katherine or the Red Centre.

ANORAK INFO
The Ghan is operated by a subsidiary of the British company Serco, which also supplies electronic tags to the Home Office and operates some of Britain's speed cameras.

USEFUL PHRASE
'She'll be apples.' Can be used as a reply to any question.

TRAVELLERS' FARE
Kangaroo tails, witchetty grubs, ants' bottoms – all are on offer at Aboriginal communities if you stop off at Katherine.

OVERHEARD
'You can tell if there's a crocodile around because they smell of vomit.'

as it is plentiful. Our first evening, we are served great bowls of Aborigine-inspired dishes such as bunya nut soup, kangaroo steak and barramundi.

Red alert

The following morning, after a series of unexplained stops in the night, there is a very different view through the widescreen windows: soggy green tropics have given way to a vista of rust-red ground, punctuated only by spiky spinifex grass, weary-looking eucalyptus trees and the occasional kangaroo bounding around in the distance. It's so vast and empty I wonder if I can see the curvature of the earth. I think back to the explorers who, a century and a half ago, were being baked alive out there, hallucinating from heatstroke and deciding whether they should drink their own urine. What a contrast it is to be seeing it now with a glass of chilled chardonnay in hand and a casual eye on the *Neighbours* episode being played on a lounge's television. It's all wonderfully meditative and I spend the day marvelling at the monumental emptiness and uselessness of the place. That evening, as the sun splits into a hundred layers of red, it becomes impossible to tell where the earth stops and the heavens begin. It could inspire a woman to poetry, if only she hadn't left her notepad at the other end of the train.

Stretching my legs later that evening, I come across a train enthusiast wielding a stopwatch and notepad. 'I'm counting the bends,' he explains. 'So, how many have there been?' I ask. 'Only one in the last four hours,' he replies. So the Ghan is not only one of the most epic transcontinental journeys in the world, it's also one of the straightest.

The next morning, the train pulls in for a four-hour stop in Alice Springs, and there's a chance to get the desert between the toes. It's 34°C in the shade – when you step off the train you experience a blast of heat not unlike opening an oven door to check a roast – and it has rained only four times in the past two years. It's at Alice that many passengers choose to leave the train and 'go bush', rejoining a few days later on the next journey south. The most compelling side trip is that to Uluru (Ayers Rock) and Kata Tjuta (the Olgas), a 275-mile, bumpy road trip west. I opt for the short bus excursion to Alice Springs Desert Park, where I learn all about Australia's vast array of toothy and tentacled inhabitants.

As the train continues south of Alice Springs, landmarks are few and far between. There are glimpses of the Flinders Ranges, the Southern Territory's largest mountain range, before the line veers off past Coober Pedy, home to 50 per cent of the world's opal production, film location for *Mad Max* and a region so hot most residents live underground in the cool air of refurbished mines. Then the line crosses the dry bed of the Finke, which is said to be the oldest river in the world, but which runs only about twice every 100 years.

It's water under the bridge: the Elizabeth River in Northern Territory

---

SIDINGS

Great Southern Rail, which runs the *Ghan*, has developed a range of 'off train' experiences, such as visiting a wildlife park, or the world's first Royal Flying Doctor Service in Alice Springs, or taking a boat cruise up Katherine Gorge (now known by its Aboriginal name Nitmiluk), a 23-million-year-old sandstone canyon with Aboriginal paintings and spectacular waterfalls. They can also arrange more elaborate options. A 60-day flexible travel pass, allowing passengers to get on and off the train as they go, provides more scope for extended sightseeing and lengthy stopovers.

There's plenty to do at either end of the journey. Just outside Darwin is Litchfield National Park, famed for its house-sized termite towers. From Adelaide, you can take a wine tour of the vineyards or a 40-minute ferry ride to the wildlife haven of Kangaroo Island.

At daybreak the following morning, the train morphs into its third climate zone – the reds and pinks of Alice are replaced by the deep yellows and golds of the grain-growing south. As the first signs of civilisation begin to appear, everything looks suddenly European. First come green, rolling hills, pleasant meadows, vineyards and rickety wooden cottages, then, as we roll into Adelaide's suburbs, snooker-green golf courses dotted with be-Pringled golfers, then office blocks and cafés. After three days in the outback,

it's a surreal sight, too clinical and clean-looking. I miss the grit of the desert.

As the train sighs into its final stop, I seize a chance to ask the driver about the unexplained nightly stops. 'That'll be the kangaroos,' he tells me. 'Messy buggers. They get caught in the headlights and end up all over the windscreen. You have to stop the train to pick them out of the grill. The camels are worse, though. They really do some damage.' Probably still getting their revenge for Harry, I shouldn't wonder.

TRAVEL INFORMATION

The train departs Darwin on Wednesdays and Saturdays at 10am and 9am, and arrives at Adelaide two-and-a-half days later. Detailed timetable and fare information are available on Great Southern Rail's website at www.gsr.com.au. For details of Platinum Service, the most luxurious way to travel, email platinum@gsr.com. For information on Darwin, visit www.tourismtopend.com.au

It's a small world

On the upper floor of a vast 19th-century warehouse beside the docks in Hamburg is one of the world's most extraordinary visitor attractions. In many other cities, the bare-brick walls would encase trendy apartments, but a much more imaginative role has been found for this large open space: a hugely ambitious construction, in miniature, of the world's most iconic landscapes, from America's Grand Canyon to the Matterhorn in Switzerland. And it is so brilliantly conceived and well executed, that it appeals to the child in all of us.

The focal point of each country is the railway, and together they add up to the largest model railway in the world, covering 1,100 square metres. But if it were simply a model railway, it would not have attracted five million visitors and made Miniatur Wunderland one of the most popular tourist attractions in Germany. Its appeal lies in the incredible detail as well as the huge scale of the models. The buildings are superbly crafted; many are faithful reproductions of well-known buildings, such as the castle of Chillon on Lac Léman in Switzerland, or the Hauptkirche St Michaelis in Hamburg.

But what gives the models another dimension is the humour and realism that have been employed in creating so many tiny vignettes of human life: 200,000 figures are scattered among sites like a campground beside a river, pop concerts, open-air cafés, football matches, a Red Bull event and town parades. There is even a fire-eater breathing flames. Numerous road accidents cause major traffic jams among the 170 computer-controlled cars, while the trains whisk past, unhindered. Behind a dam in Switzerland, the lake has been drained to reveal the ruined buildings of the village that existed before the valley was flooded, and the occasional ghost can be seen

in the church. It might sound cheesy, but the modelling has been so well done that you suspend any latent cynicism.

And when night falls, the scenes become a triumph of LED lighting. There are 300,000 tiny bulbs in buildings, on trains and in vehicles (these even have working brake lights), as well as on station platforms, ships and bridges. There are even subtle differences between the lights from houses and flats, reflecting the range of white, cream and yellow lights that most residences emit. There are orange sodium and

Mount Rushmore in miniature, top left; a baby grand canyon in the Wild West, left; Storebelt Bridge in Denmark

stop, you can even hear the Westinghouse brake pump start up.

The German model features Hamburg's main station, and many of the city's more famous buildings and structures, plus a scene in the Harz Mountains and a train ferry. Switzerland is an amalgam of the south ramp of the Gotthard main line with the spirals around the church at Wassen, the metre gauge of Graubünden and a rack section of the Matterhorn Gotthard Bahn, with supporting cablecars and even a tunnel-boring machine at work on an Alpine tunnel. Scandinavia features a brilliantly evoked Finnish mining scene under snow, and the water around the floating dock is tidal, with the water level rising and falling.

The statistics behind this hypnotically appealing world are astonishing: it has taken half a million working hours to create; 800 trains are in operation on the railways, the longest being 48 feet; there are over six miles of track and 150 push buttons that allow visitors to interact with the models; the open-to-view control centre has 40 computers, and the operators are assisted by 200 cameras, some of them relaying pictures from the front of the miniature trains.

Just allow plenty of time, especially if you have children.

Anthony Lambert

Miniatur Wunderland, Hamburger Speicherstadt, Kehrwieder 2, Hamburg (www.miniatur-wunderland.com). Book tickets in advance to avoid queueing, which can be a big problem at weekends. The nearest subway (U-Bahn) station is Baumwall. To get to Baumwall Station from the Hauptbahnhof, take the U-Bahn line U3 (the yellow line) in the direction of Rathaus/Barmbek.

white street lights, which come on with the exact flicker of the prototypes. A fairground is a kaleidoscope of flashing lights, and Las Vegas is as brash as the real thing. The day/night simulations take 15 minutes.

There are even sound effects. The police cars of each country emit the correct siren, and the Swiss PostBuses give their unique warning horn as they approach blind bends. On their slog up Wyoming's Sherman Hills, the Union Pacific steam locomotives bark their exhaust at the appropriate pace, and when they come to a

There's been a revolution in the world's trains in recent years. High-speed lines are the new buzz, and they're hauling fashionable passengers back to the tracks in their hundreds of thousands. It wasn't always thus. By the latter half of the 20th century, the train had become the dog-eared refuge of enthusiasts and railcard holders, while governments spent all their money on motorways and airports. But then the pendulum swung, as the roads overflowed, and the charisma of air travel evaporated in a plethora of no frills. Meanwhile, the new railways had been stealing up on the inside, with their exhilarating speeds, upmarket lounges, uniformed stewards and interiors designed by the likes of Philippe Starck. So suddenly the train is socially acceptable again; it's reliable, it's cool, and it carries you right to the heart of the action.

State of the Art

A toast to the future

After years of French supremacy, the British side of Eurostar has raised its game – and a star has been reborn. **By Andrew Eames**

For many years, the Eurostar was a source of British shame, a perfect example of how we Brits couldn't get our act together when it came to trains. The moment the Channel Tunnel was completed, the high-speed line from the French end of the Tunnel to Paris began to host the nearest thing to flying that most rail travellers had ever encountered. By contrast, on the British side, the 186mph Eurostar was reduced to grinding along on crash-bang railways, stuck behind slam-door commuter trains, before finally wincing to a halt in a big blue shed by Waterloo Bridge.

Mercifully, all that has finally changed, and now British travellers can hold their heads up high as they saunter towards the 9.40am service to Paris, because now the Eurostar has its own station – its own palace, more like – and a proper dedicated high-speed track for the British side. Together, the two of them have ushered in a new golden era of train travel in the UK.

That station-cum-palace is St Pancras, a giant pile of Victorian Gothic architecture on London's Euston Road, which first opened to the public back in 1868. With other big terminals at King's Cross and Euston on either side of it, St

Raise a glass: the world's longest champagne bar at St Pancras

Pancras became surplus to requirements, and for most of the 20th century it languished, underused, unloved and uncared for. It was even under threat of demolition until voices were raised – including those of poet John Betjeman – in its defence. But it wasn't until the sleek and speedy Eurostar nosed into town, seeking a London home, that it finally came into its own.

For the amount of money spent on refurbishing the building – £800 million – the rail company could have built themselves something spanking new, but thank the Lord they didn't. St Pancras today is a wonderful synthesis of ancient and modern, part Byzantine cathedral, part shopping centre, part cantilevered roof of the century. It's less a station, and more a giant temple to locomotion, all grey-girdered and orangey-brick red.

Few get to see the impressive façade (albeit unimpressively sited on drab Euston Road). Most arrive underground, spilling out into the main concourse and across a floor of speckled marble. Of St Pancras's two levels, this one is dedicated to retailing, fine foods and ticket sales. Brasseries and baguetteries bring a touch of France, but you can also buy Marks & Spencer sandwiches or a

Hamleys teddy bear. The check-in area is located in a white-pillared crypt, but there are also trains for ordinary mortals doing humdrum UK journeys down the far end.

Meanwhile, the Eurostars themselves are raised on a dais on the upper level, where they hum gently, happy to be there. So should passengers be, too, if just to appreciate the aesthetics of what is technically called the Barlow Train Shed, after engineer-in-chief William Barlow, who designed what was then (1868) the largest enclosed space in the world, and topped it with a roof that is a whopping 690 feet long and 242 feet wide. The ridge and furrow glazing contains 14,080 glass panels, giving a total glazed area the size of 38 tennis courts.

This upper level has no clutter, no advertising and no discordant colours to distract from the simple design of brickwork and steel. It does boast the (relatively discreet) longest champagne bar in Europe, but more important are the statue of Betjeman, holding on to his hat and gazing at the roof, and Paul Day's huge canoodling couple, either saying a big bronze hello or a smacker of a goodbye, under the traditional meeting place of the station clock.

White-gloved stewards and stewardesses stand by the open door of each carriage, smiling and optimistic, multilingual with a suggestion of multitalented. Their onboard announcements rotate as the journey progresses, according to the host nation of the moment.

The train's interior is grey with streaks of rusty orange, the staple colouration of boutique hotels, although some of the upholstery is beginning to look a bit tired after years of trampling feet and squirming backsides. Seats come in clumps or in singles, with tables or without, in coaches that could be family designated or (supposedly) mobile-phone free, all of which needs to be stipulated at time of booking. Certainly the coaches are so well insulated that a crying child at one end can be heard right down the other, with little ambient noise from the passing landscape to drown it out, so making the right choice is important.

What the Dickens?
Initially, there's very little to see. The train quits London through a concrete canyon, shrugging off one of the world's greatest cities in a few brief minutes, passing close to the 2012 Olympic Village along the way. The train stops briefly at a concrete-clad ditch called Ebbsfleet. Most British

Paul Day's statue of a canoodling couple at St Pancras, top left; a mustard field in Kent, below left

SIDINGS

The only major stopping point on the Paris route is the city of Lille, 30 minutes south of the Tunnel. Lille has become hugely popular with British weekenders thanks to the Eurostar, and rightly so. Thanks to its part-Flemish origins, it is far more highly decorated than most French cities. Architecture here is colourful and busy rather than monumental and severe, and interiors are warm and highly wrought. It all looks particularly splendid after dark, when coloured lights play on the belfries, the Chamber of Commerce and the Opera House, and the cobbles gleam on the central square. Despite appearances, the historic centre is within walking distance of the Eurostar station; first head for the original railway station (which is the far more attractive of the two).

Lille, with its Flemish baroque style, is a compact, Frenchified version of Brussels, the other major destination for Eurostars from St Pancras. The Belgian capital is famous for its beers, museums and Grand Place – a giant central square that looks the same as it did in medieval times and is now a UNESCO World Heritage site. Journey time to Brussels is a bit shorter than to Paris, and the Brussels Eurostar is well used by a mix of stag parties, who relish Belgian beer, and by politicians commuting back and forth to the European parliament.

In relevant seasons, the Eurostar also runs ski trains to Bourg Saint Maurice, Aime la Plagne (outbound only) and Moutiers, Disneyland Paris trains to Marne la Vallée, and long-distance services right the way through to Avignon.

passengers will have never heard of the place and be surprised that it merits a dedicated international station, but Ebbsfleet's purpose is to serve those passengers who don't want to take on the hassle of London in order to catch the international train.

Not long afterwards, the train crosses the River Medway at Rochester, a town which has a long association with Charles Dickens, although you might not want to ponder the detail, for the latter part of Dickens' life was marred by the consequences of a train crash that he experienced on the way back from France.

Suddenly the landscape improves. This is the garden of England, with orchards and even occasional vineyards, as well as some of England's most expensive property, which partly explains why it took such a long time to complete the high-speed line.

By now it will be noticeable how the Eurostar gobbles up hills; huge power means that the train no longer has to make prolonged detours to avoid inclines, as it did back in Dickens' day.

Instead, it swoops across England's southeast corner like an articulated skateboard.

Tunnel vision

Three-quarters of an hour after leaving London, you'll be slowing alongside the marshalling yards of the Channel Tunnel, with the high-sided box trucks of the car-carrying trains visible across the fences. A brief announcement, the train dips, and outside all is dark. The Tunnel transit takes around 20 minutes, although it may well seem longer to some passengers; panic attacks are not uncommon on these trains, particularly among those unaccustomed to train travel and who find the whole concept of going under the water extremely alarming.

Then the daylight returns, but with a difference: it's French. Come the evening, the tracks at this end are the focus of security patrols, as dozens of asylum-seekers do their utmost to get on trains heading north into the UK, but this daylight train heading south will be of no interest to them. For passengers, there's not a

BEST BIT

The sensation of flying on land when the train hits top speed.

TOP TIP

If you have never travelled on a high-speed train before, try to get a seat facing the direction of travel to avoid feeling strange.

PHOTO OP

Paul Day's canoodling couple under the clock at St Pancras. Or the train's long yellow snout.

ANORAK INFO

The Man in Seat 61 (a certain Mark Smith, with his excellent rail website, www.seat61. com) says that seat 61 has the best outlook.

USEFUL PHRASE

'Sacré bleu, quelle vitesse!'

TRAVELLER'S FARE

In First Class, culinary highlights include bubble and squeak or a choice of viennoiseries. The bar car has vegetable gratin and Belgian waffles. Posh children's meals are also available, but you must request these when you book.

DESIGN DETAIL

The colours and patterns of the train interiors are the work of Philippe Starck.

OVERHEARD

'Jacques, I have an awkward question. Is our au pair staying with you?'

lot to see; high-speed trains generally avoid towns and villages, and soon the Eurostar is out among largely flat agricultural land, carved up by pollarded willows, heading fast for Paris. In the train's early days, the sounding of a gentle bell used to signify when it had reached top speed, for those passengers who were interested, but these days the moment goes unrecorded, apart from in the driver's cab.

The landscapes resolve and dissolve, spiked occasionally by distant watertowers (like concrete chalices) and by Flemish church spires. The giant, ploughed fields, interrupted by poplar-lined waterways, become a succession of watercolour images, hard to watch and blurred by speed, so the passengers settle down for the long haul to Paris. They talk quietly, get on the phone or go to sleep.

On board, this mid-morning train is a cross-section of the English middle-classes, relatively well heeled and approaching retirement age, who are waxing lyrical to each other about their own lovely little corner of south-western France. The talk is of barn restorations and the difficulties of finding an architect who speaks English.

Then there's the British executive who works for a Parisian bank, on his regular mid-week commute to sit at the meeting table with his bosses. He freely admits that, in his department of 100 staff, only ten per cent fully understand what it is they do; the rest, he says, are just like him: putting on a good show.

And then there's a handful of American youngsters, for whom the whole train experience is extraordinary, ludicrous and hard to comprehend. 'What time does this ship get in?' one asks the stewardess.

Cafés and connections

After the concrete vault of the station at Lille, where the English middle classes de-train for their high-speed connections to the south, there's no more stopping before Paris. For a while the train runs alongside the main A1 autoroute,

IM Pei's pyramid at the Louvre; Gare du Nord

moving at least twice as fast as anything on the road, and then come the first signs of a big city. The canals, the warehouse distribution centres, and the villages that have unwillingly become dormitory towns.

Eventually the Eurostar has to relinquish its super-train status, and starts to share the track bed with double-decker suburban trains, whose journeys are just starting out. But we're nearly done, and with graffiti-covered walls closing in, plus a glimpse of Montmartre, we have slowed to walking pace and are gliding to a halt.

Paris Gare du Nord may not have been prettied up to the same extent as St Pancras, but it is handsome enough, and has a grittiness and an atmosphere of suppressed excitement, engendered by the meeting of international train travellers in multicultural Paris. Besides the Eurostar, the station has high-speed connections to Benelux countries and on to Germany, as well as normal trains to northern France, and it is also sitting on top of a giant suburban hub that spews out Parisians during rush hour. And unlike St Pancras, it has a range of inexpensive hotels and restaurants directly outside, in a *quartier* that is lively and welcoming. This is a place to sit with a café crème in hand and study physiognomies spilling out of one of the world's great railway interchanges, but it's also a place where you need to keep a good eye on your bags.

TRAVEL INFORMATION

There are 18 daily Eurostar services between London and Paris, and ten between London and Brussels. Some services are non-stop, but some trains make stops at Ebbsfleet, Ashford International, Calais and Lille. On weekdays, the first train from St Pancras departs at 5.25am (weekends 6.22am); the last departure is usually 8.05pm. Reservations are essential. Details on www.eurostar.com.

Start
BARCELONA
Finish
MÁLAGA
Via
ZARAGONA,
LA MANCHA,
CÓRDOBA
Journey time
6 HOURS

Spanish fly

As fast as an aeroplane, the AVE lets you breakfast in Barcelona and then cavort on the Costa del Sol. By **Peterjon Cresswell**

Only France and Japan have more high-speed train lines than Spain. This once backward system of sleepy Talgos and circuitous Cercanías today has a more extensive inter-city rail network than Germany or China.

The pride of its rail fleet, the AVE ('Bird' or Alta Velocidad Española), first took flight in 1992, the year of the Expo in Seville, home of the then ruling socialist leader Felipe González. Coinciding with the 500th anniversary Columbus celebrations, this was pioneering stuff in the post-Franco boom years. Spain was no longer an insular anomaly whose broad-gauge railway allowed no army to invade, and it no longer kept its trains at pre-war pace. Anyone who boarded the AVE felt Spain was approaching the new century as part of Europe, on the world stage.

Barcelona hosted the Olympics, support for which allowed González to connect his power base of Andalucía – the poor, backward south – with the capital, Madrid.

The Bird covered the 293-mile distance in 2.5 hours, although 'covered' is doing the Bird a disservice; it floated. Its passengers took in the free movie, while the Bird delivered them with air-conditioned ease to a region where running water, electricity and mechanised farm transport were comparative newcomers.

And then it stalled. Although the AVE continued to shuttle smoothly between Madrid's

converted Atocha and Seville's spanking new Santa Justa Station, it flew no further. Consecutive governments dithered over the budgetary and logistical nightmare of extending the line to Barcelona – Spain's economic hub, tourist magnet and doorway to France.

By the time the link finally opened between Madrid and Barcelona, in February 2008, the budget airlines had long been operating the same route over rugged Aragón. The world had moved on. There was little fanfare.

And now, a year later, without launch or ceremony, the first AVE has gone the whole nine yards, the entire length of Spain from north-west top to south-east tail: Barcelona to Andalucía. Direct. You can do a late breakfast in Barcelona and plunge into the Med in Málaga six hours later while the mid-afternoon sun is still fierce.

This alone is miracle enough. But, in between, you won't just travel; you will be greeted, ushered, and waited on as you stretch your legs, cushion your back and tuck into your meal shortly before siesta time.

BELLS & WHISTLES

BEST BIT
The heat as you step off at Málaga.

TOP TIP
Barcelona is the pickpocketing capital of Europe.

PHOTO OP
Pose with the AVE and attendant staff before it sets off.

PACK THIS
A pocket fan for Málaga.

ANORAK INFO
The first AVE trains were French Alstoms – chosen, it is rumoured, as a thank you to the French government for helping to find Basque terrorists.

USEFUL PHRASE
'Hable más despacio, por favor' ('Speak more slowly, please')

SOUVENIR
RENFE's metal cutlery comes held together with a dinky clothes peg, ideal for hanging up your cossie in Málaga.

TRAVELLERS' FARE
Lunch was pork casserole with orange-and-mustard sauce, potatoes and mangetout.

DESIGN DETAIL
The AVE bird logo is deliciously retro.

OVERHEARD
In the train bar – everything. Spain is the second-loudest country in the world after Japan.

But that's all ahead of you as negotiate Barcelona Sants – platforms 1-6 for AVE are sectioned off from the commuter chaos – for the 10.25 to sunny Málaga. A casual security search brings you to a ticket check, and your first real waft of luxuriant aftershave. Perhaps it's standard-issue along with the purple ties, but male employees of RENFE spend much time and money on their toilet before smiling gracefully at foreigners' poor grasp of Spanish.

Descend past more greeters, some in white gloves, and you will be shown your carriage as if it were your seat at the cinema. You almost expect valet parking. Gershwin rhapsodises in blue as you settle in to your wide chair (in mid-priced *preferente*), spacious chair (in cheap *turista*) or bloody great chair (in exclusive club). Passengers in both *preferente* and club are treated to free dining, to prepare you for a siesta.

Sun, sand and siestas

Today's AVE is more subdued than the pioneering experience of 1992, but some constants remain. Just after 10.30am departure, a hair-gelled RENFE hunk passes through, dishing out headphones for the loudly overdubbed Hollywood blockbuster soon to be screened. In club and *preferente*, free newspapers are distributed – you might find an *International Herald Tribune* in the mobile rack between *El Mundo* and *El País*.

Despite the table service, the smart, stand-up cafeteria does good trade. *Preferentes* save their appetite with something *para picar* – a dish of olives, perhaps – while those in *turista* may choose between sandwiches packed with tortilla, stuffed with a chunk of loin, or with thin smoky slices of Iberian ham. This will not be something shrink-wrapped, date-stamped, sanitised or bar-coded; it's that day's bread (fresh, crunchy, rustic and floury), spread with fresh tomatoes and presented with a genuine smile.

Back at your seat, the tower blocks of suburban Barcelona have given way to that horizon emptiness that Spain shares with Australia. The digital display above you registers the time, temperature and train speed of the Siemens-made S-103. A relief map hints at progress through the surrounding highlands.

At 11am, you hit Tarragona, Camp de Tarragona that is, the new station just built for the high-speed line, five miles from town. Like most stops on this route, its platforms stand Potëmkinesque surrounded by wilderness.

Shortly out of Tarragona, the clock hits 186mph, the speed at which aircraft land, and your ears pop. No worries, you are soothed with a complimentary drink at your seat. '*Benvinguts a Lleida*', welcomes the signboard at the next soulless station. You will soon leave Catalunya for Aragon, but on-board announcements continue in Catalan, Castillian and English.

As you head for Aragonese hub Zaragoza, aridity becomes apparent. Everything is being sprinkled or showered. At 1pm sharp, the

---

SIDINGS

The landscape may be a blur, but there are significant places to see if you want to break the journey. The key sight in Zaragoza is the Basilica de Nuestra Señora de Pilar, with its monumental shrine. The Virgin Mary is said to have appeared here, standing on a pillar, in the first century AD.

Ciudad Real in La Mancha has a Don Quixote Museum, which celebrates Cervantes' fictional knight, who rode through these landscapes with his loyal sidekick, Sancho Panza, tilting at windmills.

Córdoba, once the capital of southern Spain during the era of Moorish rule, is home of the beautiful mosque of the Mezquita, since converted into a cathedral.

And Málaga's most famous son, Pablo Picasso, has his own museum, containing some 200 of his works.

The fast track to Málaga

preferente menus are dished out ('granary or white bread, sir?'). 'Gourmet lunch' is accompanied by a decent Rioja Viña Real Crianza and no admonishing looks if you ask for another quarter-bottle. After clearing away the laptop-friendly, drop-down tray table, they even hand out a mightier-than-mini of Torres 10 Gran Riserva brandy as a digestif.

You pass beneath Madrid for Ciudad Real. This is the flat land of La Mancha in the heart of Quixote country. The temperature outside climbs as you touch the button to recline your seat and pull down the gauze window blind. Snooze, you're in Andalucía – it's sleepy time down south.

Just after 3pm, many alight at Córdoba, transfer station for the region. Verdant land around the Guadalquivir river gives way to two more ghost stations, Puente Genil-Herrera and Antequera-Santa Ana, followed by the last stretch, where horses graze around dirty streams, and then Málaga, arriving at 4.15pm.

Named after the local 20th-century philosopher, Málaga's María Zambrano Station is a newly opened mall, equipped with the Vid bowling alley and the Magnolia jewellery store. A begloved RENFE greeter runs across the platform to help a lady passenger with a pram. As you cross the busy road outside, a fat couple zooms by on one motorbike, music blares from somewhere and the Med beckons.

¡Andalucía! Ay, mi corazón… Your inner Strummer leaps for joy at the sheer audacity of it all: Sants to sea in six hours. That first caña of beer is going to get caned, make no mistake.

TRAVEL INFORMATION

The daily Málaga-bound AVE leaves Barcelona Sants at 10.30am. Timetable and prices at www.renfe.es. In Barcelona, both the Hotel Torre Catalunya and the Expo Hotel (both on www.expogrupo.com) are convenient for Sants Station and have rooftop pools. In Málaga, the (ahem) Hotel California (www.hotelcalifornianet.com) overlooks the beach.

Start
PARIS
Finish
NICE
Service
iDTGV
Journey time
5 HOURS

French connection

You can fly to the Riviera without leaving the ground on this high-tech train for hipsters. By **Tristan Rutherford**

Agatha Christie's *Mystery of the Blue Train* conjures up images of American heiresses and bankrupt British aristocrats on the sleeper service to the south of France. The rich and famous of yesteryear, F Scott Fitzgerald and Winston Churchill among them, were lulled down to the French Riviera in unparalleled comfort aboard the sleeper cars of the Train Bleu. This first-class-only route started in 1922, six years before the publication of Christie's novel, and mirrored the exclusively business-class air routes of today.

In preparation for the night train departure, passengers would have a Churchillian feast inside the Gare de Lyon's Le Train Bleu. This gilded establishment is still the embodiment of rococo overstatement, all velvet drapes, herringbone parquet and chandeliers in a carriage-shaped interior. Ceiling frescoes illustrate the delights of the route's winter-sun destinations; the palm trees and parasols of Monaco and Villefranche. The lavish setting is perfect for a three-hour lunch, and the €52 prix-fixe menu of foie gras de canard, roast lamb and patisserie, with a robust claret, is a good way to relax into the rhythm of a regal rail trip.

21st-century toys

That said, the passengers on today's Paris–Nice run are a very different bunch from their formal forebears. They choose sushi over steak tartare, reserved open-plan seating over dandified porters, and wireless connectivity over rubbers of bridge. French rail operator SNCF's iDTGV service offers all of these 21st-century trinkets, plus the chance to mingle with fellow first-class passengers in the bar. It's full-service concierge travel for the Star Alliance generation.

Five years ago, SNCF's raison d'être was to battle falling passenger numbers as travellers flocked to budget airlines. In December 2004, they rolled out their latest incarnation of the high-speed TGV service to its battleground states: the Riviera, Marseille and Toulouse. Research indicated that customers wanted the choice between quiet or boisterous carriages, draught beer or good coffee in the bar, not to mention printable e-tickets. The promise of slick city-to-city travel, in less time than it took to check in, board and pass security for a low-cost flight from

Gare de Lyon in Paris, top; the Provençal countryside, far left; PlayStation portables are available for hire

---

SIDINGS

The 20 train stops between Cannes and the Italian border are just a few kilometres apart and offer access to the entire Côte d'Azur. These are best explored by the local trains, which ply the scenic coast in both directions every 30 minutes. In summer, the inexpensive Carte Isabelle offers unlimited daily travel on these trains.

salles de bain. Ladies upstairs, gentleman downstairs. Although brown and charcoal grey plastic has replaced the panelled pine features of the original train, the coat hook, magazine holder and chest-high mirrors let you make your toilet in relative luxury.

Twenty minutes outside Paris and there is a barely perceptible advance of speed. The birch forests of the Ile-de-France make way for the desert-flat fields of northern Burgundy, which resemble an algae-topped lake as far as the eye can see, its obstacle-free green sheen crying out for land-speed records. For a while, we run alongside the autumnal trundle of the A6 motorway. The cars push 74mph, but the train advances past them – it's got the advantage of an additional 124mph, a speed hitherto the realm of video games. Speaking of which, a flashing bandolier of PSPs (PlayStation Portables) lies charged and ready for hire at the bar.

Things are getting lively in there. A touch of acid jazz is followed by 'Ain't No Mountain High Enough' by Diana Ross. Under the bauble lights, ladies from first class tuck into wraps, caesar salads and vodka-laced mango lassis. (The bar staff are as accommodating as they are genial.)

Headed for the future

Down the carriage, it is a post-work Friday night for those from second class, who are laughing hugger-mugger in a corner. A third group check out the DVDs for hire; *Jack Black* and *Ratatouille* among more authentic French art-house fare. *Messieurs* stare out of the windows through their *pressions* (served in proper glasses), safe in the knowledge that they are five kilometres closer to their destination with each passing minute. No traffic jams here. The shadows are long, though, with the train casting a fleeting outline across the jaggedy hills of southern Burgundy – France's answer to Derbyshire or Vermont.

A wander through to the Zap carriage is a vision of the future, far removed from the historical elegance of this route's illustrious past.

Orly or Charles de Gaulle, was essential. For the iDTGV, you can now book online for a noise-free 'Zen' or a lively 'Zap' seat, then board – and buy a drink – 20 minutes before departure. And you can carry as many bottles of liquid, knives and firearms as decency allows. As a result, iDTGV's routes boasted an 87 per cent occupancy rate in 2007, a figure that would make a budget airline boss envious.

On a recent run to the sun, the Zen first-class carriage fills up with a decorum not usually associated with Friday evening rail travel. Each set of luggage is wheeled into place well before departure, as eager faces whisper the curiously elegant phrase '*Messieurdames*' – a mangled 'ladies and gentleman', which expresses a 'hello everybody' with a hint of 'I'm also as well brought up as you are'. A minute before take-off, each occupant settles down with a copy of *Le Figaro*, *Paris Match* or the *Herald Tribune*.

The Parisian suburbs whoosh eastwards, as passengers take the opportunity to sample the

BELLS & WHISTLES

BEST BIT
Overtaking the cars outside Paris at 198mph.

TOP TIP
Silence your phone, and catch up on R&R in Zen class. Sleeping kits, with eye patches included, available from the bar.

PHOTO OP
Sunset over Burgundy fields (right side of train).

PACK THIS
A DVD from the €5 stands in Paris, in case you don't fancy the iDTGV selection.

ANORAK INFO
A TGV carried the entire cast and crew of *The Da Vinci Code* from London to the 2006 Cannes Film Festival. The trip took a mere seven-and-a-half hours.

USEFUL PHRASE
'*Pourriez-vous baisser le volume sur votre iPod s'il vous plaît?*'

SOUVENIR
'PlayStation thumb' from a 90-minute session of Splinter Cell, Wipeout or Virtual Fighter 4. Rent a PSP and you get to keep the dinky earphones.

TRAVELLERS' FARE
Ricard for chilling out, mini *saucissons* for porking out.

OVERHEARD
'Do you mind if my shih-tzu sits next to you?'

Don't forget to look up from your gadgets to gaze at the Riviera

Technology worth €100,000 has been invested in each 40-person car. A medley of iPhones and iPods, DS Lites and Blackberries light up as passengers twitter, blog and chuckle into their screens. The laptops are faddish and frivolous, a sea of Sony Vaios and silver MacBooks – necessities or fashion statements? Reading lamps illuminate newly purchased hardbacks for those not partaking in this paradisus digitalis.

One lady on a table seat has too short an attention span for any of the above. Her long, confident curls and auburn streaks make a striking impression. The seat is shared by an impeccably behaved shih-tzu – Tibetan, she explains in English, although she could likely have done so in French, Italian or Spanish (one could imagine her conversing in Via Montenapoleone, Place Vendôme and Bond Street). Madame's Christian Lacroix sweater is in keeping with SNCF ethos: the Parisian fashion designer is currently working on the design for the new TGV interiors, which will encompass family cabins, business areas and more bars.

A young businesswoman is sitting next to Madame, in white shirt and black pants. Emails are tapped out on her PC – a workaday Dell – but remain stuck in her out-box for want of an outgoing mail server. Her vigilant attention to bullet points and subheadings is a lesson in advanced Word formatting. Did she deliberately select a seat online that was close to a power socket? Oh the joy of dissecting other people's lives and habits over the course of a five-hour journey – and from the comfort of an armchair!

An hour from journey's end, and the iDTGV is hemmed in by the Mediterranean on the right, and travelling at the same speed as the A8 motorway to the left. To run a train à grande vitesse, you need a ligne à grande vitesse, and there's little space for one amid the quaint bustle of the Côte d'Azur. Each station we slowly pootle through – St Raphael, Antibes, Juan-les-Pins – still has a whiff of the old high life, the kind associated with the 1920s art deco tourist posters that once advertised the region. During that Belle Epoque, the Train Bleu had a fierce competitor in the form of the Bentley Boys, an obtuse bunch of British, moneyed, gin slingers, which included diamond magnate Woolf 'Babe' Barnato and Le Mans winner Dudley Benjafield. This posse raced their turbocharged Bentleys from Cannes northwards against the speeding train. The Great Depression took its toll on the former, while the latter got speedier still.

Nice Airport's new terminal building passes by in a blue flash as we veer away from the A8. Our plane-beating train eventually eases its length into Nice–Ville Station, faster and more graceful than its airborne rivals.

SNCF are rolling out this high-speed, high-luxury concept over the entire French network and beyond. Roll on, we say, roll on.

TRAVEL INFORMATION

The iDTGV (www.idtgv.com) concept has been rolled out over much of France. Its sister project, iDNIGHT (www.idnight.com), follows the same routes, although journey times are generally much longer. Aimed primarily at younger passengers, the service features an open carriage that hosts events including DVD screenings, DJ sets, language lessons and poker tournaments.

There are a handful of little-known hotels in Paris that can add a pretty, yet inexpensive, addition to your journey. The Hôtel de Nesle (www.hoteldenesleparis.com) in the Latin Quarter and the Hôtel du Panthéon (www.hoteldupantheon.com) by the Jardin de Luxembourg are both gems.

In Nice, the Hôtel Suisse (+33 (0)4 92 17 39 00) boasts superb views over the Mediterranean and is particularly recommended, while the Villa de la Tour (www.villa-la-tour.com), situated in the Old Town, offers year-round budget charm.

Start
MUNICH
Finish
FRANKFURT
Via
NUREMBERG
Journey time
3 HOURS

Fast and fashionable

Zoom across Germany on the ICE3, a *wünder* train that has set the pace for intelligent design. By **Anthony Lambert**

At 9.55am precisely, the Frankfurt-bound ICE3 glides out of Munich's 1960s train shed and weaves its way through the tangle of tracks that forms the approach to every major terminus. Passengers, many of them businessmen, start to unfurl their *Süddeutsche Zeitungs*, accompanied by the gentle susurration of laptops being stirred into action by conscientious owners.

Such exits from big cities are seldom a delight to the eye; the railway builders naturally chose the cheaper districts of town to lay waste and make space. But after turning north-west,

there is a tantalising glimpse of Munich's well-wooded Nymphenburg Palace park, the 18th-century summer residence of rulers of Bavaria, with its ornamental canal and a decorative bastion in the curtain wall.

Once out into the country, the line to Ingolstadt passes villages of houses with roofs so steeply pitched that they have three levels of dormer windows, vying for height with a slender church spire. As the last suburban stations are left behind, the landscape of low hills is covered by vast treeless fields and dark impenetrable forest straight out of a painting by Caspar David

Friedrich. After Pfaffenhofen, fields of hops conjure up evenings in Munich's fine beer cellars, best enjoyed out of the tourist season. Spindly wooden towers for hunters punctuate the perimeter of the woods, but by now the landscape is becoming blurred, so it's a good moment to take in the interior of Europe's finest high-speed train.

For travellers dismayed by the increasing homogeneity of the rail experience, the ICE3 (an acronym which stands for the third major design of InterCityExpress) is enough to restore their faith in intelligent design. This train does not try to copy the interiors of aircraft or of luxury buses, with their moulded plastic and moquette, but uses quality materials like wood and leather and imaginative lighting to create a distinctive environment. Though the ICE has never achieved the worldwide fame of the French *Train à Grand Vitesse (TGV)*, there is no contest when it comes to passenger ambience.

Crystal clear

ICE operation began in 1991 with the opening of the first two sections of German high-speed line, known as Neubaustrecke (NBS), which stretched between Hannover and Würzburg and between Mannheim and Stuttgart. The ICE3, with its attractively shaped sloping nose, was introduced into service in 2000, and export versions are operating in Spain, China and Russia.

Unlike its predecessors, the ICE3 has powered axles distributed along the length of the train, dispensing with the need for power cars at each end. This means that the end cars are available for seats, and the designers seized the opportunity to give passengers the popular option of sitting behind the driver with a view of his cabin and the line ahead – or behind an empty seat watching the track recede. The windows are made of two layers of glass sandwiching liquid crystal. The driver can make this opaque by cutting the power supply to the liquid crystal

Frankfurt, left

BELLS & WHISTLES

BEST BIT
Sitting behind the driver.

TOP TIP
You'll not get that top seat unless you reserve well in advance.

PHOTO OP
Taking pictures out of the windows will be tough if you haven't got a camera with a shutter speed of 1/500th second.

PACK THIS
IP3 player with the *Ride of the Valkyries*.

ANORAK INFO
Admire the surviving half-roundhouse locomotive shed at Würzburg, with a backdrop of vine-covered hills. Also note: the train has reached speeds of 228mph in trials.

SOUVENIR
Model ICE from Deutsches Museum Verkehrszentrum in Munich or the Verkehrsmuseum in Nuremberg.

TRAVELLERS' FARE
Dishes are cooked to order in proper dining cars.

DESIGN DETAIL
That liquid crystal screen behind the driver.

OVERHEARD
'*Schneller als die Polizei erlaubt!* (this is faster than the police would allow).'

should he want to block passengers' views (in the case of an emergency situation, for instance). One end car is first class and the other second, so both classes of passenger have the chance to sit in the row of seats behind the driver.

But there is technology on display outside the window, too, as the train slows near Ingolstadt, the birthplace of Audi cars, and dives between trainloads of vehicles waiting to be sent across Europe to countries that crave *Vorsprung durch Technik*. Simpler pleasures are evident in the allotments in the Ingolstadt suburbs; here, an immaculately tended piece of *rus in urbe* is a source of pride. Fussy villas fill the gap between Hauptbahnhof and Ingolstadt Nord, at the south end of the first section of Neubaustrecke.

Once you are on the high-speed line itself, it feels as though a tightly reined racehorse has been given its head as the ICE3 accelerates at an impressive rate, and passengers' eyes turn to the panel at the end of each coach, where red numerals show the speed rising steadily. Will it make the magic 300km/h (186mph)? Even at this speed, the train is rock steady, causing no anxious moments to staff serving in the restaurant car. The only drawbacks are the frequency and length of tunnels, some built solely to placate objectors to the new lines.

Emerging from a tunnel, the train passes through a pleasing landscape threaded by the River Altmühl, before it is snatched away by the next penetration of the hills in the Fränkisch Alb. Just before Nuremberg, the line crosses the broad canal linking the Main and Donau rivers.

Judgement of Nuremberg
Nuremberg's handsome historic buildings and museums lie out of sight, to the north of the Hauptbahnhof (main station). However, it was at this industrial centre that the story of the country's railways began, with the 1835 opening of the railway to Fürth, using a locomotive built

Munich is arguably Germany's most attractive large city and has a wealth of palaces, museums, art galleries, parks and churches. The Verkehrszentrum of the Deutsches Museum pays tribute to the ICE in its romp through centuries of human mobility.

Though badly bombed, Nuremberg has some outstanding museums, most notably the German National Museum and a fine transport museum with its replica of *Der Adler*. The highlights of a visit to Würzburg's Residenz are Tiepolo's fresco *The Four Continents* and the Imperial Rooms.

Frankfurt is known as a business and exhibition centre and lacks Munich's charm, particularly around the railway station, but it has an outstanding collection of German Old Masters in the Städelsches Kunstinstitut and Städtische Galerie. In the Goethe-Haus, where the writer spent his childhood, many of the original artefacts have been brought back to give a good picture of late 18th-century bourgeois life.

by Robert Stephenson in Newcastle-upon-Tyne. *Der Adler* (*The Eagle*) was shipped from England in 19 crates across the North Sea and down the Rhine, taking four-and-a-half weeks.

We're travelling considerably faster than that. Leaving Nuremberg in a westerly direction on a conventional line, at what seems like a crawl after the exhilaration of three miles a minute, the railway again crosses the Main–Donau Canal. A whole field of solar panels after Emskirchen speaks of the quest for a low-carbon economy and a second railway age, as the benefits of low-friction, steel wheel on rail reassert themselves.

Just before Kitzingen, the railway vaults over the River Main, large enough to take small ships. As the country flattens, the agriculture intensifies and a huge wind farm takes advantage of unobstructed air currents. The towers and dome on the skyline of the charming city of Würzburg tempt one to break the journey, to visit the World Heritage Site of the Residenz (an immense Baroque palace), the similarly elaborate Marienberg fortress and the *Hofkirche*.

Passing vines stretching up the hill above Würzburg, the train sets out on the last leg of the journey, taking the Neubaustrecke to Fulda as far as Rohrbach, where it curves west to join the River Main. The latter flows through high wooded hills before railway and river part company at Rohr, as the train heads through the hilly area known as the Spessart to reach Aschaffenburg.

During the remaining miles, the ICE passes the village of Dettingen where, in 1743, George II became the last British monarch to lead his troops into battle, defeating the French. Soon the impressive, modern skyline of Frankfurt captures the eye, and just before the station, the ICE makes its final crossing of the river Main.

At 1.05pm, the ultimate in German train technology eases into Frankfurt Hauptbahnhof, under the immense roof of what was once the largest station in Europe. Though rudely obscured in places by tawdry retail kiosks, a monumental stone arch makes a fitting gateway to Germany's financial capital, and an impressive finale to three hours and ten minutes of cutting-edge train experience.

TRAVEL INFORMATION

For details of the timetable, visit the website of Deutsche Bahn International (www.bahn.de and click on 'English'). There are regular trains during the day, and trains also run throughout the night. Recommended hotels at either end of the journey are the Mandarin Oriental, Munich (www.mandarinoriental.com) and the Hotel Bristol, Frankfurt (www.bristol-hotel.de)

Riding in the front

It's not just a boy thing. It seems anybody who likes trains wants to ride in the front: with the driver in his cabin, or on the footplate – anywhere to get a full sense of the train's speed, power and the surreal way in which it is led by the nose by a set of steel threads.

Of course the schoolboy's dream of 'riding in the front' (ie with the driver) has been banished by 'health and safety' culture, but what the industry takes away with one hand, it gives back with the other, thanks to modern technology. Germany's new 186mph ICE3, for example, has banks of seats directly behind the driver, who is separated from the passengers by a see-through screen (*see p77*). Meanwhile, Switzerland's latest Golden Pass trains also have seats in the front, on an upper deck above the driver's head, affording great all-round mountain views. Moreover, if you want to get a sneak preview without leaving home, there's also a webcam in a driver's compartment on the Montreux – Zweisimmen route

(www.bildersammlung.ch/bahn-webcam-goldenpass/webcam.php).

In the UK, you can ride in the front of London's automated Docklands Light Railway (DLR), enjoying the way this dibbly-dobbly little train swerves and dives through imaginary hills and valleys, surging and braking and picking its way through points. It seems a frivolous form of transport for London's financial powerhouse, but don't be tempted to make engine noises, as you're likely to be surrounded by serious executives trying to look important.

Not to be outdone by London, Paris also offers a chance to sit in the front, but under the ground. Metro Line 14 from Gare St Lazare is fully automated, and passengers who grab the front seat get the full effect of onrushing darkness, interrupted by brief flashes of stations' fluorescent lights. Sliding doors on the platforms prevent suicides; not something you want to witness when you're riding in the front.

Andrew Eames

ICE3 train

Start
TOKYO
Finish
SAPPORO
Journey time
17 HOURS

A yen for luxury

Japan is famous for its bullet trains, but the sleek Cassiopeia sleeper emphasises comfort over speed. By **Danielle Demetriou**

It is 4pm at Ueno station, Tokyo. The slow-building daily crescendo towards rush hour is gathering pace, as a grey-hued tsunami of salarymen and office ladies sweeps across the concourse. But beyond the bento box stands of fresh sushi, the steaming noodle counters, the neon lights of the convenience stores and the surging crowds of tired office workers, there's a less predictable sight.

Sitting at platform 13 is a sleek metal-grey train with a rainbow-striped logo and a double-decker structure. There is a crowd gathered here too, but they are different from the ones in the station: these are reverential, wide-eyed, digital camera-snapping, 21st-century trainspotters.

Japan has long been synonymous with cutting-edge rail travel. Jostling alongside sushi and sumo, cherry blossoms and misty mountains, neon skyscrapers and robots, its trains take pride of place among the most iconic of Japanese images. Ever since Japan proudly unveiled to the world its maiden fleet of *shinkansen* bullet trains during the 1964 Tokyo Olympic Games, the country has positively revelled in its position at the vanguard of a high-tech travel revolution.

More than four decades on, the gleaming cavalcade of sleek, safe and blink-and-you-miss-them trains remains one of the most powerful symbols of the nation's economic post-war recovery. But speed is not the only attraction, for in this fast-paced modern age, there is one Japanese train that remains something of an anomaly: the Cassiopeia.

A luxury night train that prides itself on comfort over speed, the Cassiopeia is a sleek beast that transports passengers from the skyscrapers of Tokyo through mountains, rice fields and fishing villages to the city of Sapporo on the northernmost island of Hokkaido.

The Cassiopeia takes a leisurely 17 hours and 12 minutes while travelling at a top speed of 68mph – as opposed to the 186mph bullet train – so its appeal is clearly not speed. Its charm lies in an altogether different direction: that of luxury, design and comfort, combining to create a modern appreciation of passing landscapes in traditional rail-travel style.

And so there are plush, rainbow-hued carpets, immaculate stewards, cotton *yukatas* (casual kimonos) and slippers, newspapers delivered to the door, and an on-board boutique,

as well as a dining car serving high-end French and Japanese cuisine. But the icing on the romance cake is the accommodation: it is the first Japanese train where every traveller on board is allocated one of 83 private en-suite berths of escalating degrees of luxury.

It is little surprise, therefore, that a regular prelude to the three-times-weekly departure is a cluster of trainspotters staging an impromptu photoshoot in front of the train – which gleams as good as new, despite running since 1999.

True to form, in a country where watches can be set by the trains, the Cassiopeia discreetly slides out of the rush hour chaos at precisely 16.20, as scheduled. On board, the atmosphere is one of subdued excitement mixed with a vague lack of direction at the prospect of the endless hours ahead. Swaying along the cinnamon-carpeted corridors with neat rows of rooms on two floors, I make my way to room 21 on carriage eight – and weave up the small flight of stairs before entering my home for the next 17 hours.

SIDINGS

From the moment the doors glide open, and passengers set foot on Cassiopeia's carpeted corridors, there is little doubt that few will budge from the train before its arrival the following morning. With its 4pm departure and 9am arrival, the train journey is designed to provide a full evening of leisurely eating, sleeping, window watching and stargazing in order to arrive in Sapporo relaxed and refreshed. And so there is little point in stopping off on the way – unless a passenger's idea of fun consists of swapping a warm train suite at 4am for a cold, empty platform in the Middle of Nowhere.

In contrast, the beginning and end points of the journey are major destinations. Ueno Station sits next door to one of Tokyo's main attractions: Ueno Koen park. The serene and sprawling green space brims with lotus ponds, Shinto shrines, art galleries, museums and cherry trees as well as a zoo. A lively antidote to the calm, green park is the nearby Ameyoko flea market, where hundreds of bazaar-style stalls create a bustling frenzy alongside the railway tracks.

At the other end of the journey, the wide streets and pleasantly sedate atmosphere of Sapporo belie its status as the fifth-largest city in Japan. If you arrive in February, you'll witness its famous annual Sapporo Snow Festival, where a string of elaborate ice sculptures attracts more than two million people every year. Regardless of the time of year, food should also top the agenda for any visit to Sapporo: from its ramen noodles to spine-tinglingly fresh seafood, the city features on the hit list of Japanese food-lovers.

The room is an exercise in compact design. There is a small living space surrounded by two plush seats that can be rearranged, Rubik's cube-style, into two perpendicular beds.

The carpets are deep green and the seating an abstract purple pattern, which, according to an unwritten design rule, is always used on public transport. A narrow door leads to my en-suite bathroom, a small plastic unit containing a toilet, and a complicated contraption that pulls down from the wall and doubles as a sink with a constant supply of hot water. A techno-unit to satisfy the most demanding of gadget-lovers sits on one wall, complete with a small, multi-channel television, as well as heaters, coolers, lighting and an alarm clock.

But the focal point of the spotless room lies elsewhere: a vast, gently curving window-framing a technicolour Tokyo landscape of skyscrapers and neon lights. My eyes drink in the passing cityscape until my reverie is interrupted minutes later by a high-pitched cry of 'Irashaimasseeeeeee!' ['Welcome!'].

Tokyo, tea and tofu

I open the door to find a train stewardess with perfectly coiffed hair, a brilliant smile and turquoise silk neckscarf, bearing a welcoming cup of green tea. This is the first of what later transpires to be a helpful team of cloned Stepford Wife stewardesses.

Tea ceremony over, I wander along the spotless corridors with neat glowing vending machines towards the Lounge Car at the front of the train. Here, the focus is once more on the view: a long, emerald-green sofa faces one wall of windows and violet swivel chairs are lined up on the other, while the engine carriage is viewable through the front.

Guests gathered here form a motley crew: wide-eyed honeymooning couples, father-son trainspotting teams and neatly hatted pensioners enjoying the good life, after years of toiling as overworked salarymen. 'I've wanted to come on this train for years,' says one elderly gentleman with a grey hat. 'I'm here with my son now and it's been worth the wait.'

BELLS & WHISTLES

BEST BIT
Checking into your private room, putting on your complimentary slippers and gliding calmly away from the chaos of Tokyo's rush hour.

TOP TIP
Upon arrival in Sapporo, head to a hot spring *onsen* or public *sento* bath – the perfect way to relax, wash and stretch after the long journey. Visit the tourist information centre in the station for directions.

DON'T FORGET
To draw the curtains while in a state of undress to avoid startling rural commuters as you pass through stations.

PHOTO OP
Make sure your camera is by your pillow when you go to sleep, to capture those middle-of-the-night or first-thing-in-the-morning images.

PACK THIS
Unless piped orchestral arrangements are your cup of tea, a pair of ear plugs for both the lounge car and early morning room announcements.

SOUVENIR
Mugs, model trains, playing cards, pencils – a raft of train-themed paraphernalia is available in an on-board boutique to satisfy the most hardcore of trainspotters.

Soy story: the train is known for its superb Japanese cuisine

By now, the setting sun is illuminating shafts of light through cotton-wool clouds, adding beauty to a drab scene: a seemingly endless sprawl of concrete apartment blocks, grey office towers and flashing shopping centres. As the train nudges itself northbound without any sense of haste, the sun eventually sinks behind the buildings, heralding the arrival of another highlight on board the Cassiopeia: dinner time.

By 8pm, the dining car is almost entirely filled with smiling couples and, although it may not be in quite the same class as the *Orient Express*, there is a distinctive and elegant ambience: it is decorated with library-style table lamps, white linen tablecloths and lavish table settings, and the gentle clank of creaking wheels just adds to the atmosphere. There's pink champagne for the coupled-up diners, and the menu is emblazoned with the saccharine words: 'Wishing for this journey brings you something special [sic].'

While the words 'train' and 'good food' are rarely seen in the same sentence, Cassiopeia's offerings surpass all expectations: from the four-course French menu, including beef filet and asparagus and crab salad in balsamic vinegar, to the traditional Japanese feast of rice, seafood, tofu and soups in an array of beautiful lacquerware containers.

People-watching aside, the best mealtime entertainment comes in the form of window gazing: outside, piles of snow line the tracks as the train stops briefly in the bustling neon station of Fukushima, known for its spring blossoms, before continuing its northerly pilgrimage.

Then, while tucking into my sweet 'mochi' rice pudding, a smiling steward taps me on the shoulder and pours a glass of pink champagne before gesturing towards an elegant elderly Japanese couple at the other side of the restaurant. I lift my glass in thanks; it seems that even a single female dining alone on the Cassiopeia is entitled to a touch of romance.

Back in my berth, I wrestle with the purple seating and piles of clean white bedding before a window-side bed magically manifests itself before me. Slipping into a purple cotton *yukata*, I slide into bed, resist the temptation to watch bad Japanese TV, flick off the lights – and am instantly enchanted by my view of the passing night sky through the curving window.

A giant butter yellow moon has appeared in the chill night air, illuminating a nocturnal landscape of small towns, rice fields, empty streets and lone cyclists. All of these slowly blur into one as I am rocked into sleep.

The perfect storm

An unidentifiable number of hours later I am jolted briefly awake, realise we are unaccountably now travelling in the opposite direction, and then plunge back into a world of train-themed dreams.

Sunrise incurs a less rude awakening: a silver light infuses my berth, prompting me to stare sleepily out of the window. And the sight that greets me is breathtaking: streaks of white clouds fractured with shafts of light hang above a still expanse of sea, which, in turn, is lined with piles of snow on the shore.

An island of snowy peaks, rural dairy farms and mouthwatering seafood delicacies, the northernmost Japanese island Hokkaido is a million miles from the fast-paced *Blade Runner*-style world of the capital.

It is hard to believe the still white vista before me inhabits the same universe as the frenetic Tokyo I left behind. To add to the sense of otherworldliness, I register that the train is now moving in its original direction once more – and dismiss my nocturnal apprehension as sleeping-on-train-induced confusion.

The in-room intercom system crackles to life at around sunrise, with a xylophone jingle, and a quintessentially Japanese breakfast follows, consisting of a bento box of rice and vegetables bought from a smiling trolley lady and washed down with complimentary green tea.

With only a few more hours until our final destination, I make my way down to the lounge as a perfect snowstorm gathers pace: heavy flurries of snow bluster across the small fishing towns, coastal beaches and forests.

The sense of slowly travelling back in time is compounded by the revelation that the train is now powered by a blue, Thomas the Tank Engine-style engine puffing plumes of black smoke. A young trainspotter with glasses and a yellow anorak enthusiastically confirms that I wasn't dreaming the previous night: the train always switches direction briefly in the middle of the night as the original electric locomotive is replaced with a diesel engine.

The snow continues to fall heavily as the train creeps past a steady build-up of offices, shops and apartment buildings. Eventually, finally, leisurely, the Cassiopeia pulls into the bustle of Sapporo Station, and back to reality in the form of morning commuter crowds, food halls and convenience stores. Stepping off the train and swaying slightly as I adjust to terra firma, I feel fully relaxed in the knowledge that there is no need for me to look at my watch: without a shadow of a doubt, it is precisely 17 hours and 12 minutes since we set off from Tokyo.

TRAVEL INFORMATION

There are three train departures a week. The train usually departs Tokyo's Ueno station at 4pm and arrives in Sapporo at 9am the next day, but schedules are subject to change. The official Cassiopeia website (www.jreast.co.jp/cassiopeia) is in Japanese; you can also contact Japan Rail (www.japanrail.com) or book tickets on www.accessjapan.co.uk, www.jtbusa.com and www.japantravel.com.au.

Faster than a speeding bullet

The chic new era in rail travel, as epitomised by the dynamic acronyms in these pages – AVE, ICE, TGV etc – was actually first discussed 80 years ago, when Japanese railway engineers came up with the concept of a high-speed service running on a dedicated track. But it wasn't until 1964 that the *Shinkansen* ('new trunk line') trains came into service between Tokyo and Osaka, just in time for the Tokyo Olympics. Their speed and their cone-shaped noses quickly earned the moniker by which they are now universally known: the bullet train.

It wasn't just Japan's appetite for innovation that gave birth to the bullet – it was force of circumstance. Thanks to the country's mountainous territory, the conventional (narrow-gauge) Japanese rail network was struggling to cope with demand. The only way of increasing both carrying capacity and speed was to create a dedicated standard gauge track (*see p25* **Size matters**), and to use bridges and tunnels where there once might have been gradients and curves.

The first route, known as Tokaido (Tokyo to Osaka), passes the iconic Mount Fuji. It initially travelled at speeds of up to 124mph; these days it runs at up to 186mph and has been matched (and surpassed) in speed by other high-speed rail systems around the world. But not one of these trains can as yet match the bullet train for sheer punctuality, with average arrival time within six seconds of scheduled time; or for safety, with no fatalities in 44 years of operation. The nation has since introduced several other bullet routes, with new designs and shapes of trains, but the Tokaido remains the busiest, carrying a staggering 375,000 passengers a day, with an average of six departures per hour.

Today, Japanese engineers once again hold the world speed record for rail travel with their JR-Maglev MLXO1 train; it runs on a magnetic levitation system, reducing friction to practically nil. It set a new record of 361mph back in 2003, considerably faster than the speeding bullet, but so far the Maglev has proved too costly to develop beyond the prototype stage.

The Nozomi bullet train travels the Tokaido route, from Tokyo to Osaka, in two and a half hours

In this era of globalisation, the true frontier-crossing experience is increasingly rare. No more no man's lands, midnight interrogations and slavering dogs. Thank heavens, you might say. But there should always be a frisson of excitement to the changing of nations, no matter that the journey itself may only be a dribble of ink on a map.

Crossing a border is often more than just a shift in language or currency. It could mean crossing a cultural minefield, as with the journey from Sarajevo to Ploce (*see p108*). Or it could be a journey back in time, as with the Hungarian from Berlin to Budapest (*see p96*). And borders generally have some major topographical feature, as with the Bernina Express (*see p90*), which climbs mightily to cross the Alps from Switzerland into Italy – and opens the next section in this book.

Border Busters

The armchair mountaineer

On the Bernina Express, you can scale the Swiss Alps and plunge into Italian lakes without leaving your seat. By **Andrew Eames**

The Swiss may be known for avoiding wars, but they've never sidestepped a challenge when it comes to trains. Forget that they live in one of the steepest, most topographically awkward nations on the planet; forget that the mountains yield some of the trickiest weather conditions in Europe. In the genesis of railways, somebody forgot to tell them that trains don't go up mountains: the country is riddled with ditsy little bahns, many 100 years old, which look puny and arthritic in the valley bottoms, but still manage to trundle up vertiginous rock faces with unflappable ease.

You name it, they've run a railway up it, through it and across it, by hook or by crook, by rack or by pinion, and by Albula and St Moritz. Those last two are key locations on two of the country's most spectacular trains, the Glacier Express and the Bernina Express; the former travels within Switzerland, from Zermatt to St Moritz, clambering up and down valleys and clinging to the side of the mountains like a lonely goatherd, while the latter covers much of the same route, but continues on, over the top and down the other side, leaving the ordered life of Switzerland behind and dipping down into the intoxicating pastoral world of northern Italy, finally coming to a halt among lakes and vineyards.

But they've both got a lot in common. Like the Glacier Express, the Bernina is a train of chicanery, one that bounds off cliffs and galleries of rock, does corkscrew turns inside mountains, and is recognised by UNESCO. But the Bernina trumps the Glacier in one respect: it is the highest railway crossing in the Alps.

Peaks and valleys

For a train that does all this, the Bernina Express looks surprisingly sweet in its station at Chur – a rather understated place for the oldest town in Switzerland. There's nothing understated about the train, though. Painted bright red, gleamingly clean, running on metre gauge tracks and boasting panoramic windows, it looks more of a plaything than a serious method of transport. Its passengers are well dressed, cosmopolitan, and rather well fed; they don't look like they're about to go mountain climbing.

Leaving Chur at a civilised hour (8.30am), the Bernina makes a modest start. Moving steadily alongside the baby Rhine – so different here from the barge-heavy highway it turns into in Germany – it eventually turns south, diverging from the Zermatt line after Reichenau, and heads into the lower Albula Valley. This is fertile country, dotted with fortified churches and ruined castles, some dating back to the 12th century. JMW Turner, ever the lover of dramatic landscapes, included the Ortenstein castle, perched on an outcrop of rock and highly visible from the train, in his view of the Domleschg Valley. Thusis, named after the 'torrent' where two rivers meet, is the last

A view from the bridge: crossing the Albula Valley between Preda and Bergün

Start
CHUR
(SWITZERLAND)
Finish
TIRANO
(ITALY)
Via
ST MORITZ
Journey time
4 HOURS

BELLS & WHISTLES

BEST BIT
The Albula Pass, realising that you've just emerged from the mountain directly above where you entered the tunnel.

TOP TIP
For the best views, sit on the right side if you're travelling towards Tirano.

PHOTO OP
Frankly, the best images are going to be taken from a helicopter, but if you can't manage that then try to get an image of the Landwasser Viaduct from the back of the train.

ANORAK INFO
This four-hour journey crosses 196 bridges and goes through 55 tunnels.

TRAVELLERS' FARE
There's a snack and minibar service on the train.

DESIGN DETAIL
Keep an eye out for famous Glacier Express wine glasses, with slanted stems to prevent the gradients from spilling your drink.

OVERHEARD
'Ahhh, cow poo, the Nina Ricci of the Alps.'

Eyes on the prize: passengers ogle the scenery near St Moritz, above, and Preda, top right

substantial town before the track begins a long haul upwards. Here the valley steepens quickly, and the river below, now the colour of glacier mints, disappears into a dramatic ravine. Above it, the train criss-crosses the gorge, creaking like a sailing-ship in a full-bellied wind, never satisfied with one side or the other, and resorting to tunnels before emerging for a breather at the village stop of Tiefencastel.

The next stretch is all climbing, largely through forests, with dramatic views down to the right when the trees allow. A mile after Alvaneu, the train crosses the tall, graceful arc of the Landwasser viaduct, whose 50-metre legs plunge deep into the dark of the canyon below.

Then come the Alpine villages of Filisur and Bergün, dotted with sgraffito decoration, and still with traditional barns where the cows stay in the

winter. Bergün, in particular, is a gentle, handsome place with wrought-iron balconies and cattle troughs, and traditional families selling sausages and cheese from the kitchen door.

This was once a major staging post for horse-carriages heading over the Albula Pass, and it suffered when the railway opened for business in 1903. But what the railway took with one hand, it gave back with the other. Before long, wealthy English wintersports enthusiasts staying at St Moritz discovered that the now-unused bit of roadway between Preda and Bergün was ideal for tobogganing; once they'd hurtled down the closed road, they caught the

St Moritz started life as a spa, and its popularity was assured by the arrival of British tourists at the end of the 19th century, who encouraged the development of winter sports. These days it still carries an exclusive tag, with accompanying high prices.

In the summer, there's good high-level walking from Pontresina Station to the nearby Morteratsch Glacier, and if you break the journey here, you've got enough time to catch the returning Bernina heading back for Chur in the evening.

Tirano has two railway stations, one for the metre-gauge Rhätische Bahn, and the other for the standard-gauge Italian Railways. Many people hop on a bus from here to Lugano.

train back up again, fuelling a new toboggan-based tourism industry (see p95).

Uphill of Bergün, the Bernina Express ties itself in knots, climbing and climbing. This is one of the most famous stretches of track, the bit that UNESCO gets excited about, celebrated for the audacity of its engineering, the grit of its builders and the magnificence of its views.

Glaciers, glitz and St Moritz

The train plunges repeatedly into the mountainside, completing slow, disembowelling circles in the dark, as if looking for something, before emerging in daylight, 100 metres higher.

Beyond Preda, the track's architects gave up trying to humour nature, and opted for a 3.6-mile

tunnel instead. The Albula Tunnel took 1,000 workers four years to build, and it transports the Bernina into a new landscape in the shape of the Upper Engadine, a sunny, high valley. Here the main urbanisation is St Moritz, the end station of the Glacier Express, a winter sports resort with a long tradition and a fine line in fur coats and fake tans. The Bernina Express, however, sidesteps the town: it still has some important business to complete. It runs instead along the high Bernina valley, littered with old watchtowers and framed by mountains and glaciers, before making a final push to Ospizio Bernina, the highest point on the track, at 2,236 metres.

In fact, the Ospizio's height goes almost unnoticed: there's a new landscape to occupy the eye; the lakes of Lago Bianco and Lej Nair, and their strangely lucent meltwater, in stark, treeless surroundings. This is a true watershed; these lakes are the header tanks for a river system that descends into Italy, and helps create Lake Como below. The railway, too, descends, via more hairpin turns, tunnels and avalanche shelters, but most passengers have seen enough of the armchair cinema by now; snoozing is the order of the day. But stay awake for one final flourish: as the train enters a world of rich meadows, orchards and terraced vineyards, the majestic viaduct at Brusio – which resembles two-thirds of a steeply banked colosseum – delivers the train gently to the ground.

Finally, pretending to be a tram crawling along town streets, the Express crosses a square, passes a campanile and comes to a halt alongside a station building that looks no larger than a stationmaster's house. This, then, is Tirano – and we're in Italy at last.

TRAVEL INFORMATION

In general, trains depart Chur between 8.30am and 9am, and arrive in Tirano from noon to 1pm. All necessary information is on the Rhätische Bahn website at www.rhb.ch. Reservations are required. During the summer, trains with open-topped carriages travel between St Moritz and Tirano. There are daily buses from Tirano to the lake resort of Lugano, a three-hour trip.

Postcards from the sledge

During the winter, the trains between the villages of Bergün and Preda in the Swiss Alps carry an unusual extra cargo: dozens of toboggans and their riders, departing every day, every half an hour between mid-December and mid-March. And every day, the half-hourly train down again has to suffer the indignity of being overtaken by most of them.

For Preda to Bergün is Europe's most celebrated toboggan run, and in the three short months of its operation, it hosts over 120,000 high-speed heroes, who whizz down the stretch of roadway that links the two villages. The record descent stands at five minutes and 12 seconds, while it takes the train a whopping 17 minutes. Mind you, the tobogganists travel a mere three-and-a-half miles, while the train has to go twice as far, criss-crossing the ice-blue Albula river and circling around inside the mountain itself in search of a more controlled descent between the two stations. So if you want to sip a glass of wine and look at the magnificent scenery, don't take the toboggan.

Hire places are two a penny in Bergün, and there are several varieties of toboggan, depending on expertise and ambition. There's a choice of runs too: the main traditional piste down the road, for which you need to catch the train, and a second, newer one, which involves a chairlift up to Darlux with a dazzling view, and a hair-raising set of bends on the way down.

Whichever route you choose, you're bound to have a wipeout sooner or later. Fortunately, there's plenty of time to get your breath back on the train back up to Preda, which winds itself in loops around the mountains in an eye-poppingly exhilarating bit of engineering.

One of the interesting challenges of the main piste, down the road, is how it becomes steadily faster through the day. The grand finale is coming down it after dark, when the route is lit, and the melted bits have refrozen. When the sledge's runners hit those patches of ice, it is as if somebody has lit a rocket on your rear end.

Andrew Eames

For more details, see www.myswitzerland.com

Hungarian rhapsody

From Berlin to Budapest, via Prague and a dash of paprika, the Hungaria cuts across capitals and cultures. By **Nicky Gardner**

Four capital cities in one day sounds exhausting, but there is an easy way of doing it without having to stir from the comfort of your seat, thanks to one of Europe's most illustrious daytime trains. The Hungaria leaves Berlin early every morning, just as it has done for over 40 years, and 12 hours later it slides into Budapest Keleti, having taken in Prague and Bratislava along the way.

This is a train with a strong dose of history. Throughout the 1970s and 1980s, Communist party officials used the Hungaria to travel between East Berlin and Budapest, often stopping for a night along the way in one of the several Czechoslovak cities served by the train.

But this was not just a train for apparatchiks. For a generation of Cold War Berliners, the Hungaria was inextricably linked with holidays. An early-morning departure from Berlin meant that families could be on the shores of Lake Balaton in Hungary late the same day. The Hungaria was a chance to swap Prussian austerity for the fiery warmth of paprika and a fortnight of sun.

In fact, until shortly after the political changes of 1989, the Hungaria carried sleeping cars from Malmö to Belgrade, and it was always rumoured that diplomats travelling between Sweden and Yugoslavia used the train to arrange discreet encounters with contacts in the three Warsaw Pact countries through which it passed.

Since then, central Europe has swapped communism for a market economy and political frontiers have changed. The Czech Republic and Slovakia quietly sealed a velvet divorce, while the two halves of Berlin have come together in uneasy unity. The four capitals served by the Hungaria today all now look to Brussels as they play the European game. And travellers can ride from Berlin to Budapest without ever once having to show a passport, as Germany, the Czech Republic, Slovakia and Hungary are all now part of the Schengen zone.

Goodbye to Berlin

A dozen years ago, the Hungaria comprised a multicoloured parade of rolling stock from several countries. Today, the train is formed of a rake of eight blue Hungarian carriages, new enough to have some creature comforts and yet old enough to retain a dash of style. At Hauptbahnhof, Berlin's sparkling new main station – and a veritable crystal cathedral for transport – the Hungaria looks exotic. It is a migrant from the south that creeps into the German capital late each evening, and by six the following morning is cleaned, serviced and ready to head back to the Danube.

Berliners know how to party, and an early-morning departure from the Hauptbahnhof always carries a few jaded revellers from the night before. The Hungaria has space for all –

The Catholic basilica at Esztergom is a Hungarian icon, top; Hauptbahnhof Berlin is a crystal cathedral of transport, bottom

Start
BERLIN
Finish
BUDAPEST
Via
PRAGUE,
BRATISLAVA
Journey time
12 HOURS

TOP TIP
Sit on the left of the train for the first half of the journey, but change to the right after Brno.

BEST BIT
The hour-long run from Dresden south to Dûçin through the Elbe gorge.

BEST TIME OF YEAR
Definitely not a winter foray. May, June and September are the optimal months.

PHOTO OP
The Basilica at Esztergom.

PACK THIS
A reserve supply of food and drink. Very occasionally, that all-important dining car gets left off the train 'for operational reasons', and starving from Berlin to Budapest is no fun.

ANORAK INFO
Budapest has its own celebrated Children's Railway, a seven-mile route run by children aged ten to 14. The youngsters operate the signals, flick the switches and print the tickets (but the locomotives are driven by adults).

SOUVENIR
Tokay, tokay and more tokay.

DESIGN DETAIL
Inlaid squares of yellow and beige carpet on the ceiling of the second-class carriages are decidedly eccentric, but give a nicely oriental feel. For fans of retro style, there is orange galore.

OVERHEARD
'What's this red powder they've put on my chips, Mum?'

those who missed the last train home, business folk bound for meetings in Dresden and Prague, and a few canny travellers who know that the journey from the Spree to the Danube is one of the most interesting routes through Europe.

The ride from Berlin to Budapest is a European symphony, one that has more than its fair share of great castles and cathedrals, a route that cuts through mountain gorges and crosses vast plains and then concludes by hugging the River Danube for the final run down to Budapest.

Yet unlike many symphonies, this one does not start with an allegro movement. The train is tucked away on one of the lesser platforms of the Hauptbahnhof, deep in the bowels of this multilayered station. There is no pomp on departure, and the train slips quietly away at 6.35am, somehow understanding that it really has no business to be here in Berlin.

The most striking first image of the journey is how remarkably empty the landscape is. In the light of a summer morning, the medley of lakes and forests can look deliciously beautiful, but under winter cloud, the same landscape is flat and unappealing. By the time coffee has been served, the train is dropping down into the Elbe valley, with a distant glimpse of Meissen on the right, to what is surely one of the star cities on the entire route: Dresden. You know at once that you are entering another world from gritty Berlin. There are baroque domes aplenty and lush vineyards lining the north side of the Elbe valley. By dint of some ingenious 19th-century railway engineering, the Hungaria, which stops twice in Dresden, affords brilliant views (from the left side) of the city's principal sights.

The Hungaria's connection with the River Elbe becomes an intimate one: save for one brief detour to Prague, the route follows the river valley for hours, ultimately cutting through the Moravian-Bohemian uplands to the narrow mountain valleys that lead south to the Danube.

After Dresden comes Bad Schandau, a neat German resort town and gateway to hiking trails that weave through sandstone turrets. Then, the Hungaria comes to the most appealing scenery: the Elbe gorge. The train slips without remark across the border into the Czech Republic, and trundles past Bohemian riverside villages full of timber-framed houses, tottering barns and waving children. These are the lyrical landscapes that inspired Smetana's music 'Má Vlast' (literally, My Country). But it is not all a rural idyll. There are a good few abandoned factories and smokestacks too.

A village in Slovakia, bottom left; Rathen on the River Elbe, a region known as the Saxon Switzerland, right

Goulash for breakfast

Few are the passengers who really take the Hungaria from Berlin all the way to Budapest, but, for those who do, it is possible to enjoy breakfast, lunch and supper along the way. The train usually carries a nicely old-fashioned dining car, often staffed by two elderly women who chat animatedly about Hungaria in the old days, when stern-faced officials patrolled the train during delays at borders.

The dining car serves Turkish kava as a reminder that you are heading south; it takes euros, forints and Czech koruna. Paprika comes with everything, predictably, so the menu appropriately anticipates arrival in Hungary, with a range of Hungarian red and white wines for reasonable prices. Truly dedicated fans of

paprika can even enjoy Hungarian goulash for breakfast as the trains rolls smoothly across the east German countryside, and wash it down with a bottle of sweet tokay.

The beauty of the Hungaria is that the astute traveller can map out the hours of the day by observing the changing passengers. Businessmen and shoppers bound for Prague are replaced in the early afternoon by students on their way home from college. Army reservists come and go, a woman paints her nails to perfection from Bŕieclav to Kúty; there are workers who have slipped off early from their Bratislava offices and, on the final run along the Danube valley into the Hungarian capital, couples head into Budapest for a night out. The train stops at big cities, but also at little country

SIDINGS

The opportunities for stopping off along this route are legion, with the cities of Dresden, Prague and Bratislava all obvious candidates. Another possibility is Bad Schandau, the last station at which the Hungaria stops in Germany prior to crossing into the Czech Republic. Set in the most beautiful part of the Elbe gorge, it offers easy access to the area known as the Sächsische Schweiz (Saxon Switzerland).

Real devotees of long-distance train travel can easily connect at Budapest Keleti for onward overnight connections to Greece, Bulgaria and Romania.

Night and day: Budapest Parliament, left; Buda Castle, right

stations. Kúty is one of them. The first stop in Slovakia, the ramshackle old station house on the edge of the forest oozes faded grandeur.

The most celebrated sights in the cities along the route are often out of view (Dresden is an exception). As the train approaches Prague, there is a glimpse of the rear of the castle. There is also a fleeting moment after leaving Bratislava station when you can crane your neck for a view of the Slovak capital's great Habsburg fortress, the fiercely austere Bratislavsk Hrad.

The blue Danube

Along rural stretches, the Hungaria allows for a real engagement with the passing landscape. The train rarely hurries and, according to season, passengers will get close-up views of storks' nests, the wine harvest or locals breaking the ice to fish on frozen lakes.

The train does not quite touch Austrian territory, though as the route brushes the Danube north of Bratislava, there are glimpses of Austria on the opposite bank of the river. Having hugged the Elbe for hours, the Hungaria's approach to the Danube is more diffident. It dallies with the river in the marches north of Bratislava, but then nervously veers off on to the plains again. It is only as it approaches the Hungarian border that the train turns more purposefully towards the Danube. At this point, shortly after the Slovak border station at Stúrovo, the traveller is rewarded with the most dramatic moment. We are not yet in Hungary and yet there, across the Danube on the south bank of the river, standing proud and resplendent, is a Hungarian icon: the Catholic basilica at Esztergom.

By now the Hungaria is tired, the restaurant crew are cashing up, and passengers are gathering their belongings. The train winds its way into Budapest through a maze of suburban lines busy with evening commuter traffic, and finally ends its long journey at Budapest's Keleti Station. It is a magnificent terminus, a place that seems oddly foreign and yet familiar at the same time. Sculptures of two distinguished British engineers, George Stephenson and James Watt, smile benignly at the colourful chaos on the concourse. There is a hint of the Orient, money-changers and hustlers, and just across the platform, passengers with enormous quantities of luggage are trying to negotiate their way into a train that will shortly depart for Greece.

TRAVEL INFORMATION

Book well in advance for good value. Tickets can be booked online at www.bahn.de. Look for the Europa-Spezial Ungarn fare, which requires that you specify, and stick to, the exact trains you wish to use within Germany, from Berlin as far as the first stop in the Czech Republic at Dûçin. If you wish to break your trip in Dresden, for example, you must pre-specify at the time of booking the stopover points and the exact trains that you will use. Stopovers in Germany may not exceed 48 hours. But once in the Czech Republic and beyond, you may break your journey as you wish.

A daily Deutsche Bahn train, called the Jan Jesenius, follows exactly the same route as the Hungaria, but leaves Berlin four hours later. The travel time and the fares, subject to availability, are the same, but the Hungaria is more comfortable. Meanwhile, the Metropol provides a convenient third daily direct link, leaving Berlin at tea time and rolling into Budapest for a late breakfast. Its fares are higher and depend on the class of sleeping accommodation booked.

The Hungaria arrives at 6.30pm, so it's best to book a hotel in advance. The Art'otel Budapest (www.artotels.com) is a chic hotel on the banks of the Danube, with fine views of the river and parliament building; it's ten minutes by taxi from Keleti station. The hotel works in partnership with two hotels in Berlin of the same name, both well placed for an early morning departure.

Berlin stories: from suburbia to Stasiland

Who ever heard of Ahrensfelde? It's the final destination of Berlin's suburban S7 (S-Bahn line 7) train, but for some Berliners, it's considered no man's land. 'I've never been that far,' says the man on the platform at Potsdam, Germany, on the western fringes of Berlin. His expression of horror suggests that Ahrensfelde, an eastern suburb, might be at the other end of Europe.

But then he's from Potsdam, the most orderly place on the planet. Perfect precision underpins the landscaping in the gardens at its Sanssouci Palace. Perfect precision also characterises the cream-and-red suburban trains that head east from Potsdam every ten minutes, on a roller-coaster ride through the troubled history of the German capital. So why would pristine Potsdammers travel to a huge housing estate at the other end of the line?

Suburban train journeys are a great way to feel the pulse of great cities and the people who live in them. Whether on the suburban viaducts of Berlin, Birmingham or Barcelona, most suburban train journeys have a Betjeman-like beauty: garden gnomes and blackened girders, the pot-pourri of backyards, allotments and abandoned railway sidings, and the mundane chatter and ambiguous innuendo of people on their mobile phones – hints of sex, and talk of tennis or whether the beer is in the fridge.

Despite their air of nostalgia, Berlin's suburban trains don't jolt and bounce like their fellow railways around the world. They glide,

The S7 train bridges a historic divide, crossing from Berlin's suburbs into the old East Germany

and weft of the route as we cross the old border from West Berlin to East Berlin at Friedrichstrasse. Here, citizens of a divided city once shared tearful goodbyes and shuffled like prisoners through dismal underground corridors that linked the two Berlins. Now the S7 links both parts of a formerly divided city, running along the elevated Stadtbahn tracks, with fine views of many city landmarks along the way. The carriage design has scarcely changed in 80 years, reflecting the real affection that Berliners, both east and west, have for the S-Bahn.

'I live in Ahrensfelde,' says the young woman who sees us scanning our map of Berlin, as we slip by the gentle curves of the River Spree, the art nouveau Hackescher Markt and brutalist Alexander Platz, all viewed through a graffiti-covered window. 'I hardly ever go into the west,' says the woman, as she explains why Ahrensfelde is the very best of Berlin.

The leafy neighbourhoods disappear and the atmosphere changes as the train journeys east, out past Marzahn with its curving tower blocks of vast estates and the memorial to all the Roma people killed by the Nazis. Now the busker has gone and the train is almost empty, apart from us and our map. In Ahrensfelde, a stray dog greets the train. Coffee for 50 cents is sold in the kiosk by the station platform. Russians stamp their feet to ward off the cold. And a kid with a limp sells single cigarettes to passers-by. Welcome to the other Berlin. Walls may fall, but not all suburbs are paradise.

Nicky Gardner

To ride the S7 S-Bahn from Potsdam all the way to Ahrensfelde you'll need an Einzelkarte (one way ticket) valid for zones ABC, available from machines at all stations. A Tageskarte (day ticket) allows unlimited travel throughout zones ABC on virtually all public transport.

like quiet emissaries crossing the former borders where Great Powers once stood in stonewall confrontation. S7 is one of the best, linking royal palaces in Potsdam and Charlottenburg, and passing some grim historical stops along the way: Wannsee, where Hitler's cronies pondered the Final Solution in a lakeside villa, and Grunewald. The latter is haunted by the shadows of lost Berliners on platform 17, where 50,000 folk waited for the trains to Auschwitz. Today, another generation lives here in their little leafy paradises.

From Ahrensfelde to Auschwitz, this city's soul is scarred by destinations east. Yet its very vitality comes also from the same direction. A Russian busker on the train catches the warp

Start
GÖRLITZ
Finish
ZITTAU
(GERMANY)
Via
POLAND
Journey time
1 HOUR

Borderline personality

Map the course of European history – and zigzag across the old Iron Curtain – on this train without frontiers. By **Nicky Gardner**

Görlitz is the sort of town that is hard to leave. This German city may not feature on regular tourist trails, yet it has what is arguably central Europe's most picture-perfect city centre. The Untermarkt (Lower Market Square) is sheer perfection. The early 18th-century Baroque market hall, now the Hotel Börse, makes a fine centrepiece, surrounded by a striking ensemble of Gothic and Renaissance town houses.

Görlitz may perfectly evoke pre-industrial Europe, but it has another side: it is also the archetypal railway town. It blossomed in the 19th century because of its plentiful rail connections. A carriage works was established here, and today Bombardier Transportation continues Görlitz's long tradition of railway engineering.

The route for this short journey runs south from Görlitz up the Neisse valley to Zittau, another gem of a German town with a fine Italianate square. Beyond Zittau, if you wish to tick more countries off your list, the railway continues up-valley into the mountains of Bohemia in the Czech Republic. Few other short journeys so precisely capture the convoluted 20th-century history of Europe.

Cold war memories: winter and summer, the train weaves between Germany, the former East Germany and Poland

Cross purposes

Until World War II, both banks of the Neisse river were in Germany. That all changed in the summer of 1945, when the leaders of the victorious powers met in Potsdam to redraw the map of Europe. The east bank of the Neisse was assigned to Poland, while the west remained in the part of Germany that became the German Democratic Republic. This left a knotty problem for the Neisse valley rail route, which criss-crossed from one side of the river to the other.

These are tangled territories indeed. In addition to the complicated border between Germany and Poland, the Czech Republic has little pockets of territory that jut into its northern neighbours. It may be less than 40 miles from Görlitz up the Neisse valley via Zittau to Liberec, yet in that short span, the rail route manages to cross six international frontiers (for the extra leg to Liberec, *see p106*).

The prelude to the border-hopping train ride from Görlitz is the city's fabulous main station, with a booking hall that is a feast of art nouveau. Delicate shades of blue and cream, decorative chandeliers and Romanesque windows contrast with the stern modernity of Deutsche Bahn's silver and red travel centre.

Leaving Görlitz's elegant train shed, the route dives under the main east–west line that crosses the Neisse into Poland, then skirts the bank of

BELLS & WHISTLES

TOP TIP
Travelling south from Görlitz, grab a seat on the right side for the best views of the wild Neisse valley.

BEST BIT
South of the Polish stop of Krzewina Zgorzelecka along the Neisse gorge.

PHOTO OP
The Untermarkt in Görlitz – one of the finest town squares in central Europe.

PACK THIS
Your passport/document checks are rare, but you are required to have a passport or ID card when crossing Schengen region borders.

ANORAK INFO
Görlitz's old-fashioned train shed once sheltered expresses bound for cities across Germany and beyond. Even in East German times, there were daily connections to Cologne, Munich, Kraków and Warsaw.

USEFUL PHRASE
Flawless pronunciation of Krzewina Zgorzelecka will do wonders for your street cred with the locals.

SOUVENIR
Stop off at Krzewina Zgorzelecka for ciggies and a haircut – cheaply available at the kiosks by the station platform.

TRAVELLERS' FARE
Great-value refreshments are available from the onboard attendant. Have a coffee for less than a euro! Or a glass of sparkling wine for less than two!

DESIGN DETAIL
The button you press on the ODEG trains to get the driver to stop at a request halt is hidden on the underside of the luggage rack.

OVERHEARD
'Do you have any idea what country we are actually in now?'

the river and heads south. An announcer welcomes passengers aboard and advises them that they are required to ring the bell if they wish to alight at Weinhübel.

The little stations along the line are spartan. Some, like Hirschfelde on the German side of the river, offer only a simple glass shelter for protection. Others, like Krzewina Zgorzelecka station in Polish territory – though actually no longer served by any Polish trains – are magnificent essays in dereliction.

Some of the lesser stations, like Bratków in Poland, have been decommissioned, and the train slips through without stopping. The station house at Bratków is still inhabited, however, with a goat tethered to a post at the end of the platform. But the residents no longer notice the trains that zoom past their front door.

Yet there are other people along the route whose job it is to monitor the progress of the train as it weaves in and out of Poland. Just north of Krzewina Zgorzelecka, for instance, is the first of several signal boxes along the route. Look in the face of the woman in that signal box, as she leans out of the window to nod at the passing train. It's a face that has been delineated by the rhythm of the train timetable.

Through the barricades

There was a time when these criss-crossing trains were accompanied by a bevy of border guards. Before the modern Schengen piety, which permits most European travellers to cross frontiers freely, this border was delicate. East Germany and Poland, partners in the Warsaw Pact alliance, may have professed affection for each other, but in practice relations between the two countries were cool. And after Solidarnosc (Solidarity) brought liberalism to Polish politics, the East German regime worried that Poland's wayward tendencies might wash over the border and undermine their own authority.

Krzewina Zgorzelecka Station, top, is in Poland, but only serves German trains; Görlitz, bottom, straddles Poland and Germany

SIDINGS

This short journey can be extended by continuing from Zittau further south, up the Neisse valley to Liberec in the Czech Republic. Set in the mountains, this city is famous for its extravagant town hall and winter sports. The Liberec add-on takes an extra 40 minutes and involves yet one more detour into Poland before eventually reaching Czech territory.

Devotees of narrow gauge railways may prefer instead to sample the mountain railway that heads up into the hills immediately south of Zittau. Rugged little steam engines tackle steep gradients to reach the mountain villages of Oybin and Jonsdorf. This service is not just for tourists. Steam trains run daily throughout the year and are regularly used by local residents too. Find out more on www.soeg-zittau.de.

The joy of Saxony: a scene from the Zittau Mountains

And then, after German unification in 1990, when the former East Germany was assimilated into the European Union, the Neisse valley rail route criss-crossed the outer boundary of the EU. At every border crossing, fierce barricades were erected; passengers could catch a glimpse of German border guards keeping watch on the edge of Fortress Europe. The officials have gone, but remnants of the old preventative fences are still visible, particularly along the Polish section of the route near Rosenthal – a serenely beautiful village that lies on the opposite (ie. German) bank of the river from the tracks, its timber-framed houses offset by the barbed wire of the border.

South of Krzewina, the railway clings to a ledge hewn out of the side of the Neisse valley. Nearby are the gaunt shells of old Lutheran churches in villages that were once German, but are now Polish. Before you know it, the train slides back into Germany, and arrives at Zittau. From the station, it is five minutes by bus into the town's beautiful central area.

TRAVEL INFORMATION

The Neisse valley trains are operated by the Ostdeutsche Eisenbahngesellschaft (the East German Railway Company), or ODEG for short. These are modern railcars, with heaps of glass that afford panoramic views. The run from Görlitz to Zittau takes less than an hour. Complementing the regular ODEG trains are occasional weekend steam specials, beloved of railway photographers.

The journey is best undertaken as a day trip from Görlitz. Excellent accommodation is available at the Hotel Börse (www.boerse-goerlitz.de). Buy a EuroNeisse one-day ticket that allows unlimited travel by train, bus and tram throughout these interfingering frontier regions. All schedules for this cross-border area are online at www.zvon.de.

Deutsche Bahn provides direct connections to both Görlitz and Zittau from Dresden (75 to 100 minutes). This allows the Neisse valley route to be explored as part of a triangular day trip: Dresden – Görlitz – Zittau – Dresden. Schedules on www.bahn.de. Allow three hours to explore Görlitz.

Balkan beauty

War is over, so take a peaceful trip among the verdant landscape and varied peoples of a complex region. By **Peterjon Cresswell**

Travelling through a recent war zone and one of Europe's rare divided cities may sound like a dangerous chore; this journey is anything but. Twice a day, a quaint, plush Swedish train from another era saunters along through (mainly) the unspoiled and beautiful countryside between Ploce and Sarajevo. Two decades ago, this was a regular route between two destinations within the same country, Yugoslavia.

However, since the terrible internecine war of the early 1990s, the grimy transport hub of Ploce is now in the newly independent state of Croatia, on the Adriatic coast between the Dalmatian ports of Split and Dubrovnik, offering easy access to the idyllic Croatian holiday islands of Hvar, Vis, Brac, Korcula and Mljet.

Sarajevo, meanwhile, is the capital of Bosnia-Herzegovina. Once proudly multi-ethnic, it now heads a state of mainly Bosnian Muslims and Croats, while Serbs keep to their separate state of the Republika Srpska, with its own capital (Banja Luka), currency and all.

Sarajevo is not only safe, but very civilised. But Bosnia-Herzegovina's second city, Mostar, is a different kettle of fish. Famed for the Old Bridge after which it was named, Mostar lost both bridge and the mixed community who used

Mostar, above, is a beauty, but don't mention the war

few countries in the world with an abundance of pure, clean water, but supplies ran low during the Serbian siege of the capital, which lasted nearly four years, so, as in the Middle Ages, people stuck to trusted beer to quench their thirst; pivo literally saved Sarajevo.

Landscape and landmines

Expecting a dilapidated Tito-era rust bucket, first-time travellers are pleasantly surprised when they climb into the Sarajevo–Ploce train. Formerly belonging to Swedish Rail (hence the SJ signs), its pretty carriages contain beautifully upholstered wooden interiors. Maximum comfort is gained when you operate the little lever to the side, for these are tip-back seats, of the kind you might find in an old-style cinema. Sit back and let the scenery unfold.

If you're travelling in winter, it will still be dark outside. Still, the train is busy between Sarajevo and Mostar, two hours down the line. This is another pleasant surprise, because, in neighbouring Croatia, only tourists use trains. Here in Bosnia, students, pensioners and locals

it during the bitter conflict between Croats and Bosnian Muslims. The bridge is rebuilt; the community remains separate.

Leaving Sarajevo on the 7.05am train, you should see most of the pristine Bosnian landscape by daylight, and arrive at Ploce with plenty of time to make it north to Split or south to Dubrovnik the same day. Sadly, onward train connections to those ports are Balkanesque – and best avoided. Regular buses, on the other hand, take two to three hours to reach either Dalmatian hotspot.

Sarajevo is blessed with a decent tram system and plentiful, dirt-cheap taxis. Reaching the Socialist-era railway station, just north of the centre, is easy any time of day. You may even hear the muezzin's call as you arrive. A little bar inside opens early, and coffee is a local ritual. You may order it Turkish style, served with a little, long-handled pot – watch out for the gritty bits at the bottom. You could also ask for a Sarajevsko *pivo*, the local beer served in signature fat, brown bottles. Bosnia is one of the

---

SIDINGS

Bustling Sarajevo is anything but war-torn, and most of the city centre is rebuilt. At the crossroads of east and west, it oozes history, and religion – there is a mosque, Orthodox church, Catholic church and synagogue in the centre. But there are also hotels, cafés and restaurants with modern flair.

The historic, walled city of Dubrovnik has been renovated after the bombing of 1991/92. Pricey and tourist-swamped, it is at its best out of season. Cruise ships are regular visitors, as they are at the lively port of Split, whose centrepiece is a Roman palace. Split has a fabulous Riva, or promenade, and cheap boats leave here for the main holiday islands of Vis, Brac and Hvar.

of all kinds take advantage of the low fares to avoid negotiating the treacherous roads and summertime traffic.

At some point early on, a rotund Bosnian Muslim will pass down the carriage offering cups of hot coffee and bottles of cold Löwe beer, also made by the Sarajevo brewery. (If you're making the journey in the opposite direction, your server will be delighted if you pay with Bosnian marks and not Croatian kuna.)

Pretty soon the train is dealing with the switchbacks, tunnels and viaducts that are needed to negotiate the Bjelasnica mountains, a popular ski resort in winter. Sarajevo staged the Winter Olympics here in 1984, but within ten years the facilities were devastated. Still, in winter, the snowy landscapes are wonderful, if best seen from the comfort of a train. And after March, you could not imagine a more verdant scene, with water tumbling down hillsides and bubbling up from natural springs. Looks, however, are deceptive. Parts of the Bosnian countryside are still dotted with landmines – and walkers must never stray from a main path. It's safer, then, to admire the scenery from the train.

Into the blue

After the first major stop of Konjic, the train follows the green Neretva river due south all the way to Mostar, the capital of Herzegovina, arriving around 9.25am. Although the station itself is prosaic, set on the Muslim east bank, the views pulling in and pulling out are dramatic. Mostar sprawls over the steep banks of the thin Neretva, a pleasing mess of mosques, markets and bridges, overlooked by a humungous crucifix installed by the Croats after the war. The surrounding countryside offers an arid landscape of vineyards and fig trees.

Many passengers alight here. New arrivals comprise mainly backpackers and tourists, but there are some locals. And since Mostar is a hotbed of Croatian nationalism – a world away from the more progressive liberalism of Zagreb

BELLS AND WHISTLES

BEST BIT
The scenery coming in and out of Mostar.

TOP TIP
There is little by way of food or a buffet car, so buy your own produce the day before from Sarajevo's big Kosevo market, halfway up to the national football stadium.

PHOTO OP
Mostar's rebuilt bridge.

PACK THIS
Bosnian marks and Croatian kuna.

USEFUL PHRASE
'*Zivjeli*' ('cheers!') works in both Croatian and Bosnian. '*Prijatno*' is used in Bosnian to say 'You're welcome!' or a casual 'goodbye.'

SOUVENIR
Bosnian marks feature a range of obscure heroes on tatty banknotes.

TRAVELLERS' FARE
Thick, strong, Bosnian coffee, ladled with spoonfuls of sugar.

DESIGN DETAIL
The little lever to tip back your train seat.

and Istria in the north – try to avoid the topic of politics if you're chatting to your neighbour; the scars here are recent and deep.

Three hours from Sarajevo, at 10am, the train crosses the border easily at Capljina. The stop is longer on the Croatian side at Metkovic. An English-speaking border guard exchanges pleasantries and you're in Croatia – you can sense the clear, blue Adriatic ahead.

Pazaric Station, Bosnia, in the shadow of the Bjelasnica mountains

After drifting along the flatlands of the Neretva delta, popular with birdwatchers, you pull up to the singularly unattractive terminus of Ploce. Since the war, much of Dalmatia has been spiffed up for high-end tourism – most notably in Dubrovnik. But the modernisation process has passed Ploce by. It could still be 1975, with old drunks gathered around the beer kiosk outside, and the station grey and dismal.

However, within an hour, a bus will depart from the nearby coach station, bound for the brave new worlds of either Split or Dubrovnik. If you fancy two hours of stupendous coastal scenery, this is the way to do it, but choose which side of the bus you sit on carefully: for Split, the left side offers the best views of the Adriatic; for Dubrovnik, sit on the right. With a little luck, you may even make a late boat to the islands.

TRAVEL INFORMATION

For train schedules, check www.hznet.hr. The Sarajevo–Ploce service leaves the Bosnian capital at 7.05am and at 6.18pm, arriving four hours later, and sets off from Ploce at 6am and 5pm. Sarajevo has plenty of decent hotels – the recently opened Unica (www.hotel-unica.ba) has contemporary class; the Holiday Inn (www.holiday-inn.com/sarajevo) is a landmark from the war. To stay in Mostar, try the Emen (www.pansion-emen.com), a lovely B&B right by the Old Bridge. In Ploce, the waterfront Bebic (www.hotel-bebic.hr) is an acceptable three-star.

Start
BUCHAREST
Finish
BUDAPEST
Service
PLOESTI
SIGHISOARA
ARAD
Journey time
14 HOURS

In această casă a locuit
între anii 1431~1435,
domnitorul Țării Românești
VLAD DRACUL,
fiul lui
Mircea cel Bătrîn.

On the vampire trail

From gothic castles to Dracula's grave, the Pannonia ventures deep into the heart of Transylvania. By **Peterjon Cresswell**

For many, Transylvania is a place of ghoulish deeds and mystery, of Dracula and Peter Cushing films. For Romanians, Transylvania is the third of the trinity of territories – along with Wallachia and Moldavia – that comprises this surprisingly large country in the south-eastern Balkans. For Hungarians, Transylvania is the heartland of the nation, lost in a post-World War I settlement to Romania, and bitterly missed ever since.

Modern-day Magyars bear the scars of their perceived injustice with maps on car number plates, tattoos and T-shirts. Every third taxi driver in the Hungarian capital of Budapest will bang on about Trianon, the terrible treaty named after the Versailles palace where it was signed on 4 June, 1920. 'But didn't you know? Surely you must! Look at the map on this postcard!'

Away from horror films and historic grievances, Transylvania is most of all a bucolic delight, an unspoiled land-that-time-forgot, one defined and shaped by mountains, which are pine-sloped and dotted with fearsome castles and postcard-pretty churches.

The 14-hour train journey from the Romanian capital of Bucharest to its Hungarian counterpart takes you through an enchanting landscape, where the horse-and-cart is still a standard mode of transportation. From mid-morning until mid-afternoon, perhaps observed from the window of a comfortable dining car, the scenery rarely fails to satisfy. You won't see one global brand name, one hypermarket, one penned-in field. No Tesco in untamed Transylvania. And although this is the European Union, a trip here still means funny currency and time differences.

A butcher's at Bucharest

The journey begins in Bucharest. Big, crazy and Balkan, the former Paris of the East is forever improving, but never quite catching up with the rest of Europe. And certainly pre-dawn does not see the city at its best. Around the Gara de Nord, the city's main station (rebuilt in 1944 after Allied bombing), a chorus of hoarse coughing and fearsome barking signals that the homeless – on four legs and on two – are restless.

The metro, starting at 5am, should bring you from your base in town to this shuffling hub of dark activity. Outside the station, the taxi-filled square is centrepieced by a statue depicting 'Eroilor CFR 1916-1918', a monument to fallen railway workers. For Romanians, World War I began in 1916, and the worker heroes who fell until 1918 helped achieve the restoration of Transylvania to the Romanian fold. It's a fitting start to a journey across one of Europe's most patchwork territories.

First settled by Dacians (today's Romanians), then Magyars and Saxons, Transylvania was under threat from the Turks for much of the Middle Ages as sundry royals built castles

Gothic romance: Peles Castle, top; Bucegi Mountains, left; the birthplace of Dracula in Sighisoara, far left

around this dark and mysterious region. The most notorious, Sighisoara-born Vlad III Draculea, was the role model for Bram Stoker's fictional reworking of his myth: Count Dracula.

A hard-to-spot departure board – very little is signposted in Bucharest – opposite the

information office tells you that train 374 for Praha-Krakow (Prague and Cracow) via Brasov-Curtici leaves at 6.30am from platform nine. Budapest is not mentioned, but a walk along the eight or so carriages reveals a Hungarian MÁV logo interspersed with Romanian CFR and Czech CD. All go to Budapest.

The dining car is Magyar or Romanian on alternate days. If Romanian, the 'Bar-Bistro' will be modern and functional, but limited; if it's a Hungarian *étkocsi*, expect old-style comfort and reasonable menu choice. The Romanian takes local lei; Hungarians are also happy with their forints, euros, 'anything but German marks', as Rita the genial Magyar serveuse may jokingly inform you. Alongside, the 06.38 pulls in from Sofia, later bound for Moscow. Chain-smoking, cheap-suited hustlers from the Balkans pace the platforms. It feels a long way from the West.

Before a Romanian guard in a bright red hat and navy jacket blows a loud whistle, pick up a sandwich and hot drink at the superior Coffee Right/Gregory's; other snacks are sold at various stalls. A vendor goes through the stationary train corridors selling English-language magazines ('*National Geographic*! *Playboy*!').

Dogs and Dracula
After a punctual departure, the train rattles quickly through north Bucharest, past Lake Snagov – alleged burial site of Dracula, in a monastery on an island. It then heads towards its first main stop, Ploesti. The tangles of pipelines tell you that this town was built on oil.

Inside your overheated Romanian carriage, your fellow passengers – low-paid salesmen and older locals visiting relatives – have limited conversational English or French; educated white-collar workers would drive. Backpacking interrailers fill the bar car in summer. Seats, curtains and upholstery are authentically retro brown, embellished with the cool Romanian CFR train logo of a rushing locomotive. A ticket inspector arrives early on and is never seen

Night falls
outside
Prague

again. You could probably board the train at Ploesti and make it as far as the Hungarian border without being checked.

After the train passes Campina and Breaza, dawn slowly breaks – you'll spot more stray dogs and shuffling workers on the opposite platform commuting to Bucharest.

After Breaza, the train climbs between the mountain ranges of Bucegi and Baiului – pine trees appear and waters rush down steep slopes, past abandoned quarries. Holiday chalets dot the landscape near the ski resorts of Sinaia and Predeal and the hiking getaway of the Bucegi National Park. Ahead, Brasov is the biggest town on your Transylvanian itinerary – the bar car empties here. This is the heart of Saxon Transylvania, heavily industrialised under the Communists, and one of seven walled citadels that lend the region its German name of Siebenbürgen. Fortifications loom high above, accessible by cobbled streets thronging with tourists in summer.

The jewel in the crown

Having first set its compass due north, the train veers north-west, heading for a noon appointment with the jewel in Transylvania's crown: Sighisoara. A classic Saxon citadel, Sighisoara appears dramatic and fairytale-like – many travellers feel the need to alight here to explore and soak up some romance.

From here the Pannonia heads west, just north of the Fagaras mountain range. The first main stop, Medias, is another of the historic Saxon Siebenbürgen. Then comes Blaj, a seat of Romanian learning where the language was first written in the Latin alphabet; authentic Hungarian villages such as Torockó lie to the north. By now it will be lunchtime; you can take in the ethnic mix and dramatic landscapes from the restaurant car.

The Hungarian one comprises 20 tables regularly waited on by seen-it-all Rita, happy to regale you with tales of people smuggling and expert thievery. Only recently, she was robbed of her takings by a lightning-quick pickpocket working international trains. She grabbed him, called the police, screamed at him and stripped him naked, but no money was forthcoming. When the police asked for a description, Rita failed to mention his neckerchief – the same bright neckerchief used to tie up the wallet and fling it out of the window, an easy later find a specific distance from Brasov.

On quiet days, Rita serves perfect bean soup (babFleves), thick and hearty, plus a handful of grilled meats with potatoes or rice and garnish. Full-bodied Hungarian reds can be ordered by the glass. Specials are chalked up, in Romanian, on the board – Rita is one of those Magyars with no prejudices where Romanians are concerned. During the Christmas season, she puts up

decorations, the laptop switches from pop hits to classic tunes and old-style dancing breaks out down the restaurant aisle.

Budapest or bust

Alba Iulia marks the halfway point of the journey. Originally Hungarian, and capital of the region in the 1600s, this historic town was where Saxons and Romanians gathered to witness the declaration of the union of Transylvania with the Kingdom of Romania on 1 December, 1918. The day is still a national holiday for Romanians. The train follows the Mures west, past the dull town of Deva, gateway to Corvin Castle in Hunedoara, before leaving Transylvania proper.

After pretty Lipova, the flat landscape towards the last major Romanian town of Arad prepares you for the lifeless plains of south-eastern Hungary. Arad holds a particular place in Hungarian culture – after hanging 13 Magyar generals here in 1849, the triumphant Austrians clinked beer glasses. Even today, this custom is a no-no in Hungarian bars and beerhalls.

After Arad, the Pannonia crawls to the border town of Curtici, giving customs officials, armed with ladders and torches, plenty of time to search every nook and cranny for contraband cigarettes or Moldovan migrant workers. Stray dogs await thrown titbits. A half-hour wait, and the train rolls up to Lökösháza, Hungary.

The difference is palpable. First, no stray dogs. Secondly, train signs in bright neon switch from recognisable Latin to the obscure Magyar tongue, vowels crowned with bizarre long diacritical marks, 'tempests of acute accents all swaying one way like wind-blown corn', as travel writer Patrick Leigh Fermor once described them. At each stop, the station master steps out to greet each train. The catchy jingle ('Do-la-sol-LA-mi-fa-MI') that accompanies each train announcement earns its composer, Emil Petrovics, a couple of forints in royalties.

South-eastern Hungary, 'the windy corner' to locals, is the country's least inspiring region, and the remaining three hours to Budapest feel like three days. A late-afternoon lull descends.

The Pannonia ends its 14-hour trek by pulling into Keleti station, one of Europe's great steam palaces. Despite the presence of a mall alongside, Keleti still echoes the era when Budapest was the twin capital of a great empire, and all international services for the region passed through here. If the border crossing hasn't delayed your arrival, grab a celebratory drink at the Baross platform restaurant, named after the 19th-century minister who unified the Habsburg train network.

TRAVEL INFORMATION

For train schedules, check www.elvira.hu. The *Pannonia* now leaves Bucharest at 5.50am, and Budapest at 9.13am. Three additional services run each day, but each is an overnight sleeper, so you'd see little. In Bucharest, the three-star Hotel Opera (www.hotelopera.ro) has renovated *fin-de-siècle* charm. It is centrally located near Universitatii metro stop, convenient for the Gara de Nord. Budapest's four-star Best Western Hungária (www.bestwestern.com) offers a sauna, gym and Habsburg-style restaurant opposite Keleti station. To stay in Sighisoara, try the historic Casa Cu Cerb (www.casacucerb.ro), which also has an outstanding restaurant.

The rail to Damascus

Take a nostalgia trip on the Taurus Express, a colonial ghost train from Turkey to Syria. By **Andrew Eames**

Back in the glory days of empire, of pith helmets and diplomatic bags, the continent-crossing Orient Express – London to Istanbul – had a partner train that continued its stylish journey into the Near East. This Taurus Express had a similar profile to the Orient Express; all cut glass and cummerbunds, it carried adventurers, aristocrats, ambassadors, merchants and (of course) spies, most of them heading for the imperial territories east of Suez.

Back then, the likes of Syria, Lebanon, Palestine and Iraq were yet to come into being. Since the fall of the Ottoman Empire, their territories had come under British and French control and were heading inevitably for colonial status, until World Wars intervened and colonies went out of fashion.

But in the early part of the 20th century, there was still more than enough expansionist interest to make the Taurus Express, from Istanbul to Damascus and Baghdad, one of the world's great trains. It was also a train journey with something of a murky reputation, thanks to reports of unexplained deaths on board. Indeed, it was on the Taurus that Agatha Christie's *Murder on the Orient Express* begins, with Poirot getting on the train at the Syrian city of Aleppo for a journey back to London.

These days, the Taurus Express (locally known as the Toros Ekspresi) still exists, its murder count mercifully diminished, and you can still climb out on to that platform at Aleppo and try to evoke the spirit of Poirot. The train that goes by that name sets out from Istanbul's Hydarapasa station three mornings a week, but the vast majority of its travellers are not leaving Turkey at all. For them, the destination is actually the Turkish city of Gaziantep, 27 hours to the east. But once a week, on Thursdays, the Taurus also has a Syrian sleeping car attached to the back, a sleeper that slips discreetly away from the mother train as it nears its final destination, and then hightails it over the hills across the Syrian border. This single car is the only remnant of glamorous Wagons-Lits days.

The style may be gone, but the Taurus is still a wonderful journey, with grand scenery, a tangible west–east culture shift, a nervous border crossing, and like as not an intriguing mix of passengers. What's more, the journey begins and ends in two great cities.

Come spy with me

There are few better places to start a romantic journey like this than at Istanbul's Hydarapasa station. It rises out of the Bosphorus like a proud neo-German Schloss, complete with turreted corners. Most of its passengers arrive at its gates by ferry, having just made the brief but intoxicating crossing from Europe.

Inside, in the booking office hallway, the station pillars are covered with frescoes of

Eastern promise: Istanbul's Hydarapasa station, top; Aleppo, Syria, far right; Taurus mountains, bottom

Start
ISTANBUL
Finish
DAMASCUS
Via
KONYA
ADANA
ALEPPO
Journey time
27 HOURS

phoenixes and the high ceilings with floral rosettes. The clerks sit behind a screen of etched windows under an arch of coloured glass, with customers threading towards them between railings of polished brass.

On board the train, you're quickly aware that you're one of the chosen few. The blue and white Chemins de Fer Syriens sleeping car is quite distinctive from the rest of the train, both visually and literally: its connecting doors are locked, and even the Turkish train conductors have to come round via the platform to inspect your tickets. The tracksuited car attendants are Syrian, not Turkish, and they see it as their task to maintain the privacy of their little Syria-on-wheels, their double-bogeyed diplomatic bag.

The carriage compartments have sinks and bunks, and are clean and neat, but many of the passengers spend the journey in the corridor, talking and sipping Turkish coffee provided by the tracksuited attendants. You can't help but meet your fellow travellers on a long-haul journey like this, and I shared my trip with a Lebanese

couple returning from honeymoon, a middle-aged Romanian couple attached to the Romanian embassy in Damascus, and two rather brutal-looking young Syrian 'businessmen', who could easily have been the modern equivalent of gentleman spies like Robert Baden Powell, who travelled this train in the 1930s. Pretending to go butterfly-hunting, he travelled in disguise, and came equipped with preserving jars and nets on poles; in reality, he spent his time sketching Turkish forts and marine installations (the train is now supposedly spy-free).

With or without spies, the train takes an hour to shake itself free of Istanbul. Though it travels along the edge of the Sea of Marmara, it's not always pretty, with factories, piles of slag and mountains of scrap on one side, and containers, packing cases, cranes and wharves on the other.

After about three hours, it breaks away from the Istanbul–Ankara main line, swaps electric for diesel, and climbs complainingly up through a blizzard of orange groves before descending into a narrow, steep forested valley, which smells of

Turkish delight: the Taurus Mountains

sage and thyme. For a while, it chases its tail around the top end of the valley searching for an exit. As the trees fall away, it emerges into a high, scrubby grassland, yellowed by the sun. This is the Anatolian Plateau: wide, open and forlorn.

The weather here can be severe, and in places the scouring wind has driven off the topsoil, leaving only bare standing waves of limestone and outcrops of rock, which have been weathered into disturbing shapes – the stuff of nightmares for anyone who goes out for a wander alone at dusk.

For Taurus passengers, darkness falls in mid-plateau, and passengers will see nothing of the holy and ancient city of Konya, home of the original whirling dervishes. They may, however, be wakened by the screeching descent down from the plateau towards the Mediterranean, when it'll still probably be too dark for a view of the Çukurova Plain. Unless of course the train is already substantially late, which it usually is.

Border incident

Adana, the early morning stop, is a hot, uninteresting commercial capital on an uninspiring stretch of eastern Mediterranean shore, only good for buying sesame bread from vendors on the platform. The plain on either side of the city is a flat fertile landscape of cotton fields, each with its handful of Turkish women bent double, inching forward like coloured beetles on an ochre carpet. Just past Adana is the huge airbase of Incirlik, from where US warplanes took off to patrol the northern no-fly zone during the Iraq war. The scene on the other side of the fence is like a slice of suburban America, with bungalows on lawns, letterboxes on posts, gas-guzzling pick-ups on driveways and childrens' toys parked neatly round the back.

Then the train is climbing again, at tractor speed, this time into the steep, purple-veined valleys of the Taurus Mountains themselves. Flat-roofed box houses with trellised wigs of vines are wedged against the hillsides on piles of stones,

SIDINGS

If you want to break the journey en route, the obvious place is Konya, the holy city on the Anatolian Plateau. It was founded by the Hittites 4,000 years ago, but its heyday came 3,000 years later with the rise of the Seljuk Empire, when it became the capital of the Seljuk sultanate of Rum.

Among the religious section of the Turkish population, it has a trusted reputation as a spiritual centre, but it is better known to tourists as the home of the whirling dervishes. Sultan Mevlana, a deeply thoughtful and forgiving Sufi mystic, originally devised whirling as a way of achieving meditative ecstasy and ultimate union with God, but Konya is strict about the practice these days, and it is unlikely that you will see any whirling while you're here. In Konya, whirling is only allowed once a year, at the Mevlana festival in early December.

Istanbul, the Taurus's starting point, needs no introduction, but Aleppo, its final destination, is one of the world's unsung cities. Its big attraction is a medieval labyrinthine souk, where everything you could imagine is bought and sold under gloomy brick arches, and the fetching and carrying is done by donkeys. Outside the souk, the city is almost a mini Paris, with gardens and Haussman-esque architecture, and a massive and broody citadel watching over everything. Meanwhile the city's population is a heady mix of Kurds, Armenians, Syrians, Palestinians and even Russians, and it has one of the world's most unspoiled colonial hotels in the shape of the Baron, where Agatha Christie regularly stayed.

Just outside Aleppo are the so-called Dead Cities, barely touched ruins of Byzantine civilisation.

overlooking avenues of mountain fir, eucalyptus and slender cypress. Eventually the train comes to a halt at a glorified set of sidings called Fevzipasa, where the Syrian sleeper slips the leash from the main train, and is promoted to the head of a long string of trucks instead.

After a short pause this hybrid 'express' (just you and some trucks) jogs southward across high plains, where the soil becomes a thunderous, lava black, interrupted by lozenges of green where the young sweetcorn and tobacco have started showing through.

The Turkish border station is at Islahiye, where passengers are decanted from the train and have to file through the station office, clutching their passports. While they're away, the sleeping car is loaded with an unofficial cargo of sacks and cardboard boxes, manhandled into vacant compartments under the supervision of the tracksuited attendants.

Ten minutes later, the wire fences and ditches of the border itself heave into view. This is a serious crossing, with manned watchtowers, foxholes and machine-guns at the ready. A tense silence descends on the passengers, who are unused to being held in military cross-hairs.

The first Syrian checkpoint, Meydan Ikbis, is an empty and desolate place parked on a barren high plain, several hundred feet beyond the fence. Passports have to be handed in here, while a handful of boys ferret through the sleeping car to disinter all the sacks and boxes that were loaded on the Turkish side.

Meanwhile, the Turkish diesel rumbles off back to its homeland, job done, and is replaced by a far more decrepit Syrian one, a long-snouted museum-piece, its midriff covered in webs of oil. The sleeping car is finally disconnected from the goods wagons, and the international express, by now reduced to just one coach, is ready to go. Mind you, it can only do so once the Syrian authorities are ready to return the passports, and that can take a while.

The last section of the journey is through the hills of northern Syria, Kurdish country, along track originally laid by German engineers 100

BELLS & WHISTLES

BEST BIT
A whole train for just a handful of passengers.

TOP TIP
Make friends with the Syrian driver during the border check at Meydan Ikbis and he might invite you to ride in the locomotive.

PHOTO OP
Approaching Istanbul's Hydarapasa station on the ferry.

ANORAK INFO
Every year, a retired engineer from former East Germany spends a month in Syria, repairing broken-down old locomotives.

PACK THIS
Food and drink.

USEFUL PHRASE
Ahlan wah sahlan is a phrase commonly used for 'welcome', but meant with deeper feeling, ie you're my family, so take it easy.

TRAVELLERS' FARE
The only refreshment you're likely to get is coffee and a hubble-bubble, or waterpipe.

OVERHEARD
'There will be no justice for the people of Palestine while Israel sets the parameters and inflicts the penalties.'

The final frontier: the border between Turkey and Syria near Meydan Ikbis

years ago. The soil has changed colour again, this time to the deep red of very lean meat. Rows of bluey-green olive trees march, military style, across it, climbing the hillsides and descending the valleys and repeating forever, in wave after wave. Occasionally, there's a smudge of smoke where Kurdish pruners and clippers have gathered to brew sweet tea.

And then, finally, the train reaches Aleppo, crawling through dense suburbs, yowling like a wounded beast through Palestinian refugee camps, and coming to rest in a city that is a mix of Arab, French and Indiana Jones. Step out into a station with marble floors and wood-inlaid ceilings like an upside-down backgammon set, and you know you have entered the Middle East.

TRAVEL INFORMATION

Timetable information is on the Turkish railways website at www.tcdd.gov.tr/tcdding/ortadogu_ing.htm. Another good reference is www.turkeytravelplanners.com. Foreign visitors can buy tickets in person at TCDD stations in Turkey, but it is recommended that you make reservations at least a couple of days in advance. From outside Turkey, you can book tickets through Turista Travel (00 90 212 527 7085/www.turistatravel.com). Packages are also available through Voyages Jules Verne (0845 166 7003/www.vjv.co.uk).

There is a buffet car in the Turkish part of the train, if the Syrian car attendants will let you through, but it's mainly for beer drinkers. Most people bring their own food, and you can get platform food from vendors at all the major stops.

Although the international timetable gives the *Taurus*'s end destination as Damascus, in practice it always stops in Aleppo. Onward connections to Damascus are good, however, especially the overnight sleeper. But bear in mind you can't guarantee when the train will arrive in Aleppo. There are very cheap flights between the two Syrian cities, and Aleppo's airport also has international flights, including two direct flights a week to London's Heathrow with British Midland (www.flybmi.com).

Most travellers will need to obtain a Syrian visa before getting on the train.

In some ways, a train is like a scientist, using a pipette to draw a sample from one place and then depositing it in another. If that makes rail travel sound clinical and sterile, it most definitely is not – on a train, those samples are seething with life. In South Africa (*see p160*), the rainbow nation, there'll be Zulus, Xhosas and Boers all in the same carriage; in Thailand (*see p127*), there'll be a small Buddhist shrine in the corner of the dining car; and in India (*see pp149-159*), where the nation treats its trains as travelling villages, there'll be shopping on platforms and restaurateurs roaming the aisles. For a microcosm of life's rich tapestry, you'll find it on a train.

Cultural Experiences

Make the most of London life

Start
BANGKOK
Finish
CHIANG MAI
Via
AYUTTHAYA
PHITSANULOKE
LAMPANG
Service
THE NAKORN
PING EXPRESS
Journey time
15 HOURS

Family Thais

It takes a village on wheels – with plenty of chaos and local colour – to get from Bangkok to Chiang Mai. By **Phil Cornwel-Smith**

When Thai rail engineers first slashed their way north through jungled mountains, Chiang Mai was a tributary kingdom with its own royal family, Siam was not yet Thailand, and the country was far from integrated. The Bangkok-to-Chiang Mai railway helped unite the modern Thai state.

A century ago, trains were among the many technologies that made Siam the second-most developed Asian nation after Japan. These uncolonised countries then took different tracks. While Japan feverishly upgraded to bullet trains, Thais relaxed their single-track, cannonball run and turned it into a village on wheels.

Passing a temple at Tha Chomphu

In an era of antiseptic travel, it's easy to brush aside community priorities, but here the village ways not only charm, they also function and nurture. The State Railway of Thailand (SRT) seems less like a nationalised business than a welfare service. Passengers pay pennies for long rides. Many staff live on the train or in subsidised housing at termini. Stations support an ecosystem of porters, guards and hang-around characters. Food vendors shuttle between stops several times a day. Slum shacks and markets encroach upon urban tracks, which are periodically cleared, then reoccupied, like mussels encrusting a pier.

The entire national timetable, which fits on four large-print pages, emanates from Bangkok's Hualamphong Station. Its vaulted, stained-glass hall dates back a century. Back then, the Siamese court commissioned Europeans to build landmarks in classical garb to show potential colonisers that Thais were *siwilai* (civilised). If it looks familiar, that's because architect Mario Tamagno modelled it in Liberty Style (Italian art nouveau) on Turin's Stazione Porta Nuova. Inside the station, a portrait of the modernising King Rama V looms above the platform gates. Facing him, travellers worship a replica of the Phra Buddha Chinnarat image, the original of which is housed up the line in Phitsanuloke.

But in Hualamphong, few of the swipe-carders exiting the MRT subway connect to the lower-tech, lower-class SRT. Some passengers grab an espresso at the mezzanine café. Many more picnic on mats covering the concourse, patiently awaiting their train, or their next life.

The Nakorn Ping Express to Chiang Mai, the city on the River Ping, runs six times a day. The last, Number 51, is a sleeper that maximises daylight travelling time. After it departs at 10pm, you slumber through the smooth Central Plains only to jerk awake at dawn as the train winds into the hills of Lanna – once the 'Kingdom of a Million Ricefields', now Northern Thailand.

Taking the Express 51, you are spared the palaver of readying the bunks en route. So I chain my luggage to the ladder and watch the entertainment: supersized Western backpackers squeezing down Asian-dimensioned aisles. Burdened with rucksacks, they can barely turn. Yet somehow the stewards sail through, balancing trays of coffee.

Time travel

Thai trains resemble several time capsules strung together, elephant-style, linked trunk to tail. In contrast to the retro bars in Bangkok, which artfully mismatch chairs on purpose, the SRT mixes carriages from different eras, but without the irony. From the blue leatherette berth in the second class sleeper caboose, you enter the

Backpacker in second class, left; a market at Lamphun, top; breakfast, above; vendor hawks snacks, right; Pangmuang Station, far right

second-class seating cars — a world of mustard timber panels with sash windows, fans and fully rotatable armchairs like a Victorian barbershop. Backpackers on board, who comprise half the passengers, seem oblivious to polite Thai mores; they knit limbs, share sleeping bags, stick their feet up, slurp Singha beer, and snog like it was a Pattaya short-time hotel.

Street-stall aesthetics have colonised the dining-car decor, in its improvised, everything-on-view clutter, from bulldog clips on table cloths to drink crates used as worktops. Decked in plastic flowers, it looks a bit like a Buddha shrine crossed with the staff wardrobe, and doubles as a purser's office and police hangout.

At the front, the third-class cars are a rainbow of grey. This utilitarian, but spotless, non-style dates from a simpler time when farmers boarded the train with produce, chickens and paddy-muddied feet; now that rural Thailand gets chauffeured in pickup trucks, fewer choose these vertical vinyl benches. So third class is sparsely peopled: a few migrant workers, a family dozing with their dog, a monk and a novice traveller being ascetic. Ahead, the diesel tugs us through moonlit rice fields.

Vee, a listless steward who plies the aisles with cling-filmed plates of basil-fried pork-on-rice, hails from Nakhon Sawan, a midway stop. Now aged 27, he has been working the trains since he was 17. Millions of klickety-klaks have stopwatched his decade on the rails: working, sleeping, eating and gazing out of darkened windows at the rooted majority.

Vee's vagabond career recalls an old wife's saying that lists 'rotfai reua mail likae tamruat' (railmen, postmen, opera singers, policemen) and cautions young women against marrying such roving playboys. His reality is less romantic.

Brief encounters

A Thai movie filmed on this very train, *A Moment in June*, came out in 2009. Amid steamy flashbacks, a gay couple tiff at Hualamphong before one chugs north, confiding in a traveller that he may never return. Not so much *Brief*

BELLS & WHISTLES

BEST BIT
The village-like character in the train.

TOP TIP
The right side offers the best views. Avoid Western options on the breakfast menu.

PHOTO OP
Bangkok's Hualamphong Station; sculptures at Lampang Station; views from the right side of train in Phrae and before Doi Khun Tan peak.

PACK THIS
A lockable suitcase and chain, to prevent theft and stop the suitcase from falling over; a warm top and hat in cool season.

ANORAK INFO
The Northern Line has two royal stations: the classically domed Chitrlada Station (1922) beside the King's palace in Bangkok, and the filigree teak Bang Pa-In Station (1896) for the old summer palace just before Ayutthaya.

USEFUL PHRASE
Mai pen rai (never mind) – a cliché, but people say it constantly.

SOUVENIR
Potted orchid from the plant vendor who boards at Lampang.

TRAVELLERS' FARE
The famous State Railway fried rice in the ho-hum dining car, or better local delicacies from roving food vendors.

DESIGN DETAIL
Shrine to Nang Kwak (lady beckoning prosperity) in the dining car.

OVERHEARD
'I was learning to dive in Koh Tao, when we arranged on Facebook to meet my friend in Laos. But now I am running low on time, so everyone's, like, really stoked on Chiang Mai.'

Encounter as 'Briefs Encounter'. Also set on board, *Wai Onlawon 4* features the original film's teen stars as parents visiting their wayward daughter at Chiang Mai University. CMU students are a major ridership. The university even charters a train to induct 'freshies' based in Bangkok. Fifteen hours of non-stop initiations forge bonds that last a lifetime.

On my way back through the dining car, a steward, perched atop the iced drink tub, ambushes me with archetypal Thai questions: age, origin, status, salary, Premier League club. Having established that I was single, English and hate Man-iew, he reveals that the chef, Khun Maew (Miss Cat), is unmarried. He joshes that I should give her my phone number. We chuckle,

but Miss Cat is serious – and armed with a spatula. I scrawl down my number illegibly, realising I am in the strange predicament that she will be cooking my breakfast before a first date. I am relieved when the guards lock the carriage doors after bedtime at 12.30am.

Stacked lengthwise, the unusual bunk layout minimises pitch and yaw as the wheels hunt the next rail. But unused to a vibrating bed of hinged cushions, I fail to nap. Insistently, the fans' whirr and squeaks from the bogies echo the cicada soundscape of the tropical night outside.

At 2.30am, on a trip to the steel-lined loo, I come across an Anglo-Thai couple with matching beanies, lip-rings and – surprisingly – accents (like many a young Thai indie fan, she seemingly learnt English from Oasis interviews). As they drink, smoke and negotiate cross-cultural misunderstandings, our train comes to a mysterious stop. So deserted is the wooden station that it could have been from the Thai ghost movie, *Train of the Dead*, but our stop here is all part of a delicate timetable dance.

Thai trains work well, but only to the extent that the one-eyed can see: they run on single tracks. Trains charge towards each other head-on, so timetables are dictated by the periodic need to pause in sidings while an oncoming train hurtles by. As long as the signalling is as precise as the station garden topiary, you can sleep easy.

You can't help but wake at dawn to the sounds of newly boarded vendors hollering '*gai tort, moo ping, kao niao*' – fried chicken, grilled pork, sticky rice. The need for woolly hats quickly becomes apparent. Passengers huddle in their blankets, owing to a blast of cool air from the

outermost foothills of the Himalayas. Mist swirls around valleys of rice terraces. As we climb up the rugged Yom River valley, smoke from burning rice stubble whites out the karst outcrops and sets off sneezing among the allergic. Rumours of 7am bunk evictions prove unfounded; the stewards make things shipshape while drowsers sleep in until 9am.

Bamboo and breakfast

Denchai in Phrae province heralds the start of Lanna. My neighbour, Nok, alights here to source teak carvings for her stall in Bangkok's Chatuchak Weekend Market. Leaves brush the train as we course through bamboo, teak and dipterocarp woodland, glimpsing mountain vistas in the theatrical morning light.

Miss Cat's breakfast arrives. Forewarned to avoid non-Thai menu options, I tuck into a passable rice soup. Then there's a jolt. My one-

legged table comes unfastened from the wall – and Cat's soup misses my lap by a whisker. A replacement breakfast comes courtesy of a vendor, touting grilled meat, green mango and barbecued eggs-on-a-stick (in Thailand, you never have to hunt for food; meals come to you). Then, on recalling the famous *khao pat rot fai* (train fried rice with sausage, beans, ketchup and butter), I rush to the dining car, just to try it.

At the longest stop, Lampang, sculptures enliven the platforms: miniature temples, model tunnels and a concrete horse-and-cart, the city's enduring icon. At local stations like Mae Tan Noi, the aesthetic is Alpine-esque: think bougainvillea, waterwheels and flowerbed lettering framing twee gingerbread houses. Ambulating hill tribes in costume seem oblivious to the 20th century, let alone the 21st.

Holy land: Phra Buddha Chinnarat in Wat Yai Temple, Phitsanuloke, top; a monk in Chiang Mai Station

The scenery peaks as we climb Doi Khun Tan mountain. Passengers hop to whichever seats offer the best views; the right side is best. As we teeter over trestle bridges, staff in the dining car launch home-made miniature parachutes into the gorge. Vee says they do it daily, not as a spirit offering, just for fun. After we pass an Akha tribal gateway, Thailand's longest tunnel, at almost a mile, delivers us to Doi Kun Tan Station. You can trek the national park from here, and young Thais with scarves and guitars disembark for the novelty of a jaunt in cool weather.

From there it's all downhill. And how. After its gym-like uphill workout, No 51 swoops into the Chiang Mai Valley as if riding a toboggan; slotting through the white box bridge at Tha Chomphu acts like a cold shower. Drama over, the train girds into tidying mode. Lamphun and Chiang Mai's suburban sprawl ushers us to the buffers, precisely on time.

The old town and commercial centre lie across the River Ping, and before 1921 the only route from Bangkok was by boat. The train may be slow at 15 hours, but it nevertheless represents progress from a river journey that once took six weeks.

Just as the train has brought globalised modernity to Chiang Mai, so would planned rail extensions do the same to remotest Burma, Laos and Yunnan, China. Railways spell the end of frontier, yet the Nakorn Ping Express preserves this frontier-breaching spirit.

SIDINGS

The Northern Line's great (and unmarketed) feature is that it accesses most ancient Thai cities. Some visitors ride an hour to Bang Pa-In, where cycle rickshaws pedal passengers from the half-timbered station to the eclectic summer palace. Or they alight just upriver at Ayutthaya, Siam's UNESCO-listed old capital, also on the route.

The light-luggaged can take a morning train to Lopburi for lunch, sightsee at this 1,500-year-old hub of Dvaravati, Khmer and Thai culture, then rejoin a sleeper after dinner. Beware the feral monkeys.

Phitsanuloke has Thailand's most stunning Buddha temple, Wat Yai, for the haloed Phra Buddha Chinnarat. It's also a base to explore the World Heritage Site of Sukhothai and nearby Si Satchanalai and Kamphaengphet heritage parks.

Lampang offers charming teak mansions, horse-carriage rides, exquisite fortified temples and the National Elephant Conservation Centre.

Lamphun's Dvaravati temples are best visited from Chiang Mai, which hides the ruined city of Wiang Khum Kham in its southern suburbs. Chiang Mai, capital of the north, has weeks' worth of attractions old and new.

TRAVEL INFORMATION

Check SRT timetables online (www.railway.co.th) or on the 24-hour hotline 1690. A counter at Hualamphong Station serves tourists in English. Book well ahead around cool season weekends and Thai festivals, especially New Year, Chinese New Year, Songkran and Loy Krathong.

Hualamphong Station offers food outlets, bookstores, ATMs and, considerately, Thai massage. In Chiang Mai, you'll need rest after such an intense journey. Rachamankha (www.rachamankha.com) provides an exquisite retreat, down an alley within the old town's moat. The hotel evokes the pre-train era, with its temple-inspired architecture, and the owners' use of tribal recipes and indigenous decor. Rachamankha exemplifies a neo-Lanna revival, a reminder of a culture that was lost when the likes of the Shangri-La Hotel came to Shangri-La.

Good morning Vietnam

From Hanoi to Ho Chi Minh, the Reunification Express bridges a historic divide, via some gorgeous scenery. By **Carol Howland**

Back in the buccaneering days of French Indochina, when merchant adventurers joined the military efforts of the French government in colonising feudal Vietnam, one of their most amazing engineering feats was the construction of a single-track, narrow-gauge railway from Hanoi to Saigon. Begun in 1898, the 1,560-mile track – over rivers, mountains and coastal flood plains – was finally completed in 1936. It was called the Trans-Indochinoise.

Built primarily for commercial purposes to haul freight – rubber, coal, rice, tea and coffee – the train also had a few passenger carriages to transport colonial administrators and, often, the French army, as the Vietnamese did not accept, quiescently, domination by the French. The rail line was continually sabotaged by Viet Minh resistance fighters, long before and throughout the first Indochina War (1945-54), which made travelling in those days a rather uncertain adventure. During World War II, the Japanese seized the line, and it was frequently sabotaged by the Viet Minh. Later, bombs and sabotage by both sides continued to destroy bridges and track during the Vietnam War (1965-75), which is also known as the second Indochina War. But

Market share: locals hawk their wares at Nha Trang, left, and sell bananas in Hanoi

after 36 years of constant repairs to 1,134 bridges, 27 tunnels and 158 stations, the line was proudly reopened as the Reunification Express by the newly independent Socialist Republic of Vietnam in 1976.

Welcome to the jungle

The last of the old railway carriages was replaced by a new Vietnam-built model in 2000. Don't think Orient Express – this is still very much a functional line. These days, as well as international tourists and backpackers, passengers are as likely to be local businessmen, families visiting relatives in other parts of the country and friendly young students, always eager to practise their English.

As recently as 1988, the journey from Hanoi to Saigon (now called Ho Chi Minh City, or HCMC) took 58 hours. Since 1999, that has been cut to 32 hours, but it is still not a marathon most travellers undertake non-stop (but you must buy separate tickets for each leg of the journey if you wish to hop on and hop off). Travelling the route is still something of an adventure, albeit no longer one in which you risk getting shot at or coming to a sudden halt because a bridge is out.

Five express trains depart daily, travelling in opposite directions from Hanoi and HCMC, as well as numerous slower trains. It is these expresses that collectively carry the name Reunification Express. They roll along at an average speed of 48mph through Vietnam's pretty scenery – rural villages and rice paddies, ramshackle towns, jungles and mountains, turquoise bays and white sandy beaches. It's a splendid way to see rural Vietnam.

In Hanoi, beyond the enormous fretwork grill above the entrance, the old French station remains, a classical Indochinese-style colonial building with its ochre-and-white stucco façade and black shuttered windows. Inside, the revolving fans are long gone, replaced by a dark-stained wood ceiling, concealed lighting and sleek mesh steel chairs for passengers. Snack counters sell bags of tangerines, cakes, biscuits, soft drinks and bottled water.

Foreigners can buy tickets at windows 1, 2 or 3, but most book through local Hanoi travel agents, reserving two or three days in advance as 'soft sleeper' accommodation tends to go quickly. Most break the journey along the way at the major towns where the train stops.

Boarding the 11pm train in Hanoi, passengers are subjected to scenes of mayhem. For a small tip, a station employee will take your baggage and your ticket, lead you through the crowds of well-wishers seeing off family members, and then neatly install you in your compartment. It's worth the investment.

On board, the 'soft sleeper' compartment – recommended for foreign travellers – is not exactly plush. Each compartment comprises four solid, cloth-covered-mattress bunks, equipped with a pillow, pillowcase, one sheet and a padded cover (if it's winter). There are toilets at the end of each carriage and two washbasins with a mirror; the latter are open to the passageway.

For overnight journeys, passengers of a fastidious nature might like their own 'sheet sleeping bag' – a lighter version of a regular sleeping bag – readily purchased in Hanoi or HCMC, and hand-wipes or packets of tissues. Earplugs could be useful, and maybe wellies and a nose-clip for the loo (instead of wiping, the Vietnamese spray their bottoms with a hose).

The first person to enter my compartment is a Vietnamese businessman returning from Hanoi to his family in HCMC, followed by two Aussie

The train offers tantalising glimpses of the South China Sea

backpackers who have travelled to Hanoi from China. It's late, so we make our beds and snuggle up as the train creeps south out of Hanoi. The train rumbles through the night, stopping now and then to let a northbound train pass.

As dawn filters through the curtains, we pass the 17th parallel, which marks the boundary between North and South Vietnam. (The nation was divided in 1954 through the Geneva Agreement, with the communists in the north, but then reunified in 1976.) Then, through the dirty windows, we are able to identify the Demilitarised Zone, still sparsely vegetated thanks to poisonous Agent Orange, followed by hillsides covered with military tombs and memorials.

A breakfast (or lunch or dinner) of noodles is available for minimal outlay in the wood-panelled dining car. The latter is straight out of a Wild West film set (no tablecloths or monogrammed napkins here) and crammed with Vietnamese

extras. I opt for tea and lurch back to my compartment. Most people have brought their own fruit and nibbles.

Outside the window, it's village upon village of ribbon development, Vietnamese style, until the outskirts of Hué, the beautiful former capital of Imperial Vietnam.

Down by the sea

For foreign tourists who just want a taste of the Reunification Express, but don't want to commit to the whole journey, the next 62 miles – between Hué and Danang – is the most popular leg of the railway. After departing Hué, the train cuts through a network of dykes that separate some green patches from shimmering rice paddies. The sea of green is interrupted here and there by a little crowd of family tombstones. It bends around hills and bays, through tunnels, then suddenly, the turquoise South China Sea

---

SIDINGS

Hanoi is the cultural cradle of Vietnam and, in 2010, it celebrates the 1,000th anniversary of its founding as the capital. Its Old Town, known as Thirty-Six Streets, still has family craftsmen who have followed the same trades for generations. Its beautiful lakes and pagodas still evoke the quiet spirit of ages past, despite the proliferation of motorbikes.

Next is Hué, where you can visit the exquisite red-lacquer-and-gilt palaces of the Imperial Citadel, a World Heritage Site, and take a boat along the Perfume River to the emperors' tombs – think beautifully landscaped weekend country-house temple retreats, not tombstones.

Then comes Danang, famous for its Cham Museum, which holds a collection of sculpture from the Hindu-Buddhist civilisation that flourished from the third to the 13th century. Hoi An, declared a World Heritage Site for its historic merchants' houses and Chinese community houses, is less than an hour by bus or taxi from Danang. In recent years, a series of luxurious hotels have capitalised on its nearby beach.

Nha Trang's four-mile beach is the town's magnet. There is diving near the off-shore islands, and it is the starting point for excursions to visit the ethnic minorities in the Central Highlands. At the north end of the town is a complex of restored brick Cham temples and at the southern end, one of the holiday homes of the last emperor, Bao Dai.

Saigon is now known as Ho Chi Minh City, although everyone still calls it Saigon. It is a go-getter of a city, no more than a couple of centuries old, the heartbeat of entrepreneurial Vietnam. Both Hanoi and Saigon retain numerous reminders of the French colonial era in their wide, tree-lined boulevards and elegant colonial buildings.

BEST BIT
Rounding Lang Co, just north of Danang, where the South China Sea sweeps into a lagoon framed by palm-fringed, white sandy beaches.

TOP TIP
Watch your belongings as you pass through the dark tunnels.

PHOTO OP
Snack and souvenir vendors when the train stops.

PACK THIS
A shawl for winter journeys.

ANORAK INFO
There are plans afoot to extend the track from Loc Ninh, north of Ho Chi Minh City, to Phnom Penh in Cambodia, and then to Thailand and Laos, eventually to link up with Singapore.

USEFUL PHRASE
Cam on (thank you – and no thank you!)

SOUVENIR
Silk scarves, ties, small lacquer boxes, chopsticks inlaid with mother-of-pearl, silk paintings.

TRAVELLERS' FARE
Noodles, noodles, noodles – unless you bring something else.

DESIGN DETAIL
Oddly, most carriages are painted red, white and blue – the French national colours – rather than the Vietnamese red and gold.

slips behind an idyllic white sandy lagoon called Lang Co, dotted with a few houses.

Lang Co beaches are the stuff that dreams are made of, but the high point of this leg – literally and figuratively – is just beyond Lang Co. This section is a steep crawl upward, the train pushed by a second engine through dense jungle and hilly terrain (imagine fighting in this harsh landscape) to Deo Hai Van (Ocean Clouds Pass). The latter crosses over a spur of the Truong Son Mountains that extend into the South China Sea. The French called it the Col des Nuages (Hill of Clouds) and the name doesn't lie: clouds often block the splendid view of the curved turquoise bay and white sandy beach below.

From Deo Hai Van southward, it begins to feel warmer. The pass, where summer begins, divides the semi-tropical north from the tropical south. Descending, the train passes rural village after village. Haystacks, papaya and mango trees fill the courtyards behind bamboo fences, where people go about their daily lives, ploughing with water buffaloes, transplanting rice, hauling goods in carts drawn by motorbikes, selling fruit from roadside stalls. 'Farmers' in slim boats tend their fish farms, fenced off along the coast.

South of Danang, past a few prefabricated corrugated-iron huts and runways, lies all that remains of the enormous American military base. As you pass the region, the train clings closely to the coast, flirting with the infamous China Beach, where GIs enjoyed their R&R; it also served as the backdrop for the eponymous American television series from the 1980s.

The next stop after Danang is Nha Trang, 337 miles to the south. A popular beachside resort with Vietnamese, it's a mix of luxury beachside retreats and town-centre guesthouses.

The last bit of the journey from Nha Trang to Ho Chi Minh City, round the lower rump of Vietnam, passes a few Cham towers (brick towers built by the Hindu-Buddhist kingdoms that once flourished here). These are located at Phan Rang and near Phan Thiet, the jumping-off

The blue lagoon: a beach north of Nha Trang

place for Mui Ne, a beach resort with good hotels, located seven miles away. The country is decidedly drier around here; near Mui Ne, the enormous rusty red sand dunes look like something out of the Sahara.

Between here and HCMC, fields of a strange spiky plant appear. This is the dragon fruit – a shocking-pink, scaly-skinned fruit with white pulp and tiny black seeds – and this is the only place in Vietnam where it grows.

Then the marathon journey is over, as the train hits Asian-tiger, industrial Vietnam, and a blur of factories. The temporary community that has formed on board the train has run its course. Passengers step out into HCMC's new, nondescript station, distinguished only by its red and blue plastic chairs. The colonial Trans-Indochinoise seems a distant memory in this vibrant, cosmopolitan city of entrepreneurs, dead set on style and cool modernity.

TRAVEL INFORMATION

Train timetables are in the English section of Vietnam Railways website www.vr.com.vn/ English. It is not possible to hop on and off on a through ticket from Hanoi to HCMC or vice versa. A new ticket must be purchased for each leg of the journey. There are four classes: soft sleeper (with four bunks to a compartment), hard sleeper (with no door to the compartment and six bunks), soft seat and hard seat. The first three classes are air-conditioned; only 'hard seat' is not. It is always wise to book a train journey in Vietnam several days before travelling. Train managers take a dim view of anyone who buys an entire compartment to ensure privacy – how selfish! – and may install passengers in 'your' empty bunks. Note: around Vietnamese New Year holiday (Tet), which falls late January or early February, there are no trains at all for about nine days.

Start
SHANGHAI
Finish
LHASA
Via
NANJING
XI'AN
XINING
NAGCHU
Journey time
2 DAYS

Riding high

It's up, up and away on China's mighty Qinzang railway – a train to Tibet on the top of the world. By **Gary Bowerman**

For a nation that built the world's most remarkable defensive wall, and later damned the cavernous Three Gorges section of the mighty Yangtze River, the triumph of human engineering over nature is a celebrated art. But one structural challenge appeared insurmountable to China for 40 years. Since the 1960s, Chinese scientists, engineers and government officials pored over reams of research trying to crack a seemingly intractable issue: how to build a railway across the high-altitude permafrost lands of the Tibetan Plateau.

High-profile doubters, both worldwide and within China, said that it couldn't be done. Others insisted that, science and technology aside, the Qinzang railway should not be built for ecological reasons. So when science, technology and politics combined to overcome the logistical challenges, the ethical dilemma remained: how could China justify the potentially huge environmental damage of building a railway across one of the most remote and pristine natural environments on earth?

The overwhelming forces of commercial interest and political imperative endured. In July 2006, to great national fanfare, Hu Jintao, the president of China (and a former Communist Party Secretary of Tibet), commended the launch of the first passenger train between China's capital, Beijing, and Lhasa, the capital of Tibet – a journey of some 2,500 miles. The mountainous Buddhist kingdom that China annexed following a military invasion in 1950 was now umbilically linked to a nation with which it has fought repeatedly throughout history.

A few months later, just in time for the annual China National Day holidays at the beginning of October 2006, a second long-distance Lhasa-bound route was opened. This time, the connecting line linked Tibet with China's east coast commercial capital, Shanghai.

Direct overland transport links between Lhasa and China's two largest cities served several purposes for Chinese leaders. For a start, they provided economical transportation to a mystical country (officially a 'province' of China), about which the Chinese public retains great curiosity, but little real knowledge. The result was an accessible and exciting new destination for China's emerging class of adventurous travellers. Equally importantly, the railway opened up a wealth of new trading opportunities, not just for entrepreneurs from established cities like Shanghai and Beijing, but also from the fast-developing cities of western China, including Chengdu, Chongqing and Xi'an.

The overwhelming impression – garnered from the difficulties foreigners face in purchasing a Tibet entry permit, as well as a Lhasa-bound train ticket – is that this train ride is aimed squarely at Chinese travellers.

Tibet has long been a sensitive issue for the Chinese government, and this train was never intended as an open invitation to increase foreign visitors. The 2008 riots in Lhasa – and the resulting global media coverage – have only increased China's wariness of foreign travellers seeking to enter Tibet. As always, however, perseverance pays; for this is not a journey to give up on easily.

Haute cuisine, above; a rail bridge near Lhasa, below

OXYGEN SUPPLY

A breath of fresh air: oxygen pillows for passengers, left; Tibetan pilgrims and dried donkey meat, right

BELLS & WHISTLES

BEST BIT
Traversing the Tibetan Plateau.

TOP TIP
Take a sleeper carriage – the seating areas are crowded and smoky.

PHOTO OP
In winter, snap the frozen ripples on Cuona Lake as they refract the sunlight. And Tangula Mountain cries out to be photographed.

PACK THIS
Snacks and food – the dining car menu is very limited.

ANORAK INFO
You can check the altitude on digital displays in the train's hallways; the water in the toilets has to be heated to prevent it from freezing.

USEFUL PHRASE
'Xizang', meaning Tibet in Chinese.

SOUVENIR
The official Chinese State Railways brochure, written in risible Chinglish, will induce a smile.

OVERHEARD
[Passengers looking at the mountains] 'Our skyscapers in Shanghai are higher than that.'

High achiever

As the train eases out of Shanghai Station shortly after 8pm, the sense of embarking on an epic journey is underplayed, even though 2,717 miles and 49 hours of travel lie ahead. The train, specially built in a joint venture with international train and plane manufacturer Bombardier, is functional, clean and decorated with unerring colour neutrality. There are no touches of glamour – no chandeliers in the dining car or frilled velvet curtains in the sleeper cabins. Don't expect to call room service for chilled champagne. Each cabin-bunk has an airline-seat sized plasma screen, though only state TV programmes are aired. Emergency oxygen masks for every traveller hint at the high-altitude terrain that lies ahead.

Immediately after departure, the narrow corridors between the four-bunk cabins – most of which are crammed with boxes of fruit, packets of sunflower seeds and cartons of orange juice – are soon filled up with card sharks.

As the train pulls into a dark and quiet station at Wuxi, the only sight of interest through the large windows was a new white CRH (China Railways High-Speed) bullet train slithering along the adjacent tracks. The same scenario occurs pulling into Nanjing, the Republican-era capital of China, a couple of hours later.

As sunlight emerges on day two, the train eases its way across the flat, scrubby plains of Shaanxi province, heading towards central China. The grass is parched, trees are withered and lifeless and the red-brick earth meets a low-hanging haze in the air. But as the train reaches the former imperial capital of Xi'an, there is a frisson of excitement. Scores of passengers disembark and ruddier-faced replacements jump aboard. Outside, broad concrete platforms are alive with newspaper kiosks and carts hawking fried-chicken legs and steaming pork thighs.

From Xi'an, the landscape changes totally – and the epic journey begins to catch fire. Plains become rounded mountains, which are neatly terraced and tended by agricultural workers.

Then passengers are greeted with a startling view as the train slips though a chalky causeway of spectacular ridged cliffs and deep, cracked canyons (keep your camera handy).

An hour later, the heavy clay landscape and milky, caramel, sandstone rocks appear against a pristine, azure sky. The craggy ridges endure

Tibetan horizons: the track across the Plateau, far left; a holiday park outside Lhasa, left; the Kunlun Mountains

for miles and miles, but an hour later, the mountains turn cinnamon in colour and grow taller and spikier, the peaks capped with snow.

Despite its location in the scenic province of Gansu, Lanzhou is a dreary, sooty city of power plants and aged industrial factories. It's the first stop on a long haul from Xi'an, and the ice on the tracks, briny air and impending darkness make it largely unappealing. Check a map, and you'll see that Lanzhou actually sits in north-west China, south of Mongolia's Gobi Desert and perched on the north-east corner of the Tibetan Plateau. It feels a very long way from Shanghai.

At Xining, on the edge of the plateau, the red rocks behind the station are spectacular. Scores of passengers disembark – you can tell they are locals, because each has chapped lips, wind-scaled cheeks and is wrapped in warm, embroidered Tibetan clothing. They are met by police and army guards, ubiquitous in these parts; much of the local population is ethnically Tibetan, and Chinese-Tibetan tensions run high. Soon afterwards, the train moves on – and darkness envelops the mountainous landscape.

Shortly after 8am the next morning, the sun rises theatrically over the Tibetan Plateau – and so begins the show-stopping part of the trip. The effects of altitude sickness kick in too – including shortness of breath and a dull ache in the temples. Lifting down a rucksack from the racks becomes an Olympian feat, and drinking plenty of water is essential.

Outside, the scrubby plains are bookended by dark, dimpled mountains glazed with snow and ice. A broad river meandering alongside the tracks is frozen solid, and a narrow, winding

SIDINGS

If you want to break the journey en route, the obvious place is Xi'an, home to one of China's most visited attractions: the Terracotta Warriors. Uncovered in 1974 by farmers digging a well in the red clay of central China's Shaanxi province, the 200-year-old guardians of the tomb of Emperor Qin Shihuang are a unique historical treasure. Located 16 miles east of Xi'an, the Terracotta Warriors Museum features hundreds of the reputed 7,000 warriors: life-sized and life-like, they are placed in infantry formation inside covered pits.

Most visitors to Xi'an make a beeline for the Warriors, but leave little time to explore the rest of this fascinating city. Xi'an is surrounded by solid defensive walls that were restored in the 1980s. Its central location made it a historical meeting point for traders from north, south, east and west China, as well as an ideal power base for Emperor Qin Shihuang, who ruthlessly united China's seven warring kingdoms back in 221 BC.

As the starting point of the Silk Road, Xi'an was China's capital for almost 800 years, and at one point challenged Rome in terms of size and power. Its complex history is documented at the Xi'an Museum. On show is an impressive collection of painted pottery warriors, jade Buddhist statues, stone coffins, porcelain, bronze weapons and a scale model of the imperial city. Other notable attractions include the Old City Mosque, Drum Tower, Large and Small Goose Pagodas and the handsome city walls.

The overnight train journey between Shanghai and Xi'an takes approximately 14 hours, and arrives at its destination in the morning. The onward ride from Xi'an to Lhasa is the most spectacular section of the journey – and takes about 35 hours. However, you will need to purchase individual tickets for both the Shanghai–Xi'an and Xi'an–Lhasa sections, as a single Shanghai–Lhasa ticket does not permit a stopover.

Oriental express

No other country is investing in railways like China. The nation has the third-longest railway network in the world, and it is growing fast. The engine is economic growth and a burgeoning middle class.

The current 50,000 miles of track represents seven per cent of the world's total, but carry 24 per cent of the world's traffic. The high demand has fuelled a massive investment programme: US$730 billion will be spent by 2020, on another 25,000 miles of track.

A separate, high-speed network is also developing. The top speed of these trains is 217 miles per hour, and there are now five trains an hour covering the 85 miles between Beijing and Tianjin in just 30 minutes. Fifteen years ago, there were just two trains a day from Beijing to Shanghai, a 17-hour trip. Now there are seven sleepers, taking 10 hours; in three years, the 909-mile trip should take only five hours.

Train travel can be daunting for foreign travellers, but large stations have an English window. Tickets are only sold a few days in advance from a station or a town booking office. Tickets are scarce around holidays, as millions of urban workers return home; at these times, tickets are touted (illegally) outside stations. There is no online booking, but most travel agents can obtain tickets for a small fee.

Daytime and high-speed electric trains have first class and second class. Long-distance trains offer three types of sleeper.

Before you board, look at the numbers on the ticket: for train, coach and seat. Signs show the train number, departure time and destination (in both Chinese characters and Roman script). After a security baggage scan at the entrance, you go to a numbered waiting room. Just prior to departure, the platform number is shown and the crowd stirs. But be sure you board the right train: the same number often applies to both sides of the platform. If you are in a sleeper, an attendant may ask you to surrender your ticket for a token; it will be returned to you (you need it to exit at the arrival station).

There is a metro network in ten cities, with plans to increase this to 25. Started in 1981, Beijing's network has eight lines, 123 stations and 124 miles of route. Shanghai started in 1995, but will surpass 300 miles in 2010 for World Expo. Both networks will then be longer than London's 11 lines and 248 miles.

There is an easy way of seeing China by rail. Several operators offer exclusive tourist trains, particularly GW Travel (www.gwtravel.co.uk). Tangula Trains (*see p230*, www.tangulaluxury trains.com) offer a luxury land cruise on two routes: from Beijing to Lhasa or Lijiang.

Ivor Warburton
For more information, see Duncan Peattie's Chinese Railway Timetable www.chinatt.org.

Beijing subway map

tarmac road on the opposite side – used by a few large trucks to transport goods to and from Tibet – looks treacherous.

Tangula Mountain is one of the route's landmarks, and the first sight of its spectacular glacier draws legions of camera-wielding snappers towards the windows. The rail line across the Tangula Pass, which peaks at 5,072 metres, is 'the highest in the world', according to the train brochure. As we cross, a tangible sense of national pride washes through each corridor (along with a few gasps for air).

The engineering achievement represented by the Qinghai–Lhasa section of the China–Tibet railway is undeniable. Crossing the Tibetan Plateau at an average elevation of more than 4,000 metres, the railway was built on top of permafrost. And the 1,141-mile final stretch, between Golmud and Lhasa, is, according to officials, 'the longest plateau railway with the highest elevation in the world'.

The magic of Tibet

China can be proud of such superlatives. But the environmental impact of the mega-scale project over a vast expanse of barren beauty will be debated for years ahead. For its part, the Chinese railways brochure claims China spent nearly US$200 million on environmental protection measures, and that, as a result, the railway has had 'no effect on wild animal migration or water pollution'. Constant announcements over the tannoy system boasted of 'the world's first man-made swamp built at altitude'.

These ethical issues inevitably dwell on a traveller's mind. The cultural and societal impact of China's settling of Han Chinese across Tibet – which it argues is an 'inalienable part of the motherland' – is another issue. But, as a piece of visual natural theatre, the ride across the Tibetan Plateau is mesmerising.

The set changes are constant. The earth takes on a deep ochre hue, while the sandstone hills are dotted with the first black-coated Tibetan

yaks encountered en route. Then comes another camera moment. Cuona Lake is a motionless frozen body of water whose banks are no more than 60 feet from the rail tracks. As we pass, deeply crusted frozen ridges ride the lake like surf waves suspended in motion. On the far banks, gaps in the ice refract the sunlight off the aqua blue waters. The train corridors are now packed with cooing city dwellers – and it feels like a standing ovation.

After the lake, the train ride goes downhill – literally and metaphorically. That's not to say the scenery becomes uninspiring or uninteresting – far from it. Lhasa sits at an elevation of 3,700 metres, and the physical descent was gentle. But the landscapes never again reach the heady heights of Tangula Mountain or Cuona Lake.

As we descend from the plateau heights into the Qiangtang grasslands of Tibet, the blue sky becomes cloudier and the sky seems somehow smaller. Willowy, corn-coloured plains stretch into the distance and the clouds seem almost to touch the hilltops. Two intriguing features characterise this part of the journey; fort-shaped stone Tibetan farmhouses (some occupy perilous ledges on the barren hillsides) and shaggy black yaks clumsily run away from the strange iron beast speeding down the track.

The farmhouses are intriguing, constructed with four corner turrets and coloured prayer flags atop each one. A recurrent feature is a stone wall that hems in a small yard, and earth and yak manure are spread across the walls for insulation. A yak's skull or horns usually sit above the entrance gate, and several houses are decorated with large Buddhist swastikas on the roofs and around the doors.

At Nagchu Station, there are more police than before. Clusters of Hui Muslims drag suitcases across the cold, windy platforms. Next to the station, a large, mock-Tibetan building features red roof trimming and flags planted on top. It has all the hallmarks of a Chinese municipal headquarters.

Last train to Lhasa

Soon after, the train enters 'the world's largest permafrost tunnel', emerging into a steep valley flanked by thick grasslands. As the train winds gently towards Lhasa, the vast nothingness of the Tibetan Plateau dissolves into memory. Villagers head home from the fields with long shovels carried over their shoulders, and there is an increase in the number of trucks and cars navigating the twin-track road. It is impossible not to feel a sense of sadness at the impending re-entry into human society.

Darkness has fallen by the time the train pulls into Lhasa at 9pm, two days after leaving Shanghai. As we step out, two observations are immediate – the thin air makes lugging a heavy backpack surprisingly tiring. Secondly, the evening temperature makes hats, gloves and scarves more than just functional accessories.

As we exit the spacious train station and face the dark Tibetan night, the exterior façade seems somehow familiar. The white and claret brickwork, angular walls and unorthodox palatial structure resemble a striking 21st-century interpretation of Lhasa's signature landmark: the Potala Palace. The train station merits a photo, but after you snap, be prepared for your first business negotiation: Lhasa's taxi drivers assume you do not know the city's proximity to the station – it's just a 15-minute drive to the historic Barkhor district. Bargain hard.

After you make a deal, sit back and enjoy another ride. On our trip, the real Potala Palace comes looming into view within minutes, followed by Lhasa's other architectural masterpiece: the Jokhang Temple. Even at this late hour, the Tibetan pilgrims are out in force, prostrating themselves at its front gate.

After the spacey Shanghai skyline and the über-technology of the Tibetan Plateau railway, Lhasa seems like it's in a time warp; as you enter, you feel as if you are stepping back several centuries. And that – ethical considerations, ecological controversy and politics aside – is ultimately what makes the Shanghai–Lhasa train such a memorable travel experience.

TRAVEL INFORMATION

Even before the March 2008 riots in Lhasa, travellers to Tibet needed to follow strict pre-entry bureaucratic procedures. These processes are being strictly enforced – and are subject to change at short notice. A pre-arranged visitor permit, gained through an approved travel agency (such as www.chinaspringtour.com) is required to enter Tibet. This permit will be checked by train guards, and by the police, in the train. If you are planning to travel elsewhere in Tibet beyond the capital Lhasa, a second travel permit is needed, again obtained through a tour agency. Before applying for the Tibet permit, you will need to have obtained a China visa.

The Shanghai to Lhasa departs daily, train number T164/T165. A useful website for journey planning is www.chinatibettrain.com, although the fares and schedules section is not up to date.

A couple of things are worth remembering about the train itself. While there is a buffet car, the standard of food is variable – the meaty dishes are uninspiring and unsuitable for vegetarian travellers. The bathrooms are regularly cleaned en route, but are rudimentary and the toilet is of the squat variety. There are no showers on board, but washbasins are provided. Do not drink water from the tap – bring bottled water with you. Extra supplies can be purchased at train station platforms along the way.

En route, you will notice travellers wandering the corridors slurping from steaming plastic pots of quick noodles. This is a popular travel snack in China, and if you are hungry, may be a better bet than the fare sold in the dining car. Cold Chinese and imported foreign beers are also sold on the train – but the price differential between them is significant.

India made easy

Clean, efficient and comfortable, the Shatabdi Express is a gentle introduction to a thrilling country. By **Amar Grover**

A rare moment of calm at New Delhi Station

For more than a century, the railway has been the transportation lifeblood of the Indian subcontinent. From a modest beginning back in 1853, when the first passenger train left what is now Mumbai on a 15-mile run, it has evolved into a vast, vital and much-celebrated network.

The statistics are invigorating. Indian Railways, or IR, is the world's second-largest state-owned railway. It is the world's largest commercial employer, with more than 1.4 million employees. There are 7,137 stations, and the one in New Delhi boasts the world's largest route relay interlocking system, a modern signalling device that prevents crashes. Oh, and the railway carries 18 million passengers daily – half of them seem to be milling around New Delhi Station.

From Delhi, you are spoiled for choice of destinations. You can board India's fastest train, which travels at an average speed of 68mph, and head south to Bhopal. You can join its longest train journey, from Kashmir to the Indian Ocean at the southern tip of India – a trip of three days and 2,330 miles. Opting for its most luxurious train, the Palace on Wheels, you can swan about Rajasthan, pretending that the sun never quite set on the Raj or its maharajahs. But for a manageable journey that takes you into the heart

Comfort zone: the Shatabdi's aeroplane-style interior, left, is a cut above most Indian trains; Kalka Station, top

of India, but doesn't require you to slum it, the line to Kalka and then on up to Shimla (*see p155*) in the Himalaya is a fine choice.

A safe passage through India

The daily New Delhi–Kalka Shatabdi Express heads north from Delhi across the wheat belt of Haryana state, clips the easternmost edge of the Punjab and comes to a halt at the hem of the Himalayan foothills, after a four-hour journey. Together with its cousin, the Rajdhani Express, the Shatabdi is a special service comprising India's fastest and slickest trains. They are air-conditioned, boast double-thick tinted windows, require seat reservations, and do a pretty good job of keeping the 'real' India, with its tumultuous crowds and incessant dust, at bay.

These avowedly middle-class services cater to the well-heeled and endowed. Some purists sneer, claiming they are bland and uninteresting, but only a fool would neglect this facet of a developing, aspirational India. First-time visitors will find them the gentlest introduction to national train culture, and in a country as intense as India, there's no point in sinking before you can swim.

It's a relatively straightforward passage through the portals of New Delhi Station. First, one navigates the cycle/rickshaw gridlock outside the car park, motor/rickshaw gridlock within it, and triple-parked cars going bumper to bumper. Some passengers eat and sleep on the floor of the main concourse (many with colossal mounds of baggage) and wait with the patience of Job. There are urgent queues for 'information and enquiry', and frantic lines for immediate travel tickets. Red-shirted porters stagger through the crowds, sagging under cases balanced on their heads. Through this great swirl of humanity, you stride past a couple of airport-style metal detectors, whose use is sporadic, and make for Platform One. Shatabdi is invariably a Platform One train – it's part of its prestige.

Coach positions are shown by illuminated signs hanging from the platform's rafters. Beside

BELLS & WHISTLES

BEST BIT
The sheer number and variety of people using New Delhi Station.

TOP TIP
Arrive within plenty of time.

PHOTO OP
Perch yourself on the passenger footbridges at New Delhi Station, for an overview of its seething humanity.

PACK THIS
A copy of *India Today*, whose *Newsweek*-like tone and readership perfectly reflect the respectable Shatabdi passenger.

ANORAK INFO
'*Shatabdi*' means centenary in Hindi and several Indian languages. The first such express was introduced in 1988 on the New Delhi–Jhansi run, to commemorate the birth centenary of Jawaharlal Nehru, India's first prime minister.

OVERHEARD
The squeaky pre-recorded woman's voice that names each stop over the PA system – so jaunty, you almost think she's going to break into a song-and-dance routine.

the door of each numbered coach, there are computer printouts glued to the train's exterior that list the names and ages of your fellow passengers; this is less an aid to social intercourse than simply another facet of the Raj-inspired routine of bureaucracy. Later, a black-jacketed 'TT', or Travelling Ticket Examiner, will sweep through the train with a copy of this list, ticking names against tickets.

Inside, the aircraft-style, fabric-covered seats come with footrests, a fold-down tray and a clasp designed for the bottles of mineral water that are included in the fare. It's clean, spacious and comfortable – not what you'd expect in India. The train leaves punctually at 7.40am.

The Shatabdi still seems to be leaving Delhi 20 minutes later, for this is a huge sprawling city of mostly unlovely suburbs dotted with shantytown slums. Railway police comb the carriages, placing security stickers on every item of luggage identified by passengers. We pick up speed. 'Gosh, it's a very smooth line!' exclaims a passenger, the voice inflected with both astonishment and pride. Looking up, I see a group of British rail enthusiasts.

Many consider the railways to be one of the crowning achievements of the British in India. It is. Yet amid the rosy post-colonial afterglow, it would be disingenuous to frame their construction as a benevolent gift. Railways were built for economic gain and political strategy, purely to serve the Raj. Cheap cotton, for instance, could be more easily transported and exported to the mills of northern Britain, then imported once more for distribution to a ready, if not captive, market. Mahatma Gandhi was famously – and at times bizarrely – anti-train (though he still used them to tour and politicise the country). He felt they propagated evil, exacerbated famines, and even helped defile holy places: 'Nowadays, rogues visit them to practise their roguery,' he once wrote.

In fact, you might still see a 'Rogues Gallery' at some stations – essentially a board displaying mug shots and descriptions of petty criminals. On this run, however, there is little time to investigate such curiosities. During its 164-mile journey, there are just four stops, with brief halts: this is India at its most efficient.

Tickets to ride

Before you even reach the first stop, a uniformed waiter has distributed small thermos flasks of tea with two tea bags (Taj Mahal brand, of course) and a dainty packet of Britannia's Marie biscuits. Businessmen plug in their laptops and squawk into mobiles, arranging meetings or closing deals, elderly women rearrange their woollen shawls (the air-conditioning is a bit too cool) and young couples doze.

The flat farmland of Haryana speeds past. India's breadbasket is the very picture of tranquillity. Bullock carts amble along dirt tracks, steered by wizened salt-of-the-earth farmers. Diesel water pumps puff and smoke. Small herds of dark buffalo wallow in muddy ponds. Clusters of schoolchildren in blue uniforms pause to watch the train. Villages comprise simple brick houses and a few walls painted brightly with forlorn advertisements for batteries or undergarments. The pastoral idyll is interrupted by Panipat, now an industrial centre for carpets

---

SIDINGS

You might want to break the journey in Chandigarh and explore the city's modernist layout. The City Architecture Museum explains Chandigarh's conception and construction. The city's other main attraction is its famous Rock Garden, a bizarre sculpture gallery composed of household and industrial cast-offs. Begun in 1965 by a retired Public Works Department official, it now covers 25 acres.

Twelve miles north lies Pinjore, whose Yadavindra Gardens were designed by the 16th-century Mughal governor and architect Fidai Khan. Canals, water chutes, fountains and walled quadrangles enclose three small palace-like pavilions and their extensive orchards.

Twenty-four miles north-west of Kalka, Nalagarh and its small fort hotel – perched on a hill overlooking town – make a fine and atmospheric base for overnight stops.

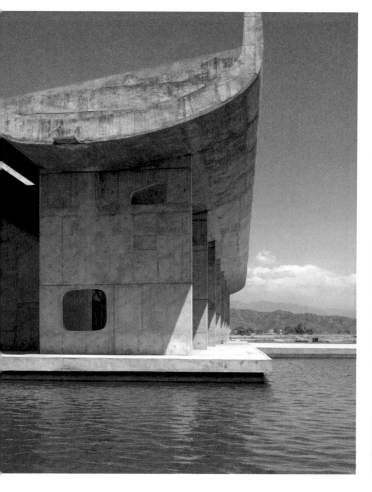

Houses of worship: Le Corbusier's Assembly Building in Chandigarh, left; Jama Masjid Mosque, New Delhi, right

and textiles. Back in the 16th century, however, it was the site of two vital battles that secured Mughal rule over north India.

The train is virtually full. Breakfast has been served (omelette for non-vegetarians, vegetable cutlet for others), with yet more tea. Here in EC class, or Executive Chair Car, you get more food, newspapers, and two-by-two seating. In CC, or Chair Car, things are just a little less spacious.

IR has its own peculiar nomenclature, which can snag the uninitiated; it might seem there are almost as many ticket classes as Hindu castes. Would, for instance, an 'SL' ticket be better than a 'II'? (Yes, since 'II' is unreserved second class, while 'SL' is a reserved berth in sleeper class). How does 'FC' compare with '3A'? (One is first class, the other is a comfortable sleeper, as it is air-conditioned and has only three tiers.) Is '3A' three times better than '1A'? (No. Although the former is a high-end option, it's three times as crowded as the latter, which is usually private; still, it is cheaper.)

These permutations apply to trains that add the suffix 'express' and 'mail' to their names, but speed in India is relative. A few are evocative – the Frontier Mail (renamed the Golden Temple

Mail in 1996 to reflect its terminus in Amritsar) was once among the Empire's most famous trains, when it linked Bombay and Peshwar; the Himalayan Queen, which covers the same route as the Shatabdi, also sounds romantic.

IR jargon, too, recalls another, vaguely Edwardian, age: some trains 'bifurcate' (and so 'amalgamate' on return). Passengers stay in Retiring Rooms; the upper classes are entitled to bedrolls. But then new Americanisms creep in too: you can officially 'detrain' or be 'wait-listed'.

Krishna meets Le Corbusier

The train glides on towards the foothills. To the east, running parallel to the train, stretches the celebrated Grand Trunk Road, an ancient route that crosses the subcontinent from Peshawar to Delhi and on to Kolkota, or Calcutta. We whisk past vast patchworks of pale green and yellow fields. You might glimpse herons perched stoically on low tree branches, or catch flashes of iridescent kingfisher blue. At Kurukshetra, you touch upon Hindu mythology. Here, allegedly, is the site of the most famous battle of the Mahabharata, the great Hindu epic, where Lord Krishna lectures one of the Pandava brothers on the eve of fighting.

Ambala, 24 miles north, is an important junction and crossroads, and the city hosts a huge air-force base, along with a major army corps. It also features – as 'Umballa' – in Rudyard Kipling's classic novel *Kim*, whose impish young protagonist is caught up in the trickery and espionage of the 'Great Game', when 19th-century Britain and Russia found their colonial frontiers edging closer. By strange coincidence, Kim Philby, the infamous British spy turned traitor, was born in Ambala and even nicknamed after Kim (but the fictional hero was no turncoat).

The line veers north-east and briefly crosses a small sliver of the Punjab. At Chandigarh, capital of both Punjab and Haryana, the train virtually empties as though some ghastly smell has seeped into the air-conditioning. Designed in the main by French architect Le Corbusier, Chandigarh's grid layout is unique in India and the city exudes an unusual combination of order and quiet prosperity. Its booming economy is the main reason for running the Shatabdi along this line, but IR wisely end the express 15 miles further on at Kalka, where the broad-gauge track finally hits the hills.

This last stage is anything but fast. Crawling along the barely perceptible incline, it is as though the Shatabdi has suddenly aged and grown tired. Kalka is, in truth, a ragged old place with nothing to recommend it. Yet there is something arresting about those first faint humps and hillocks – all ferns and damp and subtropical creeper-clad thickets – emerging through the haze, because you know they quickly evolve into some of the world's highest mountains.

The Sivalik, or Shiwalik, Hills form the southernmost Himalayan ramparts – and posed a real challenge for railway-builders. Many passengers alighting at Kalka would have it no other way: although the tortuous road is a faster and more practical way into the hills and to Shimla beyond, the narrow gauge train (*see p155*) is rather more fun.

TRAVEL INFORMATION

The New Delhi–Kalka Shatabdi Express (train 2011) departs every morning at 7.40am and reaches Kalka at approximately 11.45am. It connects with the narrow-gauge train to Shimla. Indian Railways' website (www.indianrailways.gov.in) includes timetable and fare information. To book tickets, visit the International Tourist Bureau on the first floor of New Delhi Station; pay in foreign currency or rupees (by showing a bank currency exchange receipt). Next-day tickets are usually available, except during busy holiday times.

Start
KALKA
Finish
SHIMLA
Via
BAROG
Service
KALKA-SHIMLA
RAILWAY
Journey time
5 HOURS

All the Raj

Go back in time on a colonial train to Shimla, a hill station that was once the summer capital of India. By **Amar Grover**

As the British wormed their way deeper into India during the 19th century, they found it difficult to adjust to the heat. The plains were baking, and in the months preceding the annual monsoon, the oven-like atmosphere was oppressive. There were few opportunities of escape.

But salvation was at hand, for as the Raj gradually encroached on the Himalayan foothills, the advantages of altitude became clear. Here, finally, they found a climate that more closely resembled their own. 'Hill stations', as they became known, were cool, offered curative rests, good times and perhaps the chance to find a husband or wife. None of these hill stations was more celebrated than Shimla, today the capital of the state of Himachal Pradesh. And how did the British get there? By train.

The narrow-gauge Kalka-Shimla Railway, or KSR, bears witness to those heady days when the Raj's engineering might was rigorously applied. Built between 1899 and 1903, the 60-mile route starts in Kalka's subtropical, jungly forests, at an altitude of 656 metres, and climbs up through the Sivalik Hills to Shimla's pine- and cedar-clad ridge – a height of 2,075 metres. In 2008, the KSR joined an exclusive club: it became part of the 'Mountain Railways of India'.

Comprising the Darjeeling Himalayan, the Nilgiri in Tamil Nadu and now the KSR, the three railways are collectively listed as a UNESCO World Heritage Site.

A nostalgia trip

At five hours uphill, the four daily trains are not the quickest way to Shimla. Nor, today, are the small carriages terribly practical or comfortable. Even in its early years, one writer noted '...the authorities seemed to have served an apprenticeship in the pilchard-packing industry'.

For tourists, though, the route is charming. Everything about it harks back to another age, from its indifference to speed to its retro engineering (it even uses Neale's Tokens, an old-fashioned yet proven safety system that keeps trains apart). For a mountain railway, the KSR is also a uniquely long line.

The small carriage is bustling as the 12.10pm train departs Kalka. There is much swapping of seats to unite large Indian families and placate foreign tourists; it often takes a quarter of an hour for all to settle down and start enjoying the ride. My fellow passengers comprise a group of British rail enthusiasts, a pair of Indian honeymooners who doze much of the way, a bearded saffron-robed *sadhu* and a couple of cyclists whose bikes are stored in the brake van.

The train claws up the hillside, crossing numbered culverts and tiny bridges with barely a straight stretch of line, then ducks through tunnels with the carriage lights flickering. Within a few miles you cross from the state of Haryana into Himachal Pradesh. The forest closes in sporadically and then opens up again, offering glimpses of the deepening valley, which is scattered with clusters of modern, boxy houses.

Great escape

Shimla's rise to prominence was hardly a foregone conclusion. In the early 1800s, the East India Company came to the rescue of the region's various hill states and protected them against invading Nepali Gurkhas. In return, their feudal rulers granted the company tracts of land, which came to be used as military outposts and sanatoria. British bungalows came in their wake; Shimla's first was erected in 1819.

By 1830, the governor-general had formally acquired about 4,000 acres of land from local rulers. Although one visitor quipped that it was a 'resort of the rich, the idle and the invalid', its stock was clearly rising, thanks to its comfortable climate and its gentility. It became the Raj's 'Summer Capital' in 1864 – the Viceroy Sir John Lawrence, who instigated the move, famously wrote he could do more work on a summer's day in Shimla compared to five in Calcutta – though it still often took two gruelling days to reach on the so-called 'cart road'.

From the train, you can still see some of that winding and now surfaced road, overrun with lorries, buses and umpteen private cars and shared taxis. For much of its way, though, the KSR remains aloof from the road. Its construction – financed privately by the Ambala-Kalka Railway Company – dramatically cut the travel time. But within six weeks of opening in November 1903, snow had damaged the line,

and high costs meant that, by 1905, the Indian Government was forced to take over.

No passenger, no matter how technophobic, could possibly remain oblivious to the KSR's engineering prowess. As the train climbs steadily past sleepy, time-forgotten stations, the terrain becomes more demanding. This is a railway with 988 bridges, viaducts and culverts, and 917 curves (in fact, there are so many curves and loops that you can feel disoriented). There are 102 tunnels, though another five have disappeared over the years mainly because of landslides; the region's climate is prone to torrential monsoons in July and August, and heavy snowfall in winter.

Turbans and tweed

By the time the train reaches Jabli, you will have climbed to 1,240 metres. Then, at Chir, you chug across one of the railway's largest bridges, a Romanesque viaduct with numerous arched galleries on four levels. There's a spiral loop near Sonwara, followed by a near-level stretch approaching Barog, whose mile-long tunnel is the line's longest.

Trains usually pause at Barog, which is almost the halfway point, for long enough to stretch one's legs and buy some chai (or tea) and snacks. Time, perhaps, to consider some of the odder stories behind the railway's construction. Barog is named after the British engineer charged with the tunnelling work; here, he began digging at both ends of the hill, but his alignment was out and the tunnels missed. The shame, apparently, was too much to bear, so he shot himself, and the present tunnel was begun anew. This time, the Chief Engineer was reputedly guided by Bhalku, a poor and illiterate villager, described as a local saint who also happened to possess natural engineering skills. Now regarded as something of a folk hero, and credited in the local media with shaping much of the railway's entire route, Bhalku will soon be honoured by a new, eponymous railway museum in Shimla.

The air up there: Shimla Station is nestled in the Himalayan foothills

BELLS & WHISTLES

BEST BIT
Take it as a whole.

TOP TIP
The best views are from the train's right side on the ascent, and the left on the descent.

PHOTO OP
Watch out for the galleried viaduct bridges.

PACK THIS
Kim by Rudyard Kipling beautifully evokes Raj-era India, and includes a description of arriving at Shimla.

ANORAK INFO
One steam locomotive, built in 1905, has been restored and is available for private charter on the KSR. Some of the 43 vintage steam locos now in Delhi's Rail Museum may also be revived.

TRAVELLERS' FARE
A cup of sweet chai (tea) and vegetable pakoras (fritters) at Barog station. Shimla is also the home of Lion ale; the British couldn't have a hill station without proper British beer.

OVERHEARD
'Can you Britishers still build railways like this?'

The line descends slightly as it passes through Solan and then Solan Brewery Station. They are little used now, like many of the stations on this route, as the train is losing customers to faster, more frequent, buses.

After Kanda Ghat, the line climbs steadily once more. A pair of curving, galleried viaducts neatly steers the train across deep ravines, while sunlight bathes the carriages through gaps in the forest. This being Indian Railways, no one seems to mind if you sit by an open door to soak up the exhilarating view and cooler air.

Finally, Shimla appears in the distance, a gleaming mass of buildings cresting a long ridge. One final tunnel, Invernam, heralds the approach to the line's terminus, a station that is probably among the neatest on India's entire network.

And what of Shimla? It's characterised by a dense and crowded lower bazaar and steep lanes, alleys and stairways that climb to the pedestrian-only Mall. The latter is book-ended by the striking yellow Christ Church and the Gaiety Theatre, and peaks at Scandal Point, a touristy lookout spot with a colourful history.

Today, the city divides opinions. For some, it has lost its shine through rampant development and overpopulation; for others, it is a parody of quaint Englishness. Most visitors like it – and there are not many places left in India where turbans and tweed feature so prominently on a daily stroll.

TRAVEL INFORMATION

Of the four daily departures, three are early in the morning. Train 241, at 5.15am, is a slightly faster and more comfortable service than the others. If you travel directly from Delhi on the morning Shatabdi Express, the only viable daytime connection is train 255 at 12.10pm – it reaches Shimla at 5.20pm.

Indian Railways website (www.indianrailways.gov.in) includes timetable and fare information. The easiest way to book through tickets is to visit the International Tourist Bureau on the first floor of New Delhi Station; pay either in foreign currency or in rupees (by showing a currency exchange receipt). Next-day tickets are usually available. Alternatively, simply buy your ticket at Kalka.

Start
JOHANNESBURG
Finish
CAPE TOWN
Journey time
26 HOURS

Shosholoza Meyl

A diamond in the rough

For a glimpse of the real South Africa, forgo the luxury trains and go native on the Trans-Karoo. By **Andrew Eames**

African railways are a legacy of colonialism. Originally laid for the extraction of mineral resources and agricultural produce from the continent's hinterland through to its ports, and thence overseas, they were never really intended for the internal movement of people – at least, not for the locals. African tribes may have been nomadic, but they changed their surroundings according to the seasons, on foot; they didn't change cities, on railways. So rail travel has historically been left for the long-distance carriage of heavy goods, at slow speeds, while the modern era's increasing movement of humanity has been mopped up by a quicker, and more convenient, transport infrastructure: roads.

But there is one African country that boasts a sophisticated rail network and two luxurious private train operators (Rovos Rail and the Blue Train) that promise 'breathtaking countryside' in five-star style. The experience, they say, is 'like a window into the soul of Africa'.

Meanwhile, this same country also has its own unassuming state operator, which runs regular, luridly coloured trains along the same route as those five-star cruises, for a fraction of the price. And on their trains you're far more likely to meet a cross-section of African souls.

That country is, of course, South Africa, and the route shared by the luxury rail operators and the state network Shosholoza Meyl is the 26-hour, 869-mile journey from Johannesburg to Cape Town, a stretch of track that the Shosholoza Meyl calls the Trans-Karoo.

Shosholoza Meyl is an onomatopoeic name that derives from a popular song sung by local railwaymen, and certainly South Africa's railways have played their part in the nation's history. It was beside the railway tracks near Pietermaritzburg that Nelson Mandela was arrested, in 1962, and it was from a whites-only carriage on a train that a young Indian lawyer was ejected, back in 1893, starting a lifetime of campaigning. His name was Mahatma Gandhi.

Welcome to the jungle

Johannesburg's Park Station has little sense of poetry. A taxi, bus, metro and train terminal, swilling with people, it's the kind of place where you need to keep a careful eye on your luggage. Fortunately, there is security everywhere, particularly for those passengers who penetrate down to the dingy basement where the Trans-Karoo stands, waiting for a 10.30am departure. Nobody gets near the platform without a ticket.

The train is designated as 'Tourist Class' (Shosholoza's middle grade between Premier Classe and Economy) and is composed of cabins with fold-down sleeper berths (sheets are extra), a basin in the room, and a window hatch to the corridor. It's clean, there are communal showers and toilets at the end of the carriage,

The Karoo, top

BELLS & WHISTLES

BEST BIT
The brilliant greens of the Cape Winelands, particularly after the dry browns of the dusty Karoo.

TOP TIP
Take your time over a glass of Zonnebloem Cabernet in the dining car, with its huge picture windows.

PHOTO OP
If you're patient and prepared, you can get a picture of the train passing before Table Mountain.

PACK THIS
Mosquito repellent – your window will be open and the train stops at regular intervals.

ANORAK INFO
The gauge of South African railways – 3ft 6in – is narrow; trains are therefore restricted to a maximum of 50mph. Only the new link from Johannesburg airport is broader.

USEFUL PHRASE
'Hambe Gahle', Zulu for travel safely.

TRAVELLERS' FARE
Try the beef curry in the dining car.

DESIGN DETAIL
Look for the logo engraved in the glass in the middle of the dining car windows. It's from the glass manufacturer, but be careful: you might get it floating, ghost-like, in your photographs.

OVERHEARD
'What's the difference between a tourist and a racist? Three months.'

and a dining car with picture windows and air-conditioning, which proves a godsend in late afternoon when crossing the sun-baked plains of the Karoo. And unlike on the luxury trains, where the customers are tourists from overseas, the passenger list of the Trans-Karoo is far more reflective of the land it is running through.

Rainbow nation

For my journey, I find myself in a cabin between a Zulu couple from Soweto, and a white mother taking her son to his first day in a boarding school near Cape Town. The boy is lively and talkative, and his mother a New Zealander who'd married a South African. Normally, she says, they'd fly to Cape Town, but there was Nicholas's trunk to think of, and all his tennis and cricket things. So the journey is to be a bit of mother-son bonding at this key stage in the boy's youth, while he still appreciates his mother's company.

The Zulu couple are slower to communicate, and we've been under way for half a day before I learn that Philip is a truck driver, and he is taking his wife on a holiday to Cape Town, where she's never been before. Why don't they fly? Philip gives me a sideways look, as if suspicious of my curiosity. 'We prefer to travel along the ground.'

We don't get to the Karoo until shortly before nightfall. The train takes forever to haul itself clear of the squatter camps near Johannesburg, while the symmetrical hills of former mine-workings stalk us across the horizon. At one point, skirting the township of Soweto, we rumble through a massive graveyard at a respectful walking pace. It stretches as far as the eye can see, that graveyard, and is expanding rapidly, judging by the new mounds of flower-flecked earth. The fresh graves lie rank upon rank, as if giant moles have been practising synchronised swimming just under the surface, but there is something far more deadly at work here: AIDS.

Then it is gone, and the land flattens out, emptying itself of houses and roads, of human endeavour and misdemeanour, to be replaced

by scrubland, swamp, and then warthog, zebra and impala running from the train. This is the Africa that passengers are expecting to see.

The Karoo takes shape slowly. A vast, ancient plateau fringed by stark mountain ranges, it covers nearly a third of South Africa, and was once an enormous swamp inhabited by dinosaurs, but today its baked red earth is inhabited mainly by tough merino sheep. In parts it is still green, with antelopes and warthog, but as the journey progresses, so it grows drier and hotter, and the occasional stations change too. These oases in the scrub have a certain raffish, colonial charm. This is Afrikaans (and Boer War) heartland, and at stops like Klerksdorp and Potchefstroom, once the capital of the Boer-ruled South African Republic, there are white men and women among the station staff, welcoming many of the Trans-Karoo's de-training passengers as if they were old friends.

By late afternoon, it is so hot on board that all the cabin doors are open and everyone is out in the corridor or in the dining car, the latter mainly patronised by white passengers, possibly because of the European-style menu, with the likes of lasagne and fish and chips.

Strike it rich

Many passengers are still in the dining car at dusk, when the Trans-Karoo pulls in to Kimberley. This prospectors' town boasts the biggest man-made hole in the world. Dug by 50,000 people, the giant pit yielded 2.5 tons of diamonds and vastly enriched the property owners, the de Beer family. Sadly for Cape Town-bound passengers, the Trans-Karoo only lingers for half an hour, enough for a walk to the end of the platform, but not long enough to peer into a Big Hole.

It's a rare pleasure, falling asleep in a train, especially when the air outside has begun to cool, but sleeping-car sleep is in a category of its own. Anyone who is precious about rest will find it hard, but sleeper aficionados like waking at intervals to watch lights flashing past or to find the train becalmed in a siding, and to speculate about what might be going on up ahead.

But when daylight returns, nothing has changed: the train is still jogging across the Karoo, dry, undulating and beige. But doze for too long, and the next time you open your eyes, you will be among mountains separated by pools of dazzling green into which you're plunging like a swimmer, to emerge exhilarated and refreshed.

The big hole at Kimberley

In that short moment the train has slipped off the edge of the Karoo into the valley of the river Breede, rich with orchards and vineyards. The colours of these Cape Winelands are balm for the eyes after the aridity of the plain, but the Karoo has left its calling card; all the cabin surfaces are covered in a layer of dust as a result of leaving the windows open all night.

Over egg, bacon and toast in the dining car, I tell Jill the New Zealander how I'd been warned (by white South Africans) against travelling on anything but the luxury trains, for my own safety. She tuts. 'They are their own worst enemies. They live in their own little areas, and say that the rest of the country is dangerous. But how can they possibly know when they never try?'

Beyond the very English-sounding town of Worcester, boyhood town of the writer J M Coetzee, the train leaves the verdant vineyards and squirms through several passes, squealing in protest and side-stepping furiously to avoid heavy punches thrown by the Drakenstein and Slanghoek mountains. Emerging from between the rocks like a cork from a bottle, it debouches into rolling corn lands, passing a cattle auction. Now there are Metro trains at stations – a sign, like seagulls are to ships, that the end is near.

As Cape Town approaches, there is an argument and a scuffle in the corridor. Fearing that all those pessimistic warnings about dangers on trains might prove well founded after all, I poke my head out into the corridor, and catch the eye of one of the train's security guards.

'Someone got on without a ticket,' he explains, nodding behind him to where another

---

SIDINGS

The obvious place to break the journey is Kimberley, the diamond-mining town with the aforementioned big hole, mining museum and William Humphreys art gallery.

Downtown Johannesburg is not a place to linger, with a bad reputation for street theft and little to see. But take a cursory look round before you leave, because the contrast between Johannesburg and Cape Town is remarkable: the former is black South Africa, the latter white South Africa, and it feels like two different countries.

In Cape Town, the big attractions are the trendy Waterfront area, Table Mountain, Robben Island (the prison island where Nelson Mandela was held), beaches galore, and trips into the Cape hinterland and vineyards. There's a lot to do and see.

---

guard was leading the culprit. A fare-dodger, big deal. But it's surprising to see, first of all, that they've handcuffed him – it seems a radical solution – and secondly that the fare-dodger is a young, white South African wearing designer sunglasses, surfer shorts and a feckless grin.

As the train pulls past Table Mountain and into Cape Town station, 90 minutes late, I berate myself for my own kind of prejudice. I had made the common mistake of assuming that any wrongdoing on the train would come from a predetermined side of the tracks, but nothing is ever as black and white as that.

TRAVEL INFORMATION

Berths on the Trans-Karoo need to be booked in advance, as with all Tourist Class trains. Shosholoza Meyl's website (www.shosholozameyl.co.za) carries a booking form, although it involves exchanging emails with the reservations office. Berth allocation is done in the station, and passengers' names are then posted on lists down by the platform.

Shosholoza Meyl's Premier Classe service (www.premierclasse.co.za) also runs on this route, if you would prefer to do the journey in more luxurious surroundings.

Start
CAIRO
Finish
ASWAN
Via
LUXOR
Journey time
13 HOURS

Ride like an Egyptian

Track the Nile past tombs and temples,
deserts and palm trees. By **Emma Levine**

It's a 7.30am start for the first daytime express train from Cairo to Aswan. Behind the façade of Cairo's Ramses Station, which dates back to 1898 and has blue tiles outlining the Moorish-style windows, men and women swathed in *galabiyas* clutch children and balance suitcases superbly on their heads. Tiny kiosks punctuate each of the 11 platforms, selling crisps and biscuits, and a few suited businessmen hold their briefcases, ready to board.

The French-built train has just first- and second-class carriages, with most passengers holding reservations, so there's no frantic scramble for seats. The presence of bored-looking police with large dogs is supposed to put our minds at rest, as this is one of few trains to allow foreign tourists.

The departure is delightfully gradual, the train creaking into action while the doors are still open, allowing a last few drags on cigarettes (carriages are smoke free). Reluctantly gathering speed, we travel under flyovers as the sun starts to creep through Cairo's morning smog.

At Imbaba Bridge, the train makes its first rendezvous with the Nile, the longest waterway in the world at 4,200 miles – and our companion

Ramses
Station
and Al Azhar
Mosque
in Cairo

large Cairo suburb whose highway leads straight to the Pyramids, and soon afterwards we leave Africa's largest city behind. You can almost hear the train exhale a sigh of relief as it catches the first glimpse of green fields of sugar cane, date palm trees and the occasional brick kiln.

Next to me, the besuited young Khaled retrieves his laptop. 'Who's your favourite singer?' he asks. I tell him I like Amr Diab, Egypt's equivalent of Robbie Williams. Soon, one of Amr Diab's hits emerges from the computer.

Second-class compartments, with bright red upholstery, are busy with excitable but well-behaved children sprawling on their mother's laps, or standing to gaze out of the window. And even though all carriages are air-conditioned, there is a noticeable difference between each – some are warm, others frigid.

Passengers gather to smoke in the corridors, thereby masking the unsavoury odour from the toilets. But the real smokers' meeting place, and

for the journey. Bearer of Cleopatra's royal barge, Cairo's luxury houseboats and fleets of modern cruise ships, the river has been the sustainer of one of the world's oldest civilisations, dating back 5,000 years. Without the Nile, Egypt would still be as empty as the rest of the Sahara. The river's presence, running up through the spine of the nation, ensures the country remains one of the most powerful in Africa and the Middle East.

For its part, the 546-mile rail route linking Cairo and Aswan, completed in the late 19th century to transport sugar cane from plantations to factories, forms the hub of today's 3,106-mile network. It journeys through Egypt's history and culture, close to Coptic churches, mausoleums, monasteries and burial sites. Much of the 13-hour route lies between the Nile and the Ibrahimiya Canal, which was constructed in the 1860s under the reign of Ismail Pasha and used to irrigate the sugar estates of Middle Egypt.

Jewels of the Nile

On board, the first-class compartment is composed of broad, comfortable seats that recline generously, and a few lone businessmen are quick to doze off. The train fills up at Giza, a

SIDINGS

The obvious place to break the journey – or to travel back to from Aswan – is Luxor, home to Valley of the Kings at Thebes (with the tombs of Tutankhamun and Ramses VI), Luxor Temple and the colossal Karnak Temple.

Aswan, gateway to 'the rest' of Africa, is loved for its Nile panoramas, speckled with gliding white-sailed feluccas. The two-mile walk from Kubbet Al-Hawa, over the desert hills to the ruins of Monastery of St Simeon, commands striking views. And the Old Cataract Hotel seems little changed from when it was a setting for Agatha Christie's *Death on the Nile*.

For a more unusual insight into Egyptian life, the twice-weekly market at Daraw is home to crafty trading of camels, herded from Sudan up to Cairo.

a real highlight, is the small tea bar in the middle of the train. It comprises a table-top and four bar-stools bolted to the floor, is shrouded in clouds of blue smoke, with overflowing ashtrays and jovial atmosphere. There are slim pickings on the menu: chicken or cheese sandwiches on white bread rolls, the ubiquitous Lipton's Yellow Label tea, instant coffee, bottled water and cans of Birell, the local alcohol-free lager.

At 11am, we approach Minya, once the centre of the region's cotton trade. Cotton factories, flour mills, a sugar refinery and carpet-weaving industry are mixed with fields filled with wheat and bananas; the bright colours of farm workers dot the dazzling green. This is considered the border of Lower and Upper Egypt, and it contains some of the region's greatest archaeological sites, particularly the rock-cut tombs at Beni Hassan, 15 miles south.

However, the increase in frequency of armed officers strolling through the carriages is a reminder that this tranquil town, known for its faded Italianate villas, was a hotbed of terrorist activity in the 1990s, owing to Islamic militants. Foreign tourists remain thin on the ground.

Further south, traditional dress becomes more prominent, with lots of *galabiyas* and *shaals* wrapped around heads, and fewer women at the stations. El-Balyana is the jumping off point for Abydos, where Ancient Egyptians would make a pilgrimage to the cult centre of the god Osiris.

As we trundle south, the sunny, sandy hills of the Eastern and Western deserts are just visible to the east. Then, for the most stunning

BELLS & WHISTLES

BEST BIT
The welcoming atmosphere of the buffet car, if you can take all the smoke.

TOP TIP
Bring lots of Egyptian one pound notes – they come in handy for tips and tea.

PHOTO OP
Where the train crosses a broad section of the Nile at the Qena bend, just after Nag Hammadi Station.

PACK THIS
The toilets are dire, with no toilet paper, towels or soap. Bring all of the above, with wet wipes should the water not work.

ANORAK INFO
Rail enthusiasts will love the Railway Museum at Ramses Station – www.egyptrail.gov.eg – opened by King Fuad in 1933; visit when buying your ticket. Exhibits include carriages from the original Royal train from 1859.

USEFUL PHRASE
'*Wahed shay minfadlak*' (one tea please).

SOUVENIR
A napkin from the buffet car; that rare, it's a museum piece.

TRAVELLERS' FARE
Bring your own food. There are rumours of a cooked 'dinner' made on the train, but this traveller saw no evidence of it.

DESIGN DETAIL
The fantastic swivelling chairs, which turn 180 degrees so that you can face your travelling companions.

OVERHEARD
'I love Manchester United.'

Modern meets ancient: mobile phones and Nile scenery

vista of the journey, the train crosses the sturdy bridge at Nag Hammadi, sweeping over the Nile at the broad Qena bend, with limestone cliffs rising on both sides of the valley.

The sun sets too quickly and early, beginning at around 5pm in the winter. There is no rosy-hued sky, just dusk, a darkening and draining of colour, and delicate silhouettes of slender minarets, palm trees, and stone apartment blocks. By 5.30pm, the street lights are on, with a few lorries on the highway on the opposite side of the river, and slower donkey carts laden with people trudging home from the fields.

Luxor Station, the busiest place since leaving Cairo some ten hours earlier, comes as something of a shock, with its fluorescent lights, neon advertisements and loudspeakers. Many tourists disembark here, to see the ancient Egypt found on postcards: the Luxor and Karnak temples and the Valley of the Kings.

South of Luxor, the habitual Nile valley scenery gives way to traffic, apartments with fancy balconies, and the first feeling of being in an urban area.

The train reaches Aswan at around 9pm, and the souk's bright lights wake up bleary-eyed passengers. In front of the station's main entrance, a broad boulevard stretches down to the Nile and one of Egypt's most glorious views – but that will have to wait until morning.

TRAVEL INFORMATION

Egyptian National Railways timetables are available at www.egyptrail.gov.eg. Buy tickets at Ramses Station's booking office at least two days in advance, although first-class compartments are rarely full. Foreigners are allowed only on the express train services, of which there are two in the daytime, leaving early and late mornings, plus one at night and the 'foreigners-only' sleeper train. First-class tickets are twice the price of second class, but still very reasonable.

Start
COLOMBO
Finish
BADULLA
Via
KADUGANNAWA
NAWALAPITIYA
NANU OYA
BANDARAWELA
Service
UDARATA MENIKE
Journey time
10 HOURS

Tea and scenery

Fancy a cuppa? See where Ceylon tea comes from on a train to Sri Lanka's hill country – and drink in the views. By **Royston Ellis**

This journey has its origins in a nice cup of tea. In August 1867, the first train steamed into Kandy, Sri Lanka's hill country capital; that same year, the country's first commercial tea plantation opened nearby. The two events, which lead to the prosperity for the then British colony of Ceylon, were inextricably linked. With the introduction of a railway line, it became possible to transport tea down to Colombo harbour for shipment overseas. Without it, the tea crop would not have been able to reach markets quickly. And without the thousands of tea chests carried as freight, the railway would not have been profitable.

At first the line stopped at Kandy, but then as tea production spread deeper into the hilly interior, the railway followed eastwards through forests and tea gardens to Bandarawela in 1894. And then, after a gap of 30 years, the track was finally extended all the way to Badulla.

The wooden carriages of the early steam trains were luxuriously furnished with opulent restaurant cars, and taking a trip was a grand and romantic affair. In 1924, the journey took over 14 hours. Then, in 1956, train number 15, the Udarata Menike (the Hill Country Maiden), described as 'a fast diesel-hauled express', was introduced between Colombo and Badulla. The new train reduced the journey time to nine hours for the 180mph run. Today it takes longer – at least ten hours – as speed is generally restricted to 9mph an hour. Barely an express, then, and hardly fast, although it is still diesel-hauled.

A special brew

Speed isn't everything, however. The Udarata Menike climbs from sea level to 1,911m and down again along a steep track (the gradient is 1 in 44), passing through 44 tunnels along the way. No wonder this journey delights railway buffs, but it is also a gentle way to discover Sri Lanka's breathtaking scenery. It traverses the best tea-growing country in the world; it creeps along ridges with staggering views of plunging, fertile valleys or soaring, hillside forests swathed in mist; it passes foaming waterfalls and gurgling streams, and it runs by ramshackle hamlets and terraced paddy fields.

SIDINGS

For the best accommodation in the area, leave the Udarata Menike at Bandarawela to stay at the Bandarawela Hotel (www. aitkenspencehotels.com), a splendidly retro hostelry built in 1893. The next morning, by catching the Udarata's sister train, Podi Menike, for Badulla, it is possible to view the incredible engineering feat of the Demodara Loop and the bridge of nine arches, which spans a deep ravine.

The class system

Every morning, 15 minutes before its scheduled departure time (9.30am), the six carriages that form the Udarata Menike are pulled from the marshalling yard at Maradana to the main platform, number three, at Colombo Fort Station. While passengers surge aboard, the engine is

detached and negotiates its way through a web of lines to the other end of the train. This ritual means the 44-seat, first-class observation saloon is positioned at the rear for the entire journey.

The saloon has seen better days. Many of the seats face a panoramic window, but they are worn, stuffed with rubber foam and upholstered in cloth. The decor comprises utilitarian brown plywood. There are ceiling fans, and windows can be raised to let in air. This is a good thing, as a pong from the lone, waterless toilet – corroded after years of use – pervades the air.

On time, the train jerks out of Colombo Fort Station, waved off by the green flag of the guard, who is dressed immaculately in white trousers and shirt with a black tie, his black jacket adorned with chrome buttons. He sits locked in his compartment (part of the observation car) and will only let passengers through to the rest of the train on request, for the observation saloon is a privilege not to be shared.

In its heyday, Udarata Menika used to have eight carriages, including a bar and a restaurant car. These days, it has been reduced to half a dozen, comprising a couple of second-class carriages, three ravaged third-class carriages with bench seats and the aforementioned observation saloon.

The saloon attracts the occasional tourist, but the passengers are mainly retired civil servants travelling free on pensioners' warrants, students heading for a hill-country holiday. They are a staid lot; the passengers picnicking and singing in second class seem to be having more fun, while the folk in third class sit or stand glumly for the short trips between rural stops.

After passing through Colombo's second station of Maradana, the train weaves alongside the Dematagoda running shed, yielding intriguing glimpses of rusting steam engines. It sways as the engine picks up speed, and the clatter as it rushes along a track laid over concrete sleepers makes conversation hard. Then it departs the suburbs and the scenery gradually flattens into

REST ROOM FOR CLERGY

A tea plantation at Nuwara Eliya, above; the first-class observation saloon, top right; lavatories for Buddhist monks, above right

a sea of paddy fields and plantain trees. It stops at several drab commuter stations before reaching Rambukkana, 51 miles from Colombo.

One-track mind

Here the railway slims down to a single track and the Udarata Menike pauses for permission to proceed. The station master hands the driver a purse containing the Tyer's Tablet instrument – an electric token gizmo that ensures there is no other train on the line – and the train ascends 116 metres to Kadugannawa station at 517 metres above sea level. From there, it bypasses Kandy to perform an elaborate shunting movement around the triangular station of Peradeniya, before tackling the single line up to Nawalapitiya, 86mph from Colombo.

The train's crew changes at Nawalapitiya, but the once-bustling atmosphere of this railway division headquarters has vanished. It is lunchtime and a few vendors along the platform hawk *wadey* (fat and spicy lentil cookies), spicy mango slices and packages of rice and curry. As the train heads up to Hatton, at 1,271 metres above sea level, hillsides of closely cropped tea bushes alternate with forests of tall pine trees.

As the train trundles through Poolbank tunnel – at 560 metres the longest one on the island – squeals of mock horror erupt from the children in second class. With shrieking wheels, it lurches past the swoop of St Clair Falls before pausing at the rustic stops of Great Western and Radella, dedicated to tea. At Nanu Oya Station, most passengers leave the train to catch a bus to the popular hill resort of Nuwara Eliya.

For several miles, vegetable gardens invade the scenic beauty of firs, ferns, glades and babbling brooks on the climb to Pattipola – at 1,891 metres, Sri Lanka's highest station, 138mph from Colombo. This marks the beginning of 26 tunnels to Badulla. Emerging from one, passengers in the observation car are amused by the sign on the tunnel entrance that urges slow speed because of 'weak sleepers'. It refers not to those dozing in the carriage, but to the condition of the track.

As the sun sets, the train dawdles to Idalgashina, a narrow station perched atop a ridge with a bleak and craggy landscape on one side and scalloped, formidable hills on the other. After Haputale Station, it seems to have taken a wrong turning as it wanders along the main street, sending market vendors scurrying out of its way. Passing terrain filled with orderly tea gardens that surround the military encampment station of Diyatalawa, the train slips into the outskirts of Bandarawela.

As dusk descends, so does the train: the journey from Bandarawela to Badulla covers 914 metres and takes 90 minutes. In the darkness, the train halts at stations resembling granite cottages before turning kittenish and chasing its tail down the tunnel under Demodara Station, on a piece of railway architecture called the Demodara Loop.

As the Udarata Menike finally arrives at Badulla, the end of the line, only a handful of passengers remains. They step out into a dimly lit, high-arched station, where nothing much seems to have changed since 1924.

TRAVEL INFORMATION

Tickets for Udarata Menike's first-class observation saloon can be purchased up to ten days in advance from the berth reservation office at Colombo Fort Station. In international terms, the journey is very cheap. Timetable information on http://colombofort.com/timetable.htm.

If you want to get up to the hill country more quickly, there is a fast Inter City Express train between Colombo and Nanu Oya, introduced in December 2008. There are also two Inter City express trains a day between Colombo and Kandy.

Start
LIMA
Finish
HUANCAYO
Via
GALERA
Journey time
12 HOURS

Into thin air

Scale the giddy heights of the Peruvian Andes on
a trip that will leave you gasping. By **Suzy Bennett**

It's a surreal moment. High in the Peruvian Andes, at an altitude of 4,000 metres, the door of Carriage D of the Central Andean railway glides open. There, dressed in a dazzling white uniform, stands Nurse Llelia. Under one arm, she clutches a first-aid kit; under the other, an oxygen cylinder.

'Right,' she says in Spanish. 'Who needs me?' The train has almost 1,000 metres still to climb before it reaches its highest point, and passengers are already succumbing to altitude sickness. The carriage is dotted with pale faces, mouths gasping spasmodically for air like fish out of water. Llelia Muñoz is here to treat us.

Dozens of fingers rise feebly into the air. 'Me, please,' calls one woman. Having just been sick in her handbag, and struggling for air, she plainly needs medical attention. Llelia strides towards her, unleashes the contents of her first-aid kit on to the table, gives her a piece of cotton wool soaked in alcohol and makes her take a whiff, before deftly handing her a pill. Then, the clincher: a few breaths on the oxygen cylinder. Even by Latin American standards, the Ferrocarril Central Andino (FCR) is an extraordinary railway.

Running from Lima, Peru's capital, to the mountain city of Huancayo, the FCR is one of the world's highest train lines, and its most

Carry on nurse: breathing can be difficult, but help is at hand, top left. The mining town of La Oroya, top right; lakes near Pastoruri Glacier, left

dangerous. Making a 4,829-metre ascent in just six hours, the train does not give its passengers much of a chance to acclimatise. At this altitude – more than half that of Everest – there is 40 per cent less oxygen in the air than at sea level, and bodies struggle to cope. As a point of comparison, the legal limit of a flight without oxygen is 3,600 metres; the FCR goes 1,229 metres higher than this.

Heart rates rise, breathing almost doubles; headaches, nausea and dizziness are common. In serious cases, there's a risk of pulmonary oedema or even death if left untreated. It's impossible to predict who will succumb. Elite paratroopers can be incapacitated, while their grandmothers are unaffected.

Despite the health risks, the train is packed with holidaymakers, albeit nervous-looking ones. All are apparently willing to accept the risks of making a rapid ascent to altitude, in return for a glimpse of the frozen wastes of the high Andes, one of the most extreme landscapes on earth.

The only way is up

The 12-hour journey begins at Desamporados Station, a beautiful colonial building in Lima. For the first hour, the bright red-and-yellow carriages pass through suburbs, past ragamuffins, barking dogs and startled cattle, before sweeping out into lush, open valleys terraced with ancient Inca farms. Then, the dusty blue foothills of the Andes begin to loom large and the ascent begins.

The only way the train can make its way up the sheer-sided mountain faces of the Andes is to zigzag, a laborious and disorientating process – it feels like a fairground ride that never made it past the prototype.

In fact, the construction of this line was nothing short of a miracle. Promoted by US entrepreneur Henry 'where-a-llama-can-climb, I-can-lay-track' Meiggs, it took 38 years to complete, moving at an average of just five miles per year. No fewer than 66 bridges and 59 tunnels had to be built across terrain that was constantly shifting under landslides and floods, and at least 2,000 men died in the process. In 1872, an engineer reported in the *Chicago Railroad Gazette* that one five-mile section was almost insurmountable. 'Very much of the line cannot be passed over by a biped until a road is made. He would need wings to do it,' he wrote.

It is not a journey of chocolate-box scenery. The Andes are not the neat snowy peaks you visit on Alpine ski trips. There are no chalets with window boxes and geraniums, or skiers in his-and-hers one-pieces. It's brutal, forbidding and heartbreakingly desolate. Very little can survive at this altitude – apart from the condors. The train clings to bare, crumbling precipices and spans gut-churning gorges; much of the time, the window is filled with a view of grey rock so close you could reach out and touch it. Finding blue sky requires a great deal of neck-craning.

At 2pm, the train edges into Galera, which, at 4,572 metres, was the world's highest train station until it was pipped to the post by the Qingzang line in Tibet, which is 287 metres higher (*see p140*). A sign reads 'Altura 15,681 pies' (translation: altitude 15,681 feet). But for a second, in my oxygen-deprived confusion, I thought I'd come across the world's highest, and biggest, pie shop. Those of us who are still able to stand are invited to step on to the platform on 'the roof of South America'. We totter breathlessly around outside, in the bleach-white light, hugging ourselves in the icy air, steadying ourselves on the train for support, like drunks.

BELLS & WHISTLES

BEST BIT
It may not be fun at the time, but for dinner-party conservation back home, nothing beats tales of bizarre behaviour at 5,000 metres.

TOP TIP
To avoid getting altitude sickness – *saroche* in Spanish – eat lightly, rest and avoid alcohol. Medicine is available in chemists in Lima. If you suffer from high blood pressure or heart problems, consult your doctor before travelling.

PHOTO OP
If you can still manage to walk, snap the altitude sign at Galera Station to prove you were there.

PACK THIS
Warm clothes are essential for the journey, as temperatures can drop below 0°C.

ANORAK INFO
The maximum gradient at which you can build a train line without the carriages rolling backwards is four per cent, but the gradient from Lima to the top point of the line is actually six per cent. But rest easy: the series of switchbacks provides necessary security.

USEFUL PHRASE
Dame la bolsa para el mareo (Pass me the sickbag)

SOUVENIR
Whatever you take out of the country, make sure it's not a coca leaf – you could be arrested for drug smuggling.

TRAVELLERS' FARE
Coca tea is the local way to combat altitude sickness. It's been used as a treatment by the indigenous Andean population for centuries, who say it boosts energy and helps digestion. The leaves are the raw form of cocaine, but milder. One cup of coca tea contains about 2mg of cocaine, compared to 30mg-50mg in a line. It's served throughout the journey.

A Peruvian Indian market at Huancayo

past a string of one-llama towns, waved along by red-cheeked children and wizened old women wearing traditional Andean dress: trilbies, long socks and petticoats; horsemen in flowing robes canter along a ridge above a wide lake.

A less appealing vision awaits us in the mining town of La Oroya, a place so apocalyptic it could serve as a set for *Mad Max*. Intensive mining has left bone-white scars all over the mountains, as well as belching fumes so toxic that nothing grows for a 16-mile radius. The train takes us straight through a giant smelter, where soot-blackened workers are wearing gas masks. 'Our lungs are like rocks,' one man tells me as we stop at the station. It's a reminder that this track was not built for tourists, but to transport minerals, fuel, cement and food from the mountains into the rest of Peru. So crucial is the line to Peru's economic well-being that in 1992, Peru's violent Maoist terrorist group Sendero Luminoso (Shining Path) bombed it as part of a brutal campaign, forcing closure until 2003.

During the final hour of the journey, the train coasts through the lush Mantaro Valley, which is dotted with traditional Peruvian markets and villages, and passes red-roofed Jauja, Peru's first colonial capital, founded in 1543 by Spanish conquistador Francisco Pizarro.

At Huancayo, the fun is over. This is a trip where the journey is very much the destination; Huancayo is the cultural and commercial hub of the central Peruvian Andes area and is busy, ugly and noisy. There are no other tourists here and life is distinctly un-Westernised. With altitude sickness over, I get my appetite back and head off to fill my boots. But in a land of 15,000 pies, all I can find to eat is guinea pig.

I have to concentrate on not falling over. My head is pounding, I'm dizzy and feel sick. It's every hangover I've ever had rolled into one.

Second wind

As the train lurches off again, there's a palpable sense of relief. We are heading down now, into a valley where the air is richer and warmer. People begin to feel better, but I still can't stomach lunch: guinea pig, one of Peru's specialities.

With clear heads, we enjoy open views of snow-capped mountains, flat grasslands and glacial lakes. This is classic Andes. We bustle

TRAVEL INFORMATION

The passenger service runs about twice a month all year round, with return trips two days later. Fare and timetable information is available at www.ferrocarrilcentral.com.pe. Website www.incasdelperu.org gives a detailed history of the railway, while the South American Explorers Club (www.saexplorers.org) has up-to-date travel reports about the country.

The beauty of train travel is the unhindered view. Roads attract ugliness, with all their shopping centres and distribution depots, but trains run unfettered and uncluttered through country and city, crossing gorges, bisecting plains and peering into a nation's backyards. A train's passengers are unfettered and uncluttered, too. Without the need to concentrate on the road, the brakes or the in-flight announcements, there is no reason not to drink in the view. Much of the world's most dramatic scenery, from the Alps to the Andes, is visible from a train – and in this book. And it doesn't matter if you doze off while looking; you're not going to crash, and the next time you open your eyes, you'll find that – hey presto – someone has changed the picture for you.

Scenic Spectaculars

Start
SETTLE
Finish
CARLISLE
Via
YORKSHIRE
DALES
Journey time
2.75 HOURS

Best of British

From majestic peaks to lush valleys, the Settle-to-Carlisle line
serves up a glorious panorama. By **Anthony Lambert**

No railway line in England comes close to the romantic grandeur of the 72-mile Settle-to-Carlisle line. Linking Leeds and Carlisle, but formally starting at Settle Junction just south of the eponymous North Yorkshire market town, the railway traverses the wildest parts of northern England through landscapes that have enthralled passengers since the line opened in 1876.

That it still runs is something of a miracle: it came close to never being built, and was paradoxically saved from closure by the closure proposals themselves. Originally, the Midland Railway (MR) obtained Parliamentary approval to build the line as a tactical move to force a rival to be more accommodating in sharing a parallel route. When the ploy succeeded, the MR tried to abandon the project, but Parliament – keen to promote competition – made them go through with it. So the MR were forced to make the best of a bad job – yet ended up building a superbly engineered main line through difficult country.

It was a monumental task, as passengers will appreciate as they gaze over panoramic views from lofty viaducts and burrow through the hard Pennine rocks in long tunnels. And they would have been denied the experience had British Rail triumphed with its 1983 proposal to close the

Dent Station in the Yorkshire Dales, left; Ingleborough Peak is crowned by the remains of an Iron Age fort, right

line. The threat generated so much publicity and opposition that previously empty trains suddenly filled with passengers, quadrupling the numbers. The railway was granted a reprieve in 1989, and it has since become busy with a mix of passenger trains, special excursions (many steam-hauled) and freight.

Once upon a time, you could have had lunch aboard the Thames-Clyde Express traversing this route, with fleecy white clouds of steam wafting over the train to remind you of the exertion up front on the footplate. Today, the trains that rattle over the line are largely hand-me-downs from other routes that have seen better days, but the views are what lure the passengers, whether to watch from the window or to start walks from stations en route.

Besides these tourists, the railway remains an important lifeline for small local communities, especially in winter, for the roads over the hills remain tortuous and slow. So the trains carry locals on shopping trips to towns and to the start of longer journeys from Leeds and Carlisle.

Lonely at the top

The exit from Leeds Station is shared with trains for Morecambe and Lancaster, but even this first part of the journey through the Aire Valley is full of interest. At Saltaire, for instance, you pass within a stone's throw of St Titus Salt's immense mohair and alpaca mill, which was the largest factory in the world when it was built in the 1850s. Today, it is home to the largest collection of Hockney paintings. Shortly afterwards, a plume of steam at Keighley marks the starting point of the Keighley & Worth Valley Railway, which winds up the valley past the home of the Brontë family at Haworth and on to the moorland terminus at Oakworth.

At the isolated signal-box of Settle Junction, the railway begins an almost constant climb for 15 miles at a gradient of 1 in 100, earning the sobriquet 'Long Drag' in steam days, when the fireman would be shovelling almost continuously to maintain boiler pressure. Beyond the market town of Settle, it enters the Yorkshire Dales National Park, and well-booted walkers are likely

SIDINGS

There are fantastic walks from all ten intermediate stations on the line, and some of them are described in leaflets you can pick up along the way. Settle is a delightful market town, full of narrow streets, courtyards and alleys, with two museums. In Kirkby, Stephen parish church is an eighth-century representation of the Norse god Loki, the only one of its kind in England and one of only two known to survive in all of Europe. Appleby Castle is open to visitors, and in its grounds is a collection of rare farm breeds under the auspices of the Rare Breeds Survival Trust.

Carlisle has a castle with the regimental museum of the King's Own Royal Borderers, a small cathedral, and an outstanding museum in Tullie House. Besides an exhibition on the area's railways, Tullie House has a herb garden and an exciting audio-visual presentation about the raids and feuds that blighted border life for centuries. This is also the national study centre for the whole of Hadrian's Wall, which passes just north of the city, and has an outstanding art collection with works by Ford Maddox Brown, Paul Nash, Samuel Palmer, LS Lowry, Camille Pissaro, Walter Sickert and Stanley Spencer.

Ribblehead
Viaduct

to alight at Horton-in-Ribblesdale, intent on climbing one of the adjacent Three Peaks: jelly-mould-shaped Penyghent, Whernside and Ingleborough, the last crowned by the remains of an Iron Age fort. The landscape becomes progressively wilder, the trees stunted and wind-blown and the dark stone-walled pasture gives way to coarse grasses on open moor. This is landscape on a majestic scale, the eye constantly drawn up barren hillsides to rocky escarpments and over wild fell country known only to sheep and walkers.

During the campaign to save the line, its symbol became Ribblehead Viaduct, the gently curving arc of stone that carries the line over the hollow of Batty Moss. Its desolate setting amid the Pennine hills captures the essence of the line. It is so exposed that railwaymen have had to cross it on their hands and knees in the lea of the parapet during ferocious storms, and coal was even blown off firemen's shovels. The spiritual needs of the few local railwaymen and quarry workers were met by church services held in the booking hall between 1880 and 1956.

In the dark of Blea Moor Tunnel, the line reaches the end of the long climb from Settle Junction. The tunnel absorbed over a third of the £3.3 million construction cost. Lovely views down Dentdale herald the arrival at England's highest station, Dent, at 350 metres, where the station building has been converted into self-catering accommodation that sleeps six (www.dentstation.co.uk).

How green is this valley

Garsdale, a lonely hamlet in a quiet valley, was once the junction for a railway across the Pennines to Northallerton on the East Coast main line. But only a few terraces of stone houses signify that this remote place was once a busy railway hub; today its population is a mere 200, its beauty a well-kept secret. The summit of the railway is at Ais Gill, at 356 metres, and the sharp-eyed will see maroon summit boards on

each side of the track. The great millstone-grit flank of Wild Boar Fell overshadows the line; it was hereabouts that the country's last wild boar was reputedly killed in 1464.

As the railway drops down into the valley of the River Eden, the coarse grasses give way to pasture, dotted with isolated small barns and tree-sheltered farms. Legend has it that an earlier fortification on the site of the ruined Pendragon Castle, beside the river, was the place where Uther Pendragon, father of King Arthur, was poisoned. As the valley sides diminish in height, passengers get a distant view of Lake District peaks to the west.

Once the county town of Westmorland, Appleby – the next station – is built on a loop in the River Eden, which is within walking distance from the station. From Langwathby Station, partly occupied by the Brief Encounter restaurant and café, there is another walk, to Long Meg and her Daughters, the second-largest stone circle in the country. Dating from about 1500 BC, it comprises one large and 68 small stones, supposedly representing a mother and her daughters who committed heinous acts on the Sabbath and were turned into stone.

Though journey's end is near, the line has one final flourish in the beautiful section between Lazonby and Cotehill, the prettiest part of the Eden Valley. For several miles, the river runs through a densely wooded gorge with precipitous slopes of birch and bracken dropping down to the water far below. This area is best appreciated on foot, and the ancient Nunnery Walks, near the confluence of the Eden and Groglin rivers, show off the nearby waterfalls and sandstone cliffs, which reach up 61 metres.

The penultimate stop, Armathwaite, is a pleasant Cumbrian village with a working watermill that produces woven fabrics. The scenery thereafter is pleasant, rather than spectacular, as the railway crosses the last pasture to the border city of Carlisle, and Sir William Tite's imposing neo-Tudor station.

BELLS & WHISTLES

BEST BIT
The wildest parts around the Ribblehead Viaduct, which are very exposed to the elements – and particularly dramatic on a windy day.

TOP TIP
Choose a cold, clear day in winter for the best visibility and most atmospheric conditions.

PHOTO OP
Trainspotters love this line. If you're on a steam-hauled special, you'll spot other photographers perched along the route, so snap right back.

PACK THIS
Ordnance Survey maps to help you identify topographical features.

ANORAK INFO
The Settle-to-Carlisle is featured in Microsoft Train Simulator, which depicts the line as it was in the 1920s–1940s, with the player able to drive the Flying Scotsman or British Rail Class 50 Valiant along the route.

TRAVELLERS' FARE
Snack trolleys on some trains, but best to come prepared with Wensleydale sandwiches.

DESIGN DETAIL
Many of the stations have been beautifully restored by various private organisations.

OVERHEARD
'Who in their right mind would build a railway through this?'

TRAVEL INFORMATION

There are six trains each way on weekdays, seven on Saturdays and three on Sundays. Journey time is usually about two hours and 45 minutes. Steam charters regularly operate over the line, some giving the opportunity to enjoy the incomparable scenery from a dining-car. For additional information, including departure times, visit www.northernrail.org or www.settle-carlisle.co.uk.

Inca civilisation

Make your way to Machu Picchu in the
lap of luxury. By **Edward Reeves**

Start
CUSCO
Finish
MACHU PICCHU
Service
ORIENT EXPRESS
HIRAM BINGHAM
Journey time
3 HOURS

So what makes a train journey great? One thing's certain. Size, or length, doesn't matter. On the Orient Express Hiram Bingham, which traverses the Peruvian Andes, the distance from start (Poroy Station, near Cusco) to finish (the town of Aguas Calientes) is just 58 miles, descending along a narrow-gauge track. Yet despite its brevity, it is one of the world's great train journeys, with a mind-boggling destination: the ruins of Machu Picchu.

No one knows the true history of this mysterious site. The American explorer Hiram Bingham, after whom the train is named, discovered the ruins in 1911. At the time, he thought Machu Picchu was Vilcabamba, the last refuge of the Incas, who had retreated to hidden Peru as they fled the Conquistadors in the 16th century. But the 1960s discovery of the real Vilcabamba, deeper in the rainforest, put paid to that theory. Still, Machu Picchu would have made a great hideaway, perched as it is atop sheer granite cliffs high above the Urubamba river.

To find it, Bingham had to journey through difficult terrain, cross a dangerously swollen river on an improvised rope bridge, and literally crawl up the jungle-covered mountainside; thankfully the train that bears his name today makes for a far more civilised journey.

Machu
Picchu

Even its departure time is comfortable: the train doesn't ease away from Poroy's platform until 9am, three hours after the standard PeruRail tourist service has left Cusco. But be warned: any lingering sleepiness won't survive the boarding process, as a brightly coloured Peruvian band is there to pipe passengers aboard the gleaming, blue-painted carriages. 'El Cóndor Pasa', anyone?

Cameras at the ready

Food is a big part of the Hiram Bingham experience (most of the passengers are hefty in body and wallet; thin people tend to reach Machu Picchu via the heavily oversubscribed four-day Inca Trail). It's no surprise, then, that all carriages, except the rear observation car, are set up for dining, with two- or four-seater booths. The

interior designer clearly envisaged a train packed with sophisticates in dinner suits and cocktail dresses, hence the 1920s vibe. But today, most passengers wear khakis and hiking boots. Besides, the best place to be is the observation car, which is partially open to the elements. Get in early to bag the best spot for photos (the right-hand side for the pre-brunch part of the journey). There's a bar, too, but sadly the band from the station has come along for the ride to provide music – whether you like it or not.

From Poroy, the Hiram Bingham rattles along ruler-straight tracks across the Pampa de Anta. It was on these featureless plains that the 15th-century Inca warrior Pachacutec won battles that secured Inca domination in Peru – until the Spanish arrived. Today, the plains are farmland, but 40 minutes into the journey, after the town of

flowing, and often made wider and faster by melt-water from the nearby mountains of Wakay Willka ('Tears of God') and Alankoma. The Incas took advantage of the valley's fertile soil and plentiful water to farm here; you can still see their intricately constructed terraces from the train as you pass through the town of Ollantaytambo.

Huarocondo, the train leaves the prairie and enters the dramatic, twisting gorge of the Pomatales river. Suddenly, you can see what an engineering feat this railway is, and why such a short stretch of track took so long to build (construction began in 1913 and ended in 1928).

The Pomatales is a tributary of the Urubamba, and joins it at the one-llama town of Pachar. You'll be eating brunch by now, all three courses of it. The food is international, with a couple of local flavours: an alpaca minute steak and unusually palatable Peruvian wines. Don't overdo it on the booze until the return journey, as steady feet are required at Machu Picchu: some of the unfenced paths feature lethal drops.

From Pachar, the landscape opens up as the train passes along the Urubamba river, through the Sacred Valley. The Urubamba is wide and fast

SIDINGS

At Machu Picchu, if you want to climb Huayna Picchu, the peak that overlooks the city – and you should – you must stay overnight at Aguas Calientes. Don't feel obliged to stay at the Orient Express Sanctuary Lodge by the ruins – it's expensive and you'll be cut off from lively Aguas Calientes in the evening.

Instead, try the extremely chic La Casona opposite, an 11-bedroom hotel in a restored 16th-century mansion (www.inkaterra.com). The same group has the best hotel in Aguas Calientes too, right by the train station.

Note: the first bus from the town to the ruins leaves before 6am (check the times with your hotel). Be on it, as just 400 tickets are issued for Huayna Picchu each day, on a first-come, first-served basis.

There are two cheaper services from Cusco to Machu Picchu: the Vistadome and Backpacker, which depart from Cusco San Pedro Station at 6.05am and 6.50am respectively, arriving at Aguas Calientes at 9.52am and 10.51am. On the way back, they depart Aguas Calientes at 15.25 and 17.03, arriving at Cusco at 19.41 and 21.19. If demand is heavy, extra services may be added. There are also services from Ollantaytambo in the Sacred Valley, a worthwhile destination in itself. Consider getting a cheaper service from here, and returning in luxury on the Hiram Bingham.

BEST BIT

Arriving in style in one of the world's most spectacular locations, the train having taken the strain. You'll be the envy of the footsloggers, although your inner puritan might try to make its voice heard!

TOP TIP

Don't treat Cusco as a mere base from which to get to Machu Picchu – it's a buzzing place near plenty of fascinating Inca sites.

PHOTO OP

Machu Picchu empties at the end of the day as the trains leave – if you forego the cream tea laid on for Hiram Bingham passengers, you can get a picture without the hordes.

PACK THIS

A waterproof poncho – the weather at Machu Picchu can change in an instant. And warm clothes for Cusco – it can get seriously chilly at night.

ANORAK INFO

This is a rare example of a private train operator, Orient Express, also taking responsibility for the upkeep of the track.

SOUVENIR

In Cusco, the roofs of many houses are adorned with miniature painted terracotta bulls. You can pick these up in the markets for a couple of dollars.

TRAVELLERS' FARE

The four-course dinner on the Hiram Bingham's return journey is a culinary highlight. But that might just be due to all the pisco sours you down beforehand.

The river wild

After brunch, return to the observation car, where the prime photography spot is now on the left-hand side, looking across the river. As the train enters the microclimate of the Urubamba Gorge, we have lost a thousand metres since Cusco. The lush vegetation proves it – we are descending into the cloud forest; what the Peruvians call *ceja de selva* ('the eyebrow of the jungle'). The river narrows here and becomes a torrent.

Keep an eye out for Qorihuayrachina. Here, you can't miss the long procession of hikers beginning the Inca Trail on the opposite bank of the river, their bright waterproofs marking them out against the greenery as they climb the ancient rock staircase.

After you pass Chachabamba (where you can begin the less arduous one-day Inca Trail), the river is more ferocious, foam-white water crashing against boulders the size of small houses. Hiram Bingham had to send a terrified local across the river with a rope before he could build his makeshift bridge; God knows how frightened that poor unnamed soul was.

As you near Machu Picchu, most passengers get twitchy and return to their seats for their things. But don't feel pressured to leave the observation car: the band will have stopped playing, leaving you in peace.

The train eases into Aguas Calientes, a charmingly shabby tourist town – and the gateway to Machu Picchu, 400 metres above. A bus takes you on the final 20-minute leg of the journey. Entry and a guided tour of Machu Picchu (and a cream tea in the evening) are all included in the train fare, but once is not enough. If you've time, delay the return journey for a day, so you can enjoy the site once more in the early morning, before the day trippers arrive. If not, don't worry about more hours on the train. The return leg might not have scenery (it'll be dark), but pisco sours will be poured, the band will come into their own and you can take advantage of a swell party. Now that's a great train journey.

Aguas Calientes, the gateway to Machu Picchu

TRAVEL INFORMATION

The Hiram Bingham departs Poroy Station (15 minutes' drive from Cusco) each morning apart from Sunday at 9am and arrives at Aguas Calientes at 12.25pm. The return leaves Aguas Calientes at 17.45, getting into Poroy at 21.11. Visit www.orient-express.com for more information. Timetable information is on the PeruRail website at www.perurail.com. Even if you've pre-booked long in advance, you'll have to present your passport and pay in cash the day before at PeruRail's Cusco offices at Wanchaq Station, for all services from Cusco and Poroy, including the Hiram Bingham.

Be aware that in Peru, transport strikes are a regular occurrence, especially during the peak tourism season of April to November, and that you might have to change your schedule at short notice. There are no roads to Machu Picchu, so if the trains aren't running, there's no Plan B. So use a specialist tour operator, which is likely to have experienced local staff who can think on their feet and adapt your itinerary as required. It is also sensible to ring your tour operator before departing the UK, to check if any strike action is planned during your visit to Peru.

For overnight stays in Cusco, the Monasterio is the most famous hotel (www.orient-express.com), but you should stay at the tiny and extremely chic La Casona opposite, an 11-bedroom hotel in a restored 16th-century mansion (www.inkaterra.com).

Start
LOS MOCHIS
Finish
CHIHUAHUA
(MEXICO)
Via
COPPER CANYON
AND THE
SIERRA MADRE
Journey time
14 HOURS

Treasure of the Sierra Madre

A gold mine for photographers, the El Chepe shows off the best of Mexico's mountains, canyons and rios. By **Edward Reeves**

There's a right way and a wrong way to do everything, from greeting the Queen to eating an artichoke. The same rule applies to Mexico's Copper Canyon railway. Do you start from Los Mochis, just inland from the Sea of Cortez, and travel 2,460 metres upward and 14 hours eastwards to finish the journey in Chihuahua? Or vice versa?

Conventional wisdom dictates that you begin the journey at Los Mochis or, to avoid a 6am start, El Fuerte, two hours down the line. Going up seems more dramatic (after all, Hillary and Tenzing didn't start at the top of Everest and work their way down), but there is another more concrete reason. The trains of the Ferrocarril de Chihuahua al Pacífico, known affectionately as El Chepe, can run late, meaning that if you board at Chihuahua, you risk travelling along the most dramatic sections of track in the dark. But Time Out is not a publication that listens to conventional wisdom, so we find ourselves in the waiting room at Chihuahua station far too early on a chilly January morning.

It's dark, obviously, so there's little to do but climb aboard. For the best views, ask at the ticket booth for a seat on the left-hand side. The carriages are air-conditioned, with plenty of leg room and wide, well-upholstered chairs designed to accommodate wide, well-upholstered North Americans. Come 6am, the whistles blow, the guards jump aboard (along with a couple of machine-gun toting policemen; in the 1990s, the train was raided several times by banditos), and without any ceremony, El Chepe eases through the grim, fluorescent-lit suburbs of Chihuahua.

With an hour or more till dawn, this is a good opportunity to crib up on the convoluted history of Mexico's last functioning passenger train. The story begins back in 1861, when the American engineer Albert Kinsey Owen chanced upon Topolobambo Bay on Mexico's Sea of Cortez (also known as the Gulf of California), and decided it was the perfect place to build a port to connect the Midwest United States to the Pacific. Glossing over the small matter of the mountains of the Western Sierra Madre, and the huge collection of canyons known collectively as the Copper Canyon system, Owen somehow talked the Mexican government into sharing his cripplingly expensive vision.

Building the flat sections of railroad proved easy enough, but for decades the twisty, uppy-downy bits were put off until mañana. Fifty years later there was still a missing chunk – a 160-mile-long missing chunk, to be precise, over some of the most treacherous terrain in North America. The federal government took control of the project, and somehow managed to tackle this intimidating feat of engineering in just nine years, opening the completed line, with its 39 bridges and 87 tunnels, in November 1961. Even today,

Many rivers to cross: Rio Chinipas

it remains the only viable route for cargo across the Sierra Madre, as there is still no proper road (another job for mañana).

Pining away

As dawn breaks, features of this bleak landscape will begin to be visible, and the train starts climbing and twisting into the first mountain range. Five months have passed since the rainy season, and the predominant colour is brown. It's rugged, unwelcoming territory, Apache country. It doesn't take much imagination to picture the proud warriors standing on ridges, watching in horror as the first settlers arrived, built homesteads, planted crops and started

dropping litter – practically the Mexican national sport – on the virgin plains.

Today, on those plains, the descendants of the settlers work in cellulose and viscose plants. You'll see industrial silos as you pass through the town of Anahuac, and then the polluted lake of Bustillos to the right. This is not a part of the journey you're likely to remember. Twelve miles

SIDINGS

If you want to stop en route to explore the Copper Canyon system – and you should – get off at Creel or Bachuichio rather than Divisadero; if you just want to break the journey for a night, stop at Divisadero. Within a mountain-bike ride of Creel are the peaceful camping spot of Lake Arareko, the weird rock formations of the Valley of Arareko and Bisabírachi, and the Cusararé waterfall (which can disappoint in dry season). If your schedule allows, make the four-hour drive from Creel to the Basaséachic Falls, or the six-hour drive to Batopilas, in the subtropical depths of the Urique canyon. Here you can visit the famous 'Lost Cathedral' of Satevo, the remains of a mission church of unknown origins.

For help organising treks, bike rides and canyon excursions, or to rent bikes, kayaks or camping equipment, contact Three Amigos, with offices in Creel and El Fuerte (www.amigos3.com), or El Fuerte-based tour guide Adrian Jimenez Conde (email turismofuerte@hotmail.com). Both speak English.

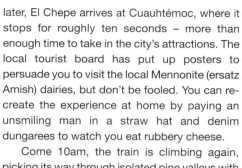

later, El Chepe arrives at Cuauhtémoc, where it stops for roughly ten seconds – more than enough time to take in the city's attractions. The local tourist board has put up posters to persuade you to visit the local Mennonite (ersatz Amish) dairies, but don't be fooled. You can re-create the experience at home by paying an unsmiling man in a straw hat and denim dungarees to watch you eat rubbery cheese.

Come 10am, the train is climbing again, picking its way through isolated pine valleys with log-cabin homesteads, chimneys smoking peacefully. Donkeys stand, staring aimlessly into space, erections with nowhere to go hanging heavy beneath their barrel-like stomachs. What are they thinking about?

The ticket inspector is doing the rounds. El Chepe always runs on time, he reassures us, at least until it reaches Divisadero. After that, the journey becomes less predictable, as going downhill can be… 'difficult'.

We cross the bridge over Rio San Pedro, and tick the stations off as we pass. Terrero, Pichachic, Ataros, Treviño, then the lumber hub of San Juanito, Mexico's coldest town. It looks it, too. Here we see our first Tarahumara Indians, a tough-looking bunch who live in the canyons and are famed for their ability to run long distances, kicking a wooden ball, drunk. Then it's another stop, at Creel, deemed a 'Magical Town' by the Mexican government, which hopes to turn it into a hub for tourists who want to explore the

Good as gold: the Copper Canyon

canyon system. An airport is planned, and even the local drug cartels are doing their bit to raise Creel's international profile, shooting dead 13 of the mayor's friends and family in cold blood.

Onwards and upwards to Divisadero, another hour along the line, during which the topography forces the track to make its famous 'Loop', doubling back on itself in a complete circle through the rocky, pine-dotted mountains. At Divisadero, the train stops for a quarter of an hour to let passengers disembark, buy ethnic knick-knacks, and take photos of the Urique Canyon. On a clear day, you'll see the silver line of Rio Urique 1,300 metres below. It'll be lunchtime by now, and this is the place to break the journey if you've only a night to spare, as we do.

Postcards from the edge

Next day, El Chepe clatters into Divisadero station over an hour late. Engine problems, explains the guard. We pull off in the pouring rain, only to stop 15 minutes later at San Rafael while

Oh Rio, Rio: the winding Fuerte

BELLS & WHISTLES

BEST BIT
The twists, tunnels and valleys from Divisadero to Agua Caliente bridge, or vice versa, depending on which end you started from.

TOP TIP
If the driver is in the mood, El Chepe will stop for a few minutes on Puente Chinipas, with views to the left over Lake Huites. Be prepared for this, because all the wannabe photographers will be competing for a door. Also be ready for the 'Temoris Switch'. Coming from Chihuahua, stay on the left, looking down on Temoris station, but as you enter La Pera tunnel (No.49), jump to the right-hand side.

PHOTO OP (OFF-TRAIN)
The train stops for 15 minutes at Divisadero, where you can disembark for a photo looking down the canyon. If you're staying overnight, walk to Piedre Volada – a round rock sitting precariously on an outcrop. Stand on it, and you can make it wobble. It's perfectly safe, apparently.

PACK THIS
A warm jumper or fleece. It can get seriously cold up in the Sierra Madre.

SOUVENIR
Chihuahua is the place to shop. Cowboy boots are a speciality, in any colour or design that you can imagine (lime green ostrich skin, for one). Starting prices work out at about £20 ($33 US).

ANORAK INFO
Sadly, Mexico has effectively abandoned the concept of passenger railways, withdrawing its government subsidy from all lines. The survivors are the commuter lines or a couple of tourist ones like El Chepe.

USEFUL PHRASE
'Excuse me, do you mind letting others have a go?' Competition for standing space by the doors is tough, but if you want good photos you have to make your presence felt.

TRAVELLERS' FARE
Food on El Chepe is expensive and mediocre, but you're not allowed to bring your own (the rule is enforced). Wait till Divisadero, where you can grab a cheap and delicious gordita or taco.

OVERHEARD
'Banditos? Aren't they the ones that come in the orange bag?'

a new locomotive is attached. It's gone 2.30pm by the time we get moving, and dusk is at six. We're racing the sun. Some quick mental calculation: the sun moves at roughly 486,000mph; El Chepe at about 40mph. The odds aren't good.

It's downhill all the way now, as El Chepe drops 2,133 metres in 122 miles, and as we lose altitude the weather gets better and better, along with the scenery. From here to the Aguas Caliente bridge over the Rio Fuerte, the stretch is the stuff of postcards, as El Chepe passes over the bulk of the line's bridges. A platoon of elderly American gentlemen is on board, armed with huge Canon cameras. Best to beat them to one of the eight doors.

As I lean out, the air is warm, and tinged with diesel smoke from the locomotive ahead. Somehow, in the space of a few miles, we've passed from a Mexican winter to an Alpine springtime, the sun reflecting off the carriages as we twist along the sides of the canyons.

Surprisingly, the rivers at the bottom of these canyons are just trickles picking their way round rocks left by the landslides that happen in rainy season. It's hard to believe such tiny streams have carved through hundreds of metres of rock, even with millions of years to do the job. They must have got the contractors in.

An overstimulated pensioner with a guidebook counts down the tunnels, which follow one another in quick succession. No. 48 is the one to look out for: El Chepe shoots out into the valley of the Rio Septentrion above Temoris station, with three levels of railroad in sight. It's quite a view, but one that's cut short by Tunnel No.49, nicknamed 'La Pera'. During its 582-mile length, El Chepe descends 30 metres and does a 180° about-turn, emerging beneath the track it's just traversed. That's some trick, and one that catches out most of the amateur photographers. Look out for the waterfall and commemorative sign made from rails, celebrating the opening of the line in 1961.

The sun is lower in the sky now, the evening light painting the rockfaces opposite the track red, gold and copper. They look good enough to eat, as if they've been drizzled with honey. It's one of those free shows Mother Nature lays on occasionally. There's much snapping of shutters, as each bend brings a new and more spectacular view. El Chepe seems to be getting faster and faster as it follows the course of the Rio Septentrion and, leaning out the window with your face in the wind, you start to feel like you're on a fairground ride. Only when El Chepe breaks sharply for Santo Niño is the spell broken.

Time is running out, along with the daylight. Damn that dodgy locomotive. But then, with exquisite timing, the valley opens up, and beneath us the Septentrion joins the Rio Chinipas at Lake Huites, as still and black as a pool of crude oil. The driver slows the train as we approach Chinipas Bridge, 102 metres above the river (which was dammed in the 1990s), and stops halfway across, with the lake to the left. It's just coming up to six o'clock, and there can be no better place to watch the sun go down.

It seems we've made it, almost. From here, there are just two more points of interest before the final destination, El Fuerte. First, the track's last and longest tunnel, No.86 (just over a mile); second the Agua Caliente Bridge, which spans a quarter of a mile over the Rio Fuerte. But now it's too dark for pictures, so everyone heads off for the dining car, and the smell of frying food mingles with the diesel.

It's 8.30pm by the time we arrive, two hours behind schedule. But El Fuerte turns out to be a postcard-perfect colonial town (and supposedly the birthplace of Zorro), so it's a good place to come back down to earth over a gin and tonic.

TRAVEL INFORMATION

El Chepe leaves Los Mochis or Chihuahua at 6am each day, and takes roughly 14 hours to reach the other end. Visit www.chepe.com.mx for timetable information. If you're travelling eastwards, catch the train at El Fuerte, at 8.30am. You won't miss anything, unless you want to see sunrise over the cactus forest. If you're starting at Chihuahua, having flown in via Mexico City from the UK, jet lag will be your friend – you'll be wide awake long before 6am.

El Chepe only usually suffers serious delays during the rainy season (June/July/August), when landslides often occur. The absolute best time to take the trip would be mid-to-late September or October, after the rains have stopped, but while the landscape will still be lush.

The hotels in Chihuahua, Creel and Divisadero are no great shakes. Compensate by staying at the idiosyncratic and romantic 17th-century Hotel Torres in El Fuerte (www.hotelestorres.com). Tour operator Bales Worldwide (www.balesworldwide.com) can make hotel and train arrangements.

Start
LA SPEZIA
Finish
GENOA
Via
THE CINQUE
TERRE
Journey time
2-4 HOURS

Bella vista

Italy's Cinque Terre is the stuff of postcards, and its colourful coastal railway is as pretty as a picture. By **Tristan Rutherford**

Central Italy is snowbound, so it is a shock to see La Spezia Station in radiant green. Palm trees run alongside the tracks in this remote outpost of Liguria, while window boxes dot the station building and Piaggio three-wheelers fill the car park. Sixty miles down the coast from the province's capital of Genoa, La Spezia is cut off from the poplars, fog and fancy cars of neighbouring Tuscany by a long train tunnel.

Market day entices elderly shoppers, who mob the midday train for the Cinque Terre discussing their morning bargains. Not for nothing are Ligurians known as the tightwads of Italy. But they are sprightly and in good spirits; before this lifeline rail route to the remote but dramatically sited villages of Riomaggiore, Manarola, Corniglia, Vernazza and Monterosso started in the 1950s, their vegetables were grown by hand on the hills, then hauled over the six-mile stretch of precipitous cliffs that separate the villages from La Spezia.

Back then, the communities were almost as isolated from one another as they were from the outside world. The literal translation of Cinque Terre is significant: not five villages, but five lands.

The line from La Spezia to Genoa follows a two-hour coastal curve north-west, but all

Get off the train at Riomaggiore for some gorgeous coastal walks

onboard are heading to the most southerly Cinque Terre village of Riomaggiore, just ten minutes but a whole world away. Shopping bags, winter gloves and the odd pair of designer shades are lost in darkness as the carriages bore straight through the limestone cliffs. The ceiling's 1980s fluorescent tube lighting fails to kick in, but that's hardly surprising, since it looks like little has been touched in the three decades since this train hit the tracks.

Eyes adjust to the five-minute blackout. The elderly passengers brace themselves: when the bright light returns, one feels a pop of the ears. A five-second exposure to the scenery, featuring a horizon-filled snapshot of grey ocean-rollers hammering the towering green cliffs, is all that's allowed before the train burrows back inside again; the vista is similar five minutes further down the line at Riomaggiore Station, which is constructed majestically over the tempestuous Mediterranean. On the platform, the local passengers join a trio of young Americans clad in hiking gear. Sensible shoes and sturdy jackets give way to the rainbow colours of Lowe Alpine

and North Face; walking between villages, instead of using the rails, is now back in vogue.

For six months a year, this trickle of hikers becomes a torrent, thanks mainly to the enthusiasm of one travel journalist. Rick Steves' *Europe through the Back Door* lifted the lid on untouched Italy in 1980. Cinque Terre remains the easily accessible 'seaside' bit on Steves' suggested 22-day itinerary, just two hours from Genoa or an hour from Pisa – a Grand Tour squished into a spring break. But the sight is still inspiring three decades later: five picture-perfect villages unblighted by modern times, their pastel-coloured hotchpotch of buildings now protected by a UNESCO World Heritage order. The area's former seclusion kept the villages unspoilt, while their current convenience keeps them rich.

Winter in Cinque Terre looks like a six-month sabbatical for some. It's still warm enough to join the café-dwelling Riomaggiore locals alfresco overlooking the flower-filled main street. A convivial scene, but times look a whole lot tougher in one of the establishment's black-and-white photos, taken in the distant days before

Love will find a way: the Via dell'Amore on the Cinque Terre coastal path, above right and right; Vernazza, bottom

SIDINGS

The Parco Nazionale delle Cinque Terre is crisscrossed with over 30 sentieri, or mountain paths, which complement the six-mile village-to-village route. These are quieter, yet more arduous, than the coastal path, passing through vineyards, citrus groves, mountain huts and churches at heights of up to 800m. Dedicated mountain bike and horseback trails also run along the cliffs. Access to the park (nominal fee) grants entry to all the coastal paths and the Riomaggiore history museum, as well as free transport on the eco-friendly local buses. Ecological concerns are taken very seriously. Riomaggiore's tourist office (+39 0187 762 187) can assist with guides and bicycle hire.

the station and harbour wall were built: in the picture, huge waves smash through the village streets where the café terrace now stands.

Riomaggiore's local history museum sums up the hardship in the days before the train. At the time of Italy's creation in 1860, coins from the new Republic's mint were worthless in these lonely climes. Imports such as clogs – though some locals simply went barefoot – were swapped with exports of oil and fruit. Particularly prized was the hard-wearing blue work cloth from Genoa, or Gênes as the port is known in French (repeat the name while thinking of blue denim trousers).

By the 1880s, emigration was rife, indeed half of all Italians leaving for the United States at this time were from Liguria, escaping with their 'jeans' from grinding poverty. The situation was exacerbated by the fact that Genoese traders paid local peasant farmers a pittance for their main export, wine. Back in those days, long before the coastal trains, locals were regarded as naive. And yet, even then, the local vintage had earned a formidable reputation among

BELLS & WHISTLES

BEST BIT
Seen from the path or the train, each multicoloured village perched above the Med has a fairy-tale beauty.

TOP TIP
Pick up the one-page Cinque Terre timetable from the tourist office with your train and park pass.

PHOTO OP
Countless. The waves crashing below the station at Manarola, as seen from the Via dell'Amore, are particularly stunning.

PACK THIS
A mask and snorkel. Each village has its own beach, with access to the national marine park.

USEFUL PHRASE
'*Mi puó prestare la sua Magic Marker*?'
For setting your love in stone on the Via dell'Amore.

SOUVENIR
Wines carrying the Cooperative Agricoltura di Cinque Terre label. The local grappa and limoncello liqueurs come in cute bottles.

TRAVELLERS' FARE
Liguria is synonymous with pesto, the green pasta sauce, composed of fresh basil, pine nuts and hard cheese, often with capers, olives and garlic thrown in.

OVERHEARD
'Pisa? No, we did it back in '98.'

oenophiles. The humanist Giacomo Braceli, visiting in 1448, raved about scenery and the wine: 'It is an authentic delight to observe mountains, not merely steep, but precipitous to the point that even birds have difficulty flying over them. Covered by vines so thirsty and more similar to ivy… here wine is made that adorns the tables of kings.' Indeed, thanks to Cinque Terre's contemporary contact with the outside world, its wine now boasts DOC status, bringing new prosperity to the local grape-growers.

A vine romance

Lofty vineyards mark the coastal path from Riomaggiore station to the platform at Manarola, forming the easiest and most popular of the five village-to-village walks. Long gone are the days of lugging bunches of grapes down the terraces to waiting *gozzi*, or fishing boats, for transport to a cantina along the coast. Now there is a rail contraption – a flexible mini-monorail on stilts,

hundreds of which stripe the terraces. Easy to lay and to operate, these inexpensive inventions can whizz bunches of grapes down the terraces, and whizz packed lunches back up them.

This part of the trip is best done on foot, as the train returns inside the limestone cliff, missing out the heady scents along the trail. The musky potpourri is spiced with olive, wild rucola, woodsmoke, pine and figs (once planted to give the grape-pickers some shade). Birdsong is everywhere – and no wonder. The Cinque Terre region set itself up as a National Park in 1999, with a philsophy that espoused environmentally friendly and organic practices – newfangled terms for what has been a longstanding way of life here. Cinque Terre missed out on the plastic-fantastic fad the first time round, becoming a pioneer in the eco-tourism and recycling game without even realising it.

The coastal path certainly lives up to its pretty name, the Via dell'Amore. Just before Manarola,

The tunnel
to Corniglia,
above; a
sign on the
Cinque Terre
coast path,
top right;
the vilage of
Monterosso,
bottom

the path narrows into a lovers' alley, a graffitied walkway bearing the passionate scribbles from the world over – 'Hilde ? Ordin', 'Sasha + Brent', 'Beppe e Silvia 03' – plus the infrequent yet touching misspelling: 'Sammy I lover you'.

Waiting to board the next train at Manarola station is a family of four New Zealanders. Their nationality (and address) is confirmed by their luggage tags. With Gore-Tex jackets and zipaway outdoor trousers, they came prepared for the elements. Sun is still shining on the snowy mountains on the other side of the gaping gulf of Genoa, as one of them takes out a camera with automatic zoom. 'I'm trying to focus in on the Pyrenees.' None of the other English-speaking passengers has the heart to correct them.

Genoa is the final destination

Fairy-tales can come true

A Spanish foursome have also got their holiday heads on as they loiter on the edge of the platform on the other side. Out of nowhere, a locomotive muscles out of the tunnel like a raging bull, its 50 containers a breakneck blur of Maersk and P&O, and the jumpy Spaniards look miffed by this 1,000-ton close shave, perhaps forgetting that they're standing next to Italy's west coast main line between Genoa and Rome.

For the run past the three remaining villages, keep your eyes glued to the window. The ten minutes of curving track from the fairy-tale redoubt of Corniglia to the bobbing boats of Monterosso is a provençal palette of burnt orange, lemon grove green and summer sky blue. The teetering buildings of the middle village, Vernazza, stand proud and vivid on a jut of land, like majestic lighthouses built on arches of rock.

Ten minutes further on, at the pre-1950s railhead of Sestri Levante, many of the passengers jump on the return train to La Spezia to repeat the harmonious kaleidoscope once again. The Spanish and New Zealanders from Manarola are changing here too; take a day trip along 30 minutes of scenic train track and you are destined to see the same people twice.

Years ago, the La Spezia-to-Sestri Levante leg took five hours in a less regular, but pioneering train. In post-war Italy, where roads were few and far between, people actually drove their cars on to Channel Tunnel-type carriages.

The train hauled these drive-on, drive-off wagons over the hilltops, instead of through the tunnels, on this now-defunct route.

The onward service from Sestri Levante to Genoa is equally dated, but by no means obsolete. Carriages are split into ten six-person compartments with reclining armchair seats; these are the comfortable workhorses of cross-county Italian rail travel. The stainless steel heater at ground level keeps the cabin cosy as flurries of snow cover the track. A touch-sensitive PC screen lies in a fellow-passenger's hand. Is he a photographer? Yes. Has he taken photos for anyone famous? '*Elle Decor*, *World of Interiors*, *Vogue*, people like this.' He's returning from the glitzy resort of Pietrasanta, near Pisa, where he photographed a millionaire's villa.

Sunset finally comes, over the equally classy resort of Santa Margherita, sister town of glamorous Portofino, just over the bay. Liberty-style mansions, castle-cum-hotels and a parade-ground-straight line of palms make up the scene, a legacy of the Roaring Twenties, when the easily reached Italian Riviera was an extension of the French. The photographer tries to point out the villa of fashion designers Dolce and Gabbana in the next bay; the contrast with homely, pastel-hued Cinque Terre is total.

A final shunt into Genoa comes in the darkness of early evening. Back in Riomaggiore, the newly prosperous inhabitants will be uncorking their wine right about now.

TRAVEL INFORMATION

Trains depart roughly every half-hour from La Spezia to Sestri Levante, calling at the Cinque Terre villages. Onward connections at Sestri Levante to Genoa are almost as frequent. Timetable at www.ferroviedellostato.it.

If you want to stay over, most of the accommodation in each of the five villages comes in the form of private apartments. The websites www.cinqueterre.com and www.arbaspaa.com, among many others, deal with holiday lettings. Of the handful of hotels inside the national park, the simple charms of the Locanda del Sole (www.locandadelsole.net) in Riomaggiore, and the more upmarket Villa Steno (www.villasteno.com) in Monterosso are particularly recommended; the latter comes with a roof terrace.

Start
NIMES
Finish
CLERMONT-
FERRAND
Via
THE MASSIF
CENTRAL
Journey time
5.5 HOURS

Magnificent Cévennes

With its classic scenes of viaducts, vineyards and valleys, the Cévenol makes a very French impression. By **Anthony Lambert**

There is a strong sense of the Mediterranean about Nîmes, and not just because of its outstanding Roman remains. Narrow streets of shuttered houses with balconies and decorative palms evoke the torrid heat of southern France. So do the landscapes that begin this journey into the desolate uplands of the Massif Central, and through the Cévennes to the Auvergne.

But first, there is a surprise for those who board the train for an 8am departure and observe the end to which the diesel locomotive is coupled. The first movement causes further consternation; surely we are going backwards? Am I on the right train? You are – all trains have to do this since the closure of a stretch of connecting track. A pilotman in radio contact with the driver guides him for several miles to the signal-box in Coubessac Yard, before heading off in the 'right' direction.

After some deep limestone cuttings, the train canters across a plain strewn with gorse, Lombardy Poplars and Aleppo pines, and dotted with embowered houses, which provide shade from summer temperatures that can reach 50°C. By Fons-St-Mamert, the first vineyards appear,

There are 1,300 viaducts and bridges along the route, including this one over the Gardon River...

and the importance of wine is emphasised by the huge cave building beside the station at St Geniès-de-Malgloirès. For mile after mile, there is little to divert the eye from vines, but by Vézénobres, they peter out, giving way to curiously desolate, scrubby country. Clues to the emptiness appear among the woodland hills: there are fragmentary remains of the coal-mines that encouraged the construction of the railway in the first place.

It was at the first stop, in the dreary town of Alès, that Robert Louis Stevenson boarded the train after his journey through the Cévennes with Modestine, the donkey and stubborn travelling companion who carried his gear. The book describing his 12-day journey, *Travels with a Donkey in the Cévennes*, was published in 1879. It has become closely identified with the region, and is considered a classic of the travel genre.

The railway becomes single track from Alès. The contours steepen and the curves sharpen with the climb into the Cévennes. A clear winter's day is ideal for this part of the journey, when the skeletal outlines of the trees do not impede the view. This is the least populated area of France, and during the winter passengers are few and far between; in fact, numbers are so low that the future of the service is under threat.

Bridging the gaps

As the frequency of short tunnels increases, so does astonishment that a railway should have been built through such difficult terrain, requiring 106 tunnels and 1,300 viaducts and bridges to complete its 186 miles. The hillsides grow so steep that they have to be terraced for agriculture, though cultivated land steadily diminishes as the train approaches one of the journey's highlights: Chamborigaud viaduct, a great arc of masonry carrying the railway between the high contours of two hills. It gives fantastic views to the east over folds of purple

BELLS & WHISTLES

BEST BIT
The Allier gorge, where the train follows the river for 53 miles.

TOP TIP
Travel first class, as it's easier to change sides for the best views.

PHOTO OP
The almost semi-circular Chamborigaud viaduct.

PACK THIS
Water and food: there is no buffet.

ANORAK INFO
Traditional mechanical signalling – as opposed to electric or computerised signals – survives at some stations, like Génolhac, which is a focal point for rail enthusiasts.

SOUVENIR
Memory of a jazz concert in the Roman amphitheatre in Nîmes.

TRAVELLERS' FARE
There's a good buffet on the station at Clermont-Ferrand.

DESIGN DETAIL
Admire the elaborate decoration on the water columns at La Bastide.

OVERHEARD
'I reckon Stevenson's donkey would go faster than this.'

hills that stretch to the horizon, while down below is the small town of Chamborigaud itself.

The high level of the railway continues to give panoramic views, with the eye suddenly arrested by a waterfall and an isolated station like Concoules-Ponteils, seemingly so remote that you wonder where its passengers come from. The huggermugger houses of the little town of Villefort fill a trench in the valley, and water cranes and towers at the station recall the time over 40 years ago when steam locomotives raised echoes through the valleys.

It pays not to close your eyes in tunnels: soon after Villefort, the train bursts out of the dark onto a viaduct across the Lac de Rachas reservoir – years ago it would have been even more dramatic, because the viaduct 'lost' half its 72m height when the dam was built and the valley flooded. Through forests of pine and larch, the train climbs along hillside ledges to the 1,023m summit at La Bastide, close to the source of the River Allier, and the watershed that separates rivers flowing into the Atlantic and the Mediterranean. At La Bastide, a single railcar waits to take a few passengers west to Le Monastier (where Stevenson first met his donkey), using one of the branch lines that diverge from lonely junctions along the route.

Beginning a long companionship with the waters of the Allier, the railway reaches Langogne, its Romanesque church protectively encircled by houses and five surviving rampart towers. During the few minutes that the train pauses here, passengers have a chance to speculate about the story behind a plaque on the station wall, commemorating the four railway staff who died in the World War I, one of whom was decorated with both the Légion d'honneur and Croix de Guerre.

Poplar culture

As though the scenery had not been captivating enough, the line delivers its *pièce de résistance* with a sustained series of stunning views along

... and this gem over Lac de Villefort

the gorges and narrow valley of the Allier, as it alternately rushes and glides north. The river's flow is frustrated by huge fallen rocks, which explains the need for the avalanche wires above the railway; these alert neighbouring stations of danger. During the winter, the still sections of the river are often covered in ice and snow; these sparkle in the sunlight as though they were embedded with diamonds.

Passengers enjoy a grandstand view: the train is almost continuously on a shelf above the water, and slows to 22 miles per hour in the long gorge. At Chapeauroux, a gracefully curving, 28-arch viaduct leads out of the village. Past Alleyras, there is another gorge, so narrow and deep that in winter, the sun hardly penetrates, leaving the trees mantled in frost and snow.

Finally, after a spectacular partnership, the track veers away from the Allier as the valley widens and flattens into a landscape of orchards and pasture, with the first sight of cows since Nîmes. After Langeac, the train climbs on to a plateau of bracken-covered heath with distant views of upland farms and woods and fields edged with poplars – a classic French scene.

At Arvant, a line trails in from Neussargues, and the appearance of digital platform indicators reflects a change in the character of the railway: from rural cross-country line to commuter feeder for Clermont-Ferrand. Volcanic plugs, for which the area is famous, appear on both sides of the line near Le-Breuil-sur-Couze, while some hills are crowned with tightly clustered villages.

The last stop is Issoire, which, in the 1570s, was at the epicentre of a merciless, centuries-long conflict between Catholics and Protestants. The town was so thoroughly destroyed that a

SIDINGS

The glorious landscapes make the region a mecca for walkers. Villefort is the best place to detrain, since Grandes Randonnés routes 44, 66 and 68 radiate from the town, where hotels can be found. Nearby is the 16th-century Château de Castanet and the Chassezac Gorge.

For architecture, Brioude has the church of St Julien, dating from 1170 and built on the site of its patron's martyrdom. It is one of the finest examples of Auvergnat Romanesque architecture, especially the polychrome masonry of the apse and ambulatory. Close to Brioude is Lamothe, known for its castle with grim dungeons.

Once you've had a good look at Clermont-Ferrand, take the time and make a special trip to Puy de Dôme, the best known of the region's volcanic plugs.

column was erected with the inscription '*Ici fut Issoire*' (here was Issoire). Nonetheless, the abbey church of St Austremoine survives from the 12th century on the east side of town.

It is a shock to arrive in the sprawling city of Clermont-Ferrand after five-and-a-half hours of near emptiness. The train clatters over the points and crossings, and the small number of winter passengers heads off into the streets of a city known as the home of Bibendum, the famous Michelin man synonymous with the tyres made in the city. For most visitors, its main attraction will be the double-spired Gothic cathedral, uniquely built out of black volcanic rock.

TRAVEL INFORMATION

Three trains a day do the whole five-and-a-half-hour journey. Information and tickets from www.raileurope.co.uk, or www.ter-sncf.com. See also www.enlightened-traveller.co.uk for more detailed information on the Cévenol railway. For accommodation, the Residence Cheval Blanc in Nîmes is close to the station (www.odalys-vacances.com).

Start
BARCELONA
Finish
PUIGCERDÁ
Via
VIC
RIPOLL NÚRIA
LA MOLINA
Journey time
3 HOURS

Homage to Catalonia

From sunny Barcelona to the snow-capped Pyrenees: a scenic day trip to the Spanish Switzerland. By **Peterjon Cresswell**

I t is not an auspicious beginning. A narrow platform crowded with commuters at Barcelona Sants Station, Spanish salarymen rushing here and there, and departure boards that are difficult to follow. Choose the right train, however, and for seven euros you can journey for three hours up into the snow-capped Pyrenees to the pretty border town of Puigcerdà. And this commuter train ends up in a different country, too, because from there you can walk into France, or stay on the train until the stop beyond Puigcerdà – the terminus at Latour-de-Carol, in La Belle France herself.

For this journey, you'll be setting out on line C3 through Zone 6 of Barcelona's Rodiales/Cercanía network, accessed from platforms 7-10 at Sants. In London, Zone 6 means suburbs like Coulsdon South or Hatton Cross. Here, line C3 through Zone 6 is the last surviving trans-Pyrenean rail route.

Once you pass your ticket through the shiny metal barriers at Sants, you're heading for ancient mountain fiefdoms, and links with all manner of idiosyncratic local railways, including the Yellow Train, whose open carriages climb to the highest station in all of France.

The end of the line: Puigcerdá

Right now, though, you're in a tunnel, the long tunnel that runs under the main hubs of Barcelona and doesn't bring you out into the world of lorry-choked motorways until 15 minutes later. Already, hills are visible, but it will take the best part of an hour before the houses become significantly more sparse.

The train itself is as plain as can be. Dressed in the standard RENFE commuter livery of red and white, it lacks the two-deck convenience of the Paris RER, and the random range of characters that may occupy the Berlin S-Bahn. Iggy Pop would not wail about 'the city's ripped backsides' on this one. Smart teenagers clutching ring-bound files gossip, while older locals bid farewell with a sturdy Catalan 'adéu!' as the train thins out after each stop. It's easier to follow these stops using the train's red tickertape digital display board than by trying to decipher the muffled announcements in Catalan.

An old-school, moustachioed RENFE collector comes by to greet regulars and validate your ticket with a museum-piece ticket puncher, produced from one of the innumerable pockets in his waistcoat.

After Montcada, industrial commuterville gives way to pleasant little communites: La Garriga, for example, by the edge of the Montseny Nature Park, a town of pretty churches and natural thermal waters.

As the train passes smaller spots, and you pass the hour mark, dogs try to chase you away as if you were the postman. A local trainspotter spends his day standing and waving at passing trains. Streams of clear water begin to rush, highland tunnels become more frequent and, after the popular jump-off point of Vic, the gateway to the Pyrenees, mobile-phone reception blinks in and out. You're now leaving Zone 6, and entering mountain country.

SIDINGS

The Monestir de Santa María, ten minutes' walk south-east of Ripoll, was founded in 888 by Wilfred the Hairy. The Benedictine monastery and its priceless library burned down in 1835, but the striking Romanesque west portal remains.

Towards Puigcerdà, the adventure park at La Molina (www.lamolinaparkaventura.com) offers Tarzan jumps, climbing, snowboarding and rope walks for most ages – children from the age of four can take part in activities.

Skiing in the Pyrenees is far cheaper than in the Alps. Beginners and families are best suited to the slopes around Núria, terminus of the Cremallera 'Zip' train. For more details, see www.epyrenees.com. La Molina (www.lamolina.cat) is a well-equipped ski centre.

The Cremallera 'Zip' rack railway up to Núria was built in 1931 alongside the old mule trail and runs daily (except in November) between Ribes-Enllaç (across the platform at Ribes de Freser on the Puigcerdà line) and the ski slopes at Núria. About eight trains a day make the 40-minute journey (E9; www.valldenuria.cat). Núria is also known for its religious sanctuary, which dates back to the 7th century and is a famous place of pilgrimage.

After Puigcerdà, the train carries on for another six minutes over the border to Latour-de-Carol. To walk from the middle of Puigcerdà to France takes only about 15 minutes – and there are no border controls these days. Just over the border, the Yellow Train (train jaune; tren groc) runs from Latour-de-Carol, an extension of the main Villefranche-de-Confient to Mont-Louis line. Its open carriages offer dramatic views, particularly when it climbs to Bolquère-Eyne, the highest railway station in France. See more on www.trainstouristiques-ter.com.

Scenes from a chocolate box

Over the rocky, twisting Freser river, you head north towards the iconic Catalan stronghold of Ripoll and borderland of the Cerdanya/Cerdagne. Backpackers and strapping men with labradors board the train. Some two hours into the journey, look for the snowy peaks in the direction of 11 o'clock!

At Ripoll, you're in the heart of the Catalan Pyrenees, as evidenced by the nearby presence of the Monastir de Santa María, a historic Benedictine monastery and the most notable sightseeing attraction on the journey.

By now, snow-topped peaks surround you. The Freser valley rises to 1,000 metres. At the top is Ribes de Freser, which has two claims to fame: as a hiking stronghold, and a transit point for those wishing to take the Cremallera ('the Zip'), Catalonia's last railway that climbs up to Núria, Spain's highest station. At 1,964 metres, it is twice the elevation of the departure point.

At this point, you are just five stops from Puigcerdà. In winter, Planoles and Toses are firmly in skiing territory – and in the Cerdanya, which is divided equally between France and Spain. Catalans refer to the Spanish side as Baixa ('Lower') Cerdanya; for the French, their side is, naturally, La Cerdagne Française. Puigcerdà became capital of the Spanish side after the Treaty of the Pyrenees in 1659. This also awarded Roussillon to France, and gave nearby Llívia to Spain. Surrounded by French territory, the latter town is still a historical anomaly, the Kaliningrad of the Pyrenees.

By the time you reach La Molina, you're at 1,700 metres. This resort, in partnership with much higher Masella, has been rebranded as Alp 2500 – the largest ski area in the Pyrenees. The train clunks through tunnels, and sheer drops appear immediately under your window. Chalets dot the landscape, Toblerone scenes stretch either side of you, and the penultimate station in Spain is even called Urxt-Alp, in a strange case of topographical schizophrenia.

BELLS & WHISTLES

BEST BIT
The view from the funicular at Puigcerdà across from the station.

TOP TIP
Be careful on the crowded narrow platforms at Sants – trains pass in and out quickly. The Puigcerdà train is also far shorter than the platform – you may have to run to catch it.

PHOTO OP
Ask nicely and the RENFE train conductor with the magnificent waxed moustache will let you take his picture.

PACK THIS
Food and drink for the journey – there's nothing on board.

ANORAK INFO
Llívia, a Spanish town surrounded by France, was kept by Spain in the 1659 Treaty of the Pyrenees, which only entitled France to claim villages. Buses run from Puigcerdà.

USEFUL PHRASE
'No ho entenc' ('I don't understand')

TRAVELLERS' FARE
La Cantina bar at Puigcerdà Station sells huge sandwiches for the return journey. These great *entrepans* come with cheese and bacon, chorizo and anchovy, among others.

DESIGN DETAIL
The red circle with a white semi-circle – the logo of the Cercanía/Rodiales train network.

OVERHEARD
'Està estirat!' (There's not a cloud in the sky)

Our Lady of Núria Sanctuary in the Pyrenees

You are now coming into Puigcerdà ('Poocherdah' says the tannoy), three hours out of Barcelona Sants. When you alight at the quaint little station, it's a breath of fresh air, literally. Outside the station are a pair of hotel restaurants; before you is a public playground, and just ahead you can see a little funicular gliding up and down. Stride the five minutes to its station terminus, wait another five minutes and the 12-person carriage will arrive. Press '1', as if in a hotel lift, and your free taxi will take 90 seconds to ascend.

At the top, a small open platform allows a lovely view of the Pyrenees. Scale five steep sets of interlaced stone staircases and you're right at the top of Puigcerdà, and moreover you're right at the main square, Plaça de l'Ajuntament. On the right-hand side, round a corner, is the tourist office; to the left, bars and restaurants beckon from the main street. French voices mingle with Catalan sounds all around you, and this is where your journey ends – and perhaps another, over the border, begins.

TRAVEL INFORMATION

At Barcelona Sants, ticket machines stand by the platforms marked 7-10 Rodiales/Cercanías. Red line C3 is for Puigcerdà. More information is available from www.renfe.es/cercanias.

For this journey, a handy train to catch would be the 9.17am from Sants, arriving into Puigcerdà at 12.31pm. This itinerary would allow good time to look around, and then return the same day.

Cheaper hotels around Sants include the Catalonia Roma (www.hoteles-catalonia.com). Once you reach Puigcerdà Station, the adjacent hotel-restaurant Tèrminus (www.hotelterminus.net) offers very convenient bed and board.

Start
STOCKHOLM
Finish
NARVIK
Via
LAPLAND
Journey time
21-24 HOURS

Northern exposure

Through lakes and Lapland, fjords and fur, join in the reindeer games on the night train to Norway. By **Nicky Gardner**

During the peak of Stockholm's evening commuter rush, a rake of carriages backs into the city's main station. The train nudges up between commuter services bound for suburbs of the Swedish capital; across the platform, the city slickers head home. But another kind of passenger heads for the train bound for Lapland and beyond. People wearing fur hats and sheepskin coats, soldiers on their way to military bases in the far north, and families with skis. This overnight service is a Swedish institution, and one of Europe's most engaging rail journeys.

The train leaves Stockholm around 6pm, bound for Narvik on the coast of Norway, with a route that slices through Lapland and crosses the Arctic Circle along the way. Few other night trains offer such a heady sense of adventure, albeit much of it in the imagination, for in truth the first dozen hours of the journey are mainly a matter of watching the birch trees get smaller and the snow get deeper.

Frozen assets

It is not long before urban Sweden is left behind. Outside the window, the view is of rocks and

A snowy stretch in Lapland

forest: pines and birch trees with a tumble of lichen-covered granite boulders that poke up through the last remnants of winter snow. Every now and again, there are glimpses of lakes shimmering in the evening sunshine. Dusk comes, but seems to linger forever.

For those with fatter wallets, there are well-appointed sleeping cars and a good restaurant car. Expect reindeer stew, creamy mashed potatoes, Swedish beer and decent wines served by an ebullient attendant who has crossed the Arctic Circle more than a thousand times. The decor is a feast of fake mahogany, retro table lamps and blue and gold upholstery, all presided over by images of the Swedish royal family adorning the wall – an atmospheric spot to linger over a slow dinner.

Around nine in the evening, the train pauses at some country wayside halt. No one boards or alights, and nothing stirs in the churchyard that lies beside the tracks. In this village of the dead, all you see is a church – its pale shade of pink catches the gleaming sun in summertime – and gravestones. '*Saliga äro de vilkas väg är ostrafflig*,' reads the inscription from a psalm on one of the stones. 'Happy are those whose way is perfect' – a good omen for train travellers. There is a jolt as the train starts to move north again, and the smiling bartender in the restaurant car serves up another round of beer.

Proper night never really comes, there's just a dreamy bluish twilight. Outside, little changes: it's a non-stop blur of rocks and forests. But eventually the trees thin out, the birches shrink and the snow becomes even deeper. The lakes freeze. Those who stir in the small hours stare out into the dim of the northern night and might glimpse moose, deer or a fox. During the wee small hours, the cast changes, with some passengers leaving and others joining the train at remote stations along the way.

At six in the morning, the bartender is already up and about and there is a smell of fresh coffee. The clutter of humans curled up under blankets begins to stir. A young man gently repositions an ice axe that seems to have crept under the seats and caught itself on his leg during the night. The train slithers to a halt in Älvsbyn, a place where winter snow has been bulldozed into neat piles. Men in fur coats chat on the platform, their breath making a hoary mist that hangs steady in the still air. A white van delivers the morning newspapers directly to the train, and within a few minutes every table in the restaurant car has a copy of *Norrländska Socialdemokraten*, a local daily. There is news of the spring thaw, adverts for flights that hop over the Arctic Circle and obituaries for men and women who lived long lives and never left their northern homeland.

Soldiering on

The train jogs on through the forest and soon arrives in Boden. Here the snow has long since blown away. A stop of 20 minutes gives passengers the chance to emerge from their sleeping cars and taste the bitter cold of a clear northern morning. A man wearing a Stetson stands on the station platform. A handful of soldiers alight from the train; others sit in a jeep beside the tracks, for Boden is a Swedish military outpost. It was a bastion that during the Cold War years reminded the Soviet Union that Sweden was prepared to defend its borders, even in the

far north. Boden has lots of concrete and a brutal architectural style; had the Russians ever invaded, they would have felt entirely at home.

The next stop is Kiruna, Sweden's northernmost city, and one of the inspirations for this line. It was the mineral wealth of Kiruna's iron ore that prompted the construction of the railway from northern Sweden over the mountains to Norway. English investors provided the capital — on the condition that the marine terminus of the railway on the Ofot Fjord should be named after the then English monarch: Victoriahavn. The company went bankrupt and English aspirations to create an Arctic monument to their Queen were quickly eclipsed as Swedish and Norwegian engineers moved in to finish the task. Victoriahavn was renamed Narvik, and the entire route across the mountains to the Norwegian port was completed in 1902.

It is an extraordinary journey. The stretch from Boden to Narvik takes a little over six hours,

BELLS & WHISTLES

TOP TIP
The extra cost of the sleeping berth is worth the additional outlay. A night in regular seated accommodation is not recommended.

BEST BIT
The run down into Narvik from the Swedish-Norwegian border at Riksgränsen.

PHOTO OP
Deep snow as the train lingers at Riksgränsen in the crystal cold of a spring morning.

PACK THIS
The *Bradt Guide to Lapland* by James Proctor gives a good overview of the part of the route that lies within the Arctic Circle. Also, during the summer, take midge repellent.

ANORAK INFO
The route to Narvik is often dubbed the most northerly railway in the world. Sadly, this is not quite the case. At least three passenger routes in Russia are further north.

DID YOU KNOW?
Gällivare, the first train stop north of the Arctic Circle, is home to an unusual religious sect. For the 'pietistic revivalists of Firstborn Laestadians', Gällivare has a pull akin to that of Rome for Catholics.

DESIGN DETAIL
Dine under the watchful gaze of King Carl Gustav and Queen Silvia, whose portraits are in the restaurant car. One wonders if they approve of all the bingeing on reindeer.

and with every mile that passes, the landscape gets better and better, a medley of lake and sky.

The Arctic Circle

After breakfast, there is the anticipation of the Arctic Circle. How odd that we ascribe such significance to a particular line! Old hands on the route affect to ignore this arbitrary rite of passage. 'But it's not arbitrary at all,' protests a bespectacled student from Edinburgh in the restaurant car. 'The Arctic Circle is a loxodrome, the precise line of which is determined by the obliquity of the ecliptic.' He turns out to be quite an expert. 'Had you realised that the Arctic Circle

Reindeer in Lapland, above; a sculptural tribute to the navvies at Kiruna Station, Sweden, right

moves? At the moment, it is shifting north a few metres each year. Variations in the tilt of the Earth's axis – a sort of astronomical wobble – cause the move.'

Reindeer must understand all about loxodromes and the obliquity of the ecliptic. As soon as a sign indicates that we are entering the Arctic Circle, a small herd appears, standing sentinel in the snow beside the railway line. These are the first reindeer we see on the long trip north, excepting the ones on our plates.

At Kiruna, a Sami woman joins the train. She is weatherbeaten and has a deeply expressive face. Wrinkles that tell of three-score winters spent in the far north, eyes that sympathetically survey the restaurant car, and clothing that is well attuned to the climate: dark brown leather trousers, and a long sheepskin coat in a delicate shade of bluish-grey that reaches almost to her ankles. Notwithstanding her age, this is a creature of exquisite grace, and all eyes are on her as she carefully positions her coat on an empty chair, sweeps back her long hair, sits down and orders breakfast.

Cold comfort

There is a lyrical quality to these northern landscapes, ever more so as the railway skirts the shoulders of mountains and creeps up narrow valleys where the hillsides tilt sharper and sharper. For over 30 miles, the train runs along the south shore of Torneträsk, a magnificent glacial lake that is frozen for more than half the year. Black dots on the ice mark the spots where fishermen have carved holes in the hope of catching tonight's supper.

The railway traverses some of Europe's wildest country, and for the modern traveller enclosed in the cosseted comfort of the train, it is hard to imagine the hardships endured by those 19th-century navvies who, for a dozen years, laboured to build the railway line.

The Lofoten island of Moskenesoya in Norway,

SIDINGS

Narvik wins no prizes for grace or charm. The waterfront on Ofot Fjord is dominated by the freight terminal, at which iron ore is loaded on to ships. Better to head on to the Lofotens, a scatter of rugged islands of breathtaking beauty. A direct bus on Route 760 (Lofotenekspressen) leaves Narvik for Svolvær a couple of hours after the night train from Stockholm arrives. Find out more on www.loftoten.info.

For skiers and mountaineers, the winter resorts of Abisko and Riksgränsen – both stops on the route – afford easy access to the slopes and backcountry hiking. Both communities rely on the railway for their survival. At Riksgränsen, you can arrange a Siberian husky tour.

Abisko is a year-round lakeside resort, and marks the northern end of a Swedish long distance footpath, the Kungsleden. Riksgränsen is located rather higher, and has a fierce winter climate. Snow lingers here well into mid summer, offering the prospect of skiing under the midnight sun.

For something decidedly different, stop off en route at Kiruna and spend a night at the ice hotel in nearby Jukkasjärvi (see www.icehotel.com).

In Abisko, a major resort on Torneträsk Lake, most of the passengers alight. The Scottish student accompanies them, fearful that his plans to identify rare Arctic lichens might be thwarted by the deep snow. Now it is just the Sami lady with the magnificent sheepskin coat who keeps watch in the restaurant car. As the railway heads into the hills at the west end of Torneträsk, there is a little cemetery of simple white crosses beside the tracks with the remains of the navvies who died, some from accidents, others from typhus.

The journey that started so serenely in Stockholm culminates with a crescendo of magnificent scenery as the train enteres Norway at Riksgränsen, then drops down to the coast. At the border, the train tunnels through deep snow, and begins the long and winding descent to the Ofot Fjord. Avalanches and landslides play havoc with the line; the route has been rebuilt many times. On the right, there is a glimpse of the old Norddal bridge, which once carried the railway, but is now a national monument. Then come views of a great fjord below, more tight curves and steep drops until, bang on train, the sleek carriages of the night train from Stockholm come gently to a halt at their final destination.

TRAVEL INFORMATION

The train departs every day, and is often referred to as the SJ Norrland and sometimes as the Norrlandståget (even though this name was officially dropped in 2008). It is operated by SJ Norrlandstrafik, a subsidiary of Statens Järnvägar (Swedish State Railways). Fares and schedules are available on www.sj.se.

During the summer months, a private rail operator, Veolia, runs additional services from southern Sweden to Narvik, following the same route. The Veolia trains, dubbed the Lapplandståget, originate in either Göteborg or Malmö. From both cities, the journey to Narvik takes approximately 29 hours. Fares from Göteborg or Malmö are only slightly more than those on the SJ trains from Stockholm. Details on www.veolia-transport.se.

Throughout the winter-sports season, especially during school holidays, and during the mid-summer period, it is best to reserve seats or sleeping berth accommodation well in advance.

Highland fling

On the Caledonian Sleeper, you can go to sleep in central London and wake up to the sight of Scottish lochs. By **Andrew Eames**

In the early stages of this book's production, contributors were canvassed about which routes they'd nominate for inclusion within its pages. Among the raft of suggestions there was one that occurred time and time again: the sleeper train from London to the Highlands of Scotland. Everyone suggested it, and practically everyone wanted to travel on it, no matter that most had already travelled on it before.

It is easy to see why it got so many votes. In terms of transport effectiveness, the Fort William sleeper (sometimes called the Deerstalker) carries passengers to the heart of a region where air travel is still a poor relation. In terms of social usefulness, the train serves communities that sometimes don't even have any roads. In terms of aesthetics, it swaps a sprawling metropolis for some of the most unsullied and breathtaking wilderness scenery in the whole of the northern hemisphere. And in terms of time taken, it enters a dimension of its own, for while the journey is overnight according to the timetable – usually around 11 hours, depending on the season – in reality it seems to begin in the 21st century, and end at any time in the previous 75 years. This really is a journey that winds back the years.

To emphasise the time-travel element in the whole experience, there's also a chance of making an additional journey, from Fort William to Mallaig, on the only scheduled train in Britain that is still pulled by a steam locomotive – the Jacobite Express. And from Mallaig, you can go on to complete the whole misty-eyed, romantic and awesome threesome, by catching a ferry over the sea to Skye. Taken together, the sum of all these parts creates an experience that is far greater than simply taking a train journey.

Goodbye to all that

For all that, this smog-to-bog journey couldn't start in more unprepossessing surroundings. Euston Station was built in the late 1960s and doesn't belong in the same breath as London's great railway cathedrals such as Paddington, Kings' Cross or St Pancras. Its utilitarian lobby could be the front end of a tax office, and there's certainly no sign of any trains, not even in picture form. It is almost as if the planners believed that locomotives and coaches were things to be ashamed of, to be hidden away in a dingy low-ceilinged train shed, far from anything welcoming such as humanity, hot coffee and Sock Shop. Passengers must seek out their trains down long ramps into a basement, like rabbits disappearing down a rabbit hole. And yet here, from 8.30pm every evening (except Saturdays), stands the longest train in the UK, ready to embark on one of the country's greatest journeys.

Once they've found the right platform, Fort William-bound passengers have to walk nearly the whole distance of the quarter-mile, 16-coach train to find their berths, and herein lies another of the train's great mysteries, for when they wake up in the morning, those same passengers will find themselves in a mere stub of a train, just four coaches strong. The rest will have been discarded, just as a rocket sheds its stages on its journey to outer space.

In reality, the train as it stands in Euston Station is a holy trinity of sleepers, a three in one,

A train for all seasons: early spring on Loch Rannoch, top; winter on Rannoch Moor, right

Start
LONDON
Finish
FORT WILLIAM
Via
PRESTON
Journey time
13 HOURS

which is subdivided once across the Scottish border into sections that are bound for Fort William, Inverness and Aberdeen. Fortunately, there's a cabin attendant to hand to make sure everyone ends up on the right one.

Dream machine

Once aboard, the interior is welcomingly warm and quiet, but it isn't particularly decorative. These sleeper coaches are mostly around 30 years old, although they have been refurbished and re-upholstered many times. In the bunk-bedded compartments, there is little scope for

hide and seek, and no hiding the functionality of the metal bolts holding the bunks, the coat-hangers on the partition wall, the sink under the lid by the window, and the his 'n' hers toilets down the corridor, which itself is too narrow for more than one person at a time. Essentially, the Caledonian Sleeper is all the same as it was 30 years ago, with little attempt at luxury beyond the crisp white sheets.

The difference is in the lounge car, down the corridor, where sofas and designer chairs are gathered to create a convivial atmosphere not often encountered on trains. Here passengers can scoff paninis or ciabattas, and even sometimes – a foretaste of what's to come – haggis and neeps. Coffee comes in a proper silver coffeepot, and there'll be a packet of shortbread and a sprig of heather on the tray. This is where the regulars on the service gather, and swap stories about shenanigans in the City or problems on the line, and are served by frosty, statuesque Poles or cheery (and dumpy) Glaswegian wifeys. There's often an interesting cross-section of society to be found here; families going up to see granny, business travellers on a weekly commute, overseas visitors curious about the service, and the landlords of large Highland estates, taking clients north for a bit of shooting.

In fact, the Deerstalker owes a lot to blue-blooded travellers; for many years it was the transport of choice for aristocrats with hunting estates, and it was they who formed a powerful lobby in Parliament when the future of the service was threatened through the 1990s. One of the early-morning stations, Corrour, is still privately owned by a very wealthy Scandinavian family, and trains only stop there by request.

After the lounge car, it's time to try to sleep. There's nothing to match the sensation of stretching out in your bed while hurtling through the dark, through a nation at rest. Inside, it is cosy, rhythmical and reassuringly womb-like. Outside, lights flash past, and it's always intriguing to try to glimpse a clue or two as to where you actually are. Sleeping car sleep is in a category of its own; your mind has rested, but your body has gone the distance, absorbing all the bumps and points. A delightful synthesis of sleep and travel.

With grandparents from the Isle of Skye, I have completed this route many, many times, and I have always woken up several times, keen to keep abreast of how we're going and where we are. And although it has always been a short night in terms of the number of hours slept, I wouldn't want it any other way.

View from a bridge

Certainly, nobody should still be asleep when the (by now much truncated) train emerges into the Highlands proper, at Crianlarich at around 7.30. Early wakers lying back in bed watching the lurching landscape unroll beyond their cabin

BELLS & WHISTLES

BEST BIT
Waking up with the Highlands rocking and rolling outside your cabin window.

TOP TIP
Arrange with your cabin attendant to have your breakfast in the lounge car, rather than your cabin.

PHOTO OP
The Auch Gleann viaduct (the Glenfinnan viaduct for the Mallaig line), but ideally you'd need to be on the other side of the valley to capture it at the moment it is being crossed by the train.

PACK THIS
A wee dram to get you in the mood.

ANORAK INFO
The Mallaig line still has a couple of old-fashioned semaphore signals, while the signalling across Rannoch Moor is all radio-controlled.

USEFUL PHRASE
Learn the difference between 'uh-oh, a stag party' (ie probably best to avoid the lounge car) as opposed to 'oh-ho, a party of stags' (look out of the window or you'll miss them).

OVERHEARD
'Dad, I just saw a midge overtaking the train!'

To complete the experience, make a connection at Fort William with the train out to Mallaig, which is the fishing and ferry port for Skye. If you make this 90-minute journey in the summer season, you will have the option of the steam-hauled Jacobite Express, which is run by a private company, but travels along the national network. This route, too, is spectacularly beautiful, with the train often running along the edges of lochs.

The first highlight is the crossing of the Caledonian Canal, which runs all the way across from the Moray Firth; if you look back at this point you should also, finally, be able to see the top of Ben Nevis. The train then runs along the side of Loch Eil, with views across to the Moidart hills. When the tide is out, the foreshore here is covered in acres of bladderwrack; when it's in, the water comes almost up to the line. The Jacobite's only stop is at Glenfinnan, famous as the place where Bonnie Prince Charlie first raised his standard after coming ashore from France, and started his campaign (which so nearly succeeded) to be king. Glenfinnan, or at least its curving, arched railway viaduct, has also achieved more recent fame in the Harry Potter films, with the Jacobite becoming the Hogwarts Express, although you'd find scant mention of that in the small museum and shop on Glenfinnan station, which is run by train enthusiasts.

You will, however, hear tell (and be able to buy postcards) of the filming of *Local Hero*, which used a small chapel by the side of the line and some of the wonderful beaches at Traigh, up just beyond Arisaig. At this point the water beside the train is actually no longer a loch, but the sea, and the land opposite is a peninsula, or even the so-called 'cocktail islands' of Rhum, Eigg and Muck, the first of the Hebrides. And then as the train turns north, the Isle of Skye itself heaves into sight, and the tips of the Cuillin Mountains will be visible on a clear day.

As for Mallaig, it is a cheery, blowsy little place, with plenty of fishing- and ferry-boat activity. Plenty to watch if you've got time to waste before catching a boat or a train.

window would have caught tantalising glimpses of Loch Lomond as the train runs through the parish of Arrochar, hunting out the ridges in order to climb a particularly tortuous section of the line, where 37 navvies (mainly Scots, Irish and Poles) died during construction work.

By Crianlarich, most of the climbing is done and the forests of pine, ash and rhododendron will have fallen away. The station buildings on the platform, and all along the line, are incongruous bungalows, with sash windows and net curtains that appear to have been transplanted from some distant urban housing estate.

At Crianlarich, a branch line veers off for Oban, ferry port for Mull and the Outer Hebrides, but the Fort William line crosses the river valley and growls on up the other side, onwards through Tyndrum, by which time any passenger with any interest in the aesthetics of wild country should be in the lounge car, drinking in the view through the picture windows. In winter, the shoulders of these mountains will be frosted with snow, and the deer will be down in the valleys, dotted against a white background. In summer, climbers and walkers will already be out and about, colouring the heather in orthodox colours.

By now, the Deerstalker itself will have slowed to barely more than a jog-trot, particularly over the distinctive arching viaduct at Auch Gleann. That's because the locomotive is simply too heavy for bridge-crossing at any speed; indeed, from here on in, the train does a good impression of an elephant on a unicycle – wobbly, uncertain, and far too powerful for what lies

The Jacobite Express crossing the Glenfinnan Viaduct, above; Glenfinnan Monument in the West Highlands, top right; Mallaig, bottom underneath. The comparatively lightweight day trains are far better suited to the line.

Brave hearts and great lochs

For most of the journey, the railway is never too far from a valley-hugging road and the occasional hamlet, but after Bridge of Orchy it breaks away from all civilisation, and strikes out alone across the welter of bog and rock that is Rannoch Moor. For travellers who appreciate the power and glory of wild country, there is nothing quite like this stretch of deeply inhospitable land, but you'd be a fool to try to cross it on foot without making elaborate preparations beforehand.

The A82 to Fort William nips across the moor's western flank and dives to safety down Glen Coe, but the railway weaves right across the middle. Back in 1894, the track-layers had to contend with horrendous conditions and unforeseen difficulties when they first pioneered this stretch. At times, the ground was so boggy that the track had to be laid on a floating raft of logs, where it is still ironed flat by passing trains.

Nevertheless the moor has two stations. One, at Rannoch, was originally little more than a remote base for railway workers, and the rail-laying manager's house is now a small hotel (the Moor of Rannoch, www.moorofrannoch.co.uk). The other, at the aforementioned Corrour, is a remote walkers' and stalkers' stop which has absolutely no road access, but with a wonderful youth hostel (www.syha.org.uk) on the shores of nearby Loch Ossian; Corrour also featured in a memorable scene in the movie *Trainspotting*.

It is ludicrous that these isolated stations, with practically no local populations, have a direct sleeper service from London, but ludicrously wonderful too, if you're attracted to this kind of thing. Only the brave and the well-prepared dismount here. There's fishing in the sandy-shored Loch Laidon, by Rannoch, where the ripples over shallow rocks look like otters playing. There's walking, too, on the Road to the Isles, a former drover's track which keeps to high (and dry) ground, and goes all the way to Ullapool. From up here, Rannoch's lochs appear to be bits of sky fallen to ground, and the occasional train, puny among all this immensity, looks like a metal caterpillar crawling across the moor's face, stopping momentarily to release another nutcase or two.

After Corrour, the train descends rapidly, sliding down beside lonely Loch Treig as it slips unnoticed around the back of Ben Nevis. Sadly, the highest mountain in the UK is too close to be properly viewed through the train windows; as we creep in to Fort William, it's swallowed up once again by a landscape of rivers and trees.

And sadly, too, the final destination is as prosaic as the starting point. Fort William Station has all the charisma of a school science block, and the town has failed to capitalise on the great location under the shadow of Ben Nevis, between mountain and sea. But this is still light years away from London and a gathering point for adventurers, a place to stock up on crampons – and have a bucket of chips – before setting off into the unknown.

TRAVEL INFORMATION

Caledonian sleepers are run by First Scotrail (www.scotrail.co.uk/caledoniansleeper/index.html). Timetable details are available from National Rail Enquiries (www.nationalrail.co.uk). The ticket prices include a complimentary breakfast on board. The Jacobite Express runs daily from May until October (for more details, see www.steamtrain.info).

The Alexandra Hotel (www.strathmorehotels.com), opposite the station in Fort William, is comfortable and well maintained. The Morar Hotel (www.morarhotel.co.uk), within a couple of miles of Mallaig, has wonderful views out to the islands.

Destinations
INDIA
AFRICA
EUROPE
CANADA
CHINA
THAILAND
MALAYSIA

Rooms with a view

Hop aboard a moving hotel for a luxury 'train cruise' – and get spoiled rotten while you see the world. By **Andrew Eames**

A suite on the Rovos Royal

Now here's a question to tease the travel-savvy: where in the world can you cycle one mile, skip for one mile, run for a mile, and then get off the running machine having done a total of at least 15 miles? And to make things even more confusing, the slower you did your various bits of 'training', the further you would've gone while you were doing them.

The perplexing answer to this riddle is 'all over India', and the clue is in the word 'training', because you will have just completed your exercise in a gym – on a train. In this case, a luxury hotel train called the Deccan Odyssey, which has double rooms with en suite bathrooms, a bar, dining car, library, business centre, spa and gym, just like any hotel. The only difference is that this train-hotel moves so that you don't need to, unless of course you are a fitness fan, in which case you can move too. (In fact, if you're on a running machine in a train gym, there's every chance that you will set a cross-country personal best, before you've even broken into a sweat.)

The Deccan Odyssey (www.maharashtra tourism.gov.in, www.gwtravel.co.uk), which runs on a loop between Mumbai and Goa (plus other

less frequent routes), is one of a growing band of hotel trains around the world. Sometimes called train cruises, or just luxury trains, these mobile hotels are stylish and comfortable, and ideally suited for spectacular and challenging destinations like India, where there's so much to see and experience, but where local hotel accommodation and food can be patchy in quality once you leave the cities. With the likes of the Deccan, you get to ramble cross-country, seeing everything and sleeping in a different place every night, but you only need to unpack once, always sleep in the same bed, and you can rely on a lunch and an evening meal that won't test your digestive system.

While they all operate in stunning settings, these luxury trains have idiosyncrasies. In the matter of on-board design, some go for a regional flavour, others for a boutiquey finish, but the majority recreate some glorious bygone era, the Golden Age of train travel, when diplomats and aristocrats crossed continents in style, slept in Wagons-Lits and were served five-course meals on silver trays.

Most of the time, these trains are privately operated, which means you won't find them listed on national railway timetables, and their cabins will be made available through international tour operators and websites, not from railway ticket offices. And generally their itinerary is complemented by an enticing range of side trips, which are included in the price, to such an extent that sometimes the train becomes like a mother ship, while most of the sightseeing day trips are done by feeder buses.

Just occasionally, too, the same actual train can have more than one name, depending on the routes that it works. Such is the case with the Deccan Odyssey, which gets rechristened when it departs from its normal Mumbai–Goa circuit, and sets off cross-country as the Viceroy of India, on a 15-day epic to Calcutta, via Jaipur, Delhi,

Inside the Rovos Royal, left; a Rovos train passes Mossel Bay, on South Africa's Garden Route, right

Bharatpur Nature Reserve and Varanasi, before sighting the Bay of Bengal, 1,430 miles after setting off from the Arabian Sea.

Wheels of fortune

The Deccan is not alone in India. As with the Viceroy, it crosses the terrain worked by one of the most longstanding and successful hotel trains in the world: the Palace on Wheels (www.palaceonwheels.net), which works a seven-day route around Rajasthan from Delhi to Jodhpur, Jaipur, Jaisalmer and Udaipur, with side trips to Mughal forts and palaces.

Further south, there's a new, Indian rail-based option in the form of the Golden Chariot (www.goldenchariot.org), again a sumptuous hotel train with spa and gym, which begins its journey in Bangalore and runs around through Mysore and the historical sites of Belur, Shravanabelagola, Halebidu and world heritage site Hampi, and ends up in Goa.

Across in Europe, the most famous of these luxury train cruises is the Venice Simplon Orient Express (VSOE), whose journey from London to Venice is covered elsewhere in this book (see p26). Its Orient Express parent company (www.orient-express.com) also operates the very exclusive Royal Scotsman on a variety of circuits of the Scottish Highlands, castles, gardens and distilleries; dinner is always on board, and very often served while the train is 'stabled' in a siding overnight (www.royalscotsman.com).

The VSOE has a new competitor in Europe in the shape of the Danube Express (www.danube-express.com), which runs a variety of itineraries largely in the eastern side of Europe, some of them on the route of the original Orient Express to Istanbul. But while the VSOE's guiding principle is the re-creation of a familiar classic, the Danube Express takes a similar approach to the Indian trains, in that it introduces passengers to parts of Europe that they might otherwise not

have contemplated, presumably because they believed travel there would be to be too difficult and local services to be too primitive. Most of the train's itineraries start from Budapest, and head east into Transylvania, south to Bulgaria, or north to Poland and the Baltic States.

Not every luxury train is completely self-contained. The Transcantabrico, for example, which runs across the north of Spain from Santiago de Compostela to León, offers accommodation and breakfast on board, but takes its passengers to a different specialist local restaurant for dinner when it makes its overnight stops (www.transcantabrico.feve.es). Its route is through green Spain, across the plains of Castilla y León to the seas of Cantabria.

To boldly go

Many thousands of miles to the west, on the other side of the Atlantic, guests of Canada's Rocky Mountaineer also spend a fair amount of time away from the train itself, although in their case, they sleep in local hotels, while spending most of the day on board the train, gazing at mountains, waterfalls and wildlife, with a good chance of seeing a moose or a bear from the train window. The classic Rocky Mountaineer journey is from Vancouver to Banff in three days, although the operator offers a range of other packages (www.rockymountaineer.com).

Across the Pacific to Asia, the concept of the luxury train hotel as a method of exploring difficult terrain is also taking hold. New to China are Tangula Luxury Trains (www.tangulaluxury trains.com), operating on the ultra-high railway between Beijing and Lhasa (see p140-p145), and using specially adapted rolling stock with oxygen pumped into the compartments.

Also operating partly in China, and all the way across Russia, are two more trains from G W Travel (www.gwtravel.co.uk). The Shangri-La Express is at the core of itineraries around China and Tibet, and the new Golden Eagle Trans-Siberian offers a 15-day journey between Moscow and Vladivostok, but in more comfort than the traditional backpacker route.

For a shorter and more accessible Asian trip, there's also the colonial-style Eastern & Oriental (www.orient-express.com), on its regular run between Bangkok and Singapore, through Thailand and Malaysia, with sidetrips to Penang and the famous bridge over the River Kwai. The food on this service is especially good, reflecting several popular regional cuisines, and this is another train from the Orient Express group.

And finally there's Africa, where two particularly well-known luxury trains make regular round trips. In South Africa, the Blue Train (www.bluetrain.co.za) runs a scheduled service back and forth between Pretoria and Cape Town, a 26-hour journey across the Karoo Desert. Effectively the same route as featured in the Trans-Karoo chapter (*see p160*), this is a journey completed in high style, in elegant suites with

luxury lounges and fine dining. It also has one or two key stops en route, which give passengers more of a flavour of the passing nation.

Rovos Rail also covers the same route across the Karoo, running between Cape Town and Pretoria in (if it's possible) even more sumptuous style, sometimes employing old steam locomotives. Rovos (www.rovos.co.za) also offers occasional trips along South Africa's gorgeous Garden Route, or through Botswana and Zimbabwe to Victoria Falls, and even a 14-day epic to east Africa and Dar es Salaam, passing through parts of Africa that would make many an independent traveller feel nervous.

But that is the beauty of the hotel train; it opens up new worlds for the traveller, by giving them access to unfamiliar and spectacular places, and it does so in comfort and style.

The Blue Train crosses the Karoo in South Africa

The coming of railways revolutionised society, widening horizons and colonising nations, giving even the poorest slum-dweller the chance to see lakes, mountains and sea. But then came roads and cars, and the axe fell on many unprofitable branch lines. Yet those lost trains were often so seminal to local history, and their routes so scenic, that many communities brought them back, as private operations run by enthusiasts and volunteers. For some, these beasts of oil and steam bring back fond memories; for others, they are a source of wide-eyed fascination that the world was ever thus.

Heritage Railways

Start
WERNIGERODE
Finish
QUEDLINBURG
(GERMANY)
Via
THE HARZ
MOUNTAINS
Journey time
5 HOURS

Primal steam

Old-fashioned coal powers this train through the forests and mountains of the former East Germany. By **Anthony Lambert**

The smell of pine resin mingles with the occasional whiff of hot oil and coal. And your ears are filled with the rapid staccato bark from the chimney of one of the most demonstrative and evocative machines ever made by man, working hard just a few feet away. Cool mountain air alternates with heat from the black smokebox, framed by three large lamps that illuminate the track on winter nights. To the right is the kind of cat's cradle of pipes and metalwork that no self-respecting British locomotive engineer would ever have allowed to interrupt the lines of his designs; below you are two lamps and just above the rails is a bright red snowplough. You are in the Harz Mountains, which span the borders of Lower Saxony, Saxony-Anhalt and Thuringia, in what was East Germany not so long ago.

There are few places anywhere in the world where you can experience the charisma and power of the steam locomotive at such close quarters as you can here, standing on the balcony of the leading coach of a historic train. For the Harz Mountains are the setting for one of the great daily steam spectacles of Europe, as the huge tank locomotives of the Harzer Schmalspur-Bahnen (HSB) tackle the steep gradients. And the HSB is unique in being the only surviving steam-worked narrow-gauge network of any size, the sole representative of thousands of railways that once served sparsely populated areas throughout the world.

This 86-mile network serves the towns and villages of the mountains and carries over a million passengers a year, many up through rolling forests to the 1,142-metre summit of the Brocken, setting for a scene in Goethe's *Faust* and off-limits until German reunification because of a Soviet listening post. Thankfully, no roads reach the Brocken, so the railway does a brisk business with skiers in winter and walkers and tourists the rest of the year. Many schoolchildren, commuters and shoppers rely on rail; the southern part of the line is also used by local trams.

Saved by the bell

Most visitors begin their journey at one of the three stations with connections to the Deutsche Bahn national network: Wernigerode and Quedlinburg in the north, and Nordhausen in the south. Nordhausen was bombed heavily during World War II because of the V2 factory, but Wernigerode and Quedlinburg are astonishing survivals. Street after street of newly restored half-timbered façades give them a medieval appearance, accentuated by the cobbles underfoot and the absence of cars in the pedestrianised centres. The contrast with their appearance before the Iron Curtain came down is astounding; a visitor to one of these towns back in the 1980s would wonder when a can of paint had last been used.

Wernigerode is the heart of the HSB. The locomotive workshops and largest engine shed are located beside Westerntor Station, which is closer to the town centre than the main terminus. The well-equipped workshops maintain the 17 steam locomotives, built in 1954–56 by Lokomotivbau Karl Marx (and still used today) and eight historic locomotives, the oldest dating

Steaming
through
the Harz
Mountains

BELLS & WHISTLES

BEST BIT
Riding on the open balcony of the leading coach, right next to the locomotive.

TOP TIP
Three- and five-day tickets give passengers unlimited travel, necessary if you want to get the best out of the Harz.

PHOTO OP
The line up the Brocken has the most open spaces.

PACK THIS
Scarf, gloves and hat for balcony-riding in cooler months.

ANORAK INFO
Four of the older locomotives are Mallets, with two cylinders on each side, a design pioneered by the Swiss engineer Anatole Mallet.

SOUVENIR
You're spoiled for choice in the HSB shops.

TRAVELLERS' FARE
There are buffet cars on some trains, as well as an excellent restaurant in the station at Drei Annen Hohne.

OVERHEARD
'Double, double-toil and bubble, let's hope we get no engine trouble!'

from 1898 (used on special occasions). The lengthy trains on the main line to Nordhausen and on the branch to Brocken contain a variety of coaches including bar and buffet cars, and even open carriages during the summer. The latter are quickly colonised by railway buffs and photographers, who make a pilgrimage to the railway from all over the world.

Bell clanging for the level crossing, the Goliath of narrow-gauge steam locomotives eases the train past Wernigerode's 13th-century West Gate and alongside a road, calling for more whistling and clanging. Soon the train is out of the town and the bark of the locomotive's exhaust resounds from the woods on the twisty 1 in 30 climb up to the first junction at Drei Annen Hohne. This is the busiest station on the HSB, with its own bar and restaurant; three trains often meet here, with north- and southbound trains crossing a train heading up the Brocken.

Most passengers take the last option, curious to visit the mountain that has played such a prominent role in German literature and legend. It is best known for its association with Walpurgis Night on the eve of May Day, when witches and warlocks were said to meet to share stories of the year's evil doings. To reach the summit, the railway climbs almost continuously at a gradient of 1 in 30 and resembles a corkscrew up the hill giving passengers panoramic views in all directions. At the top, you can wander round the summit and visit the museum, which reveals the varied roles this mountain has played across the centuries. You may also witness the phenomenon that has become known all over the world as a 'Brocken spectre' – when the low sun projects a shadow on to mist or cloud, creating a ghostly form.

Meanwhile, down below, the southbound train leaves Drei Annen Hohne to meander across a forested undulating plateau of upland meadows, before reaching the track summit – just after the half-timbered station at Elend. Clearings in the forest allow long views across the occasional field of cereals, and there is a profusion of wildflowers in spring.

Benneckenstein, where the station building now has a flat for rent (*see below*), is the start of the descent to Nordhausen. A change may be necessary at the junction of Eisefelder Talmühle, situated in foxgloved woods, where the line from Quedlinburg comes in from the east. The train pauses at tiny halts among the trees to collect passengers for Nordhausen, where the HSB terminates at a platform shared with town trams.

Fewer passengers venture east from the junction of Eisefelder Talmühle, but it is a rewarding journey. The train climbs the narrow, steep-sided valley of the River Behre to reach a clearing in the forest for the lonely station of Birkenmoor, used mostly by walkers. Dropping down to the junction of Stiege, where a line proceeds to a terminus at Hasselfelde, passengers with time to spare can walk through the town to a lakeside castle begun in 1202. A willow-shaded river and grazing cattle keep the railway company on the way to the neatly laid-out village of Strassberg and its prominent church tower. Yet another line wanders off at the junction of Alexisbad, to the small town of Harzgerode, where trains terminate beside the 16th-century castle.

Leaving Alexisbad, there is a classic stretch that runs through Drahtzug to Mägdesprung, where 'tasteful articles in cast iron' were once made at an ironworks founded by Prince Frederick Albert of Anhalt; the remains can still be seen from the train. Whistling furiously for a level crossing, the locomotive roars up the steepest gradient on the line, skirting artificial lakes and orchards on the approach to Gernrode.

Some passengers get off here to see the glory of Gernrode, its outstanding Romanesque church; the rest continue on the last section of line through an open, agricultural landscape to reach Quedlinburg, famous for its cobbled streets of timber-framed houses, museums and 16th-century castle.

Slow the journey may have been, but such railways served regions where few were in a hurry and a value was placed on having the time to talk to friends and acquaintances from down the line.

TRAVEL INFORMATION

HSB (www.hsb-wr.de) has all timetable and fare information, albeit mostly in German. Go to the Deutsche Bahn (www.bahn.de) website for information about how to get there. British volunteers have created a holiday home out of the station house at Benneckenstein, which can be rented for a minimum of seven nights (www.wanderlustcentre.net).

Start
DURANGO
Finish
SILVERTON
(COLORADO)
Via
THE ROCKY
MOUNTAINS
Journey time
3.5 HOURS

The wild west

For a showdown in a one-horse town, hitch a ride on a pioneer train through the Colorado Rockies. By **Anthony Lambert**

Rich brown smoke wafts from the smokestack of the squat black locomotive that is sitting outside the roundhouse in Durango, Colorado, its stable-mates facing the turntable that will orient the day's locomotive on to its train.

At the platform, those who fancy a taste of what it was once like to travel America in a private railroad car ease themselves into the plush, well-upholstered seats, looking forward to standing on the observation platform at the rear and giving presidential waves to passers-by. Most passengers fill deluxe class or await morning pastries around a table in first class in their historic, clerestory-roofed, yellow-and-black carriages. Meanwhile, hardier souls take their seats in open-sided gondolas.

This scenario is played out most days of the year at the headquarters of the Durango & Silverton Narrow Gauge Railroad (DSNG). It is a remnant of the wonderfully characterful network of Denver & Rio Grande Railway (DRG) lines that once threaded the Rocky Mountains, linking mining and sheep-rearing agricultural communities. With narrow tracks of 914mm climbing to over 3,048 metres, brave feats of construction were required to forge a passage through difficult back country. And those acts of

The train hugs the edge of canyons and rivers, and is powered by a coal fire

bravery have left a legacy for travellers. Today, the DSNG is one of the great tourist railways of the US, offering a 90-mile round trip through the San Juan Mountains. The largely unspoilt scenery and period atmosphere has made it a natural choice for films such as *Denver & Rio Grande*, *How the West Was Won* and *Butch Cassidy and the Sundance Kid*.

A real cliffhanger

Kids and adults alike cluster round the colossal locomotive, which dates from the 1920s and was built to operate over mountainous terrain, delivering the brute power needed to heave trains of silver ore up fearsome gradients. The distinctive thump of a Westinghouse brake pump and the sizzle of hot oil combine with the smell of steam, oil and coal smoke to give visitors a taste of mankind's most demonstrative machine. For some, this heady combination becomes a lifetime's addiction.

The admirers scurry for their seats, the engineer gives two long blasts on the whistle and sets the bell ringing. As steam enters the bulbous cylinders, the ten-coach train eases out of the 'depot', as Americans like to call their railway stations. This is a good moment to scoff those pastries and drink coffee, for the flat exit from

Durango, alongside Highway 550, is a dull prelude to one of the world's great rail journeys. But things look up from the moment the train stops beside the water tank at Hermosa to prepare for the climb ahead.

The railway then enters the San Juan National Forest, where evergreens rise up steadily taller hills, before burrowing into a narrow pass to reach Rockwood. As the train hugs the rock walls of Rockwood Cut, which introduces a seemingly perilous section of line, heads turn to the landscape, and first-time passengers let out a gasp at the panorama. Far below, the Animas River, or the Rio de las Animas Perdidas, wends its way among a jumble of boulders at the foot of many landslides.

Plainly, a lower level route through the valley would have been utterly impossible. The only option was to blast a high shelf in the canyon sides. Men had to be lowered on ropes to drill a hole, which they packed with explosives. Having lit the fuse, they shouted to be hauled up and hoped they made it over the lip of the cliff before the charges went off, or they would have been blown to pieces.

The result of all that endeavour is a shelf of rock winding round the mountain, with a sheer cliff above and a sheer drop 300 metres down to the water. The train gingerly picks its way round the sharp curves, giving passengers time to take in the drama of the gorge. The curves are so tight that in the days of 20-boxcar freights, the engine at the front and the caboose at the back of the train could appear to be moving in opposite directions. Stories that the rear brakeman could lean across to get a light from the fireman are, however, apocryphal.

Silver lining

In an astonishingly short distance, the railway is suddenly level with the river – the same one that passengers were gazing down at moments before. It is not that the train has ceased climbing, as the staccato bark from the front end testifies, but that the river pitches down the valley at an even steeper angle than the railway. But now the two keep company all the way to Silverton. It was hereabouts that the 'lost souls' gave the Rio de las Animas Perdidas its name, when a group of 18th-century Spaniards in search of gold tried to ford the river, and were never seen again.

BELLS & WHISTLES

BEST BIT
Animas Canyon at the highest point above the river.

TOP TIP
Ride in the open gondolas for the best views.

PHOTO OP
Special winter photography trips are offered – when the steam condenses in the cold air, the visual effects are dramatic.

PACK THIS
Layers of clothing, hat, sunglasses and sunscreen, especially if you're travelling in a gondola.

ANORAK INFO
The locomotives weigh 143 tons – more than most standard-gauge locos.

SOUVENIR
Engineer's blue- and white-striped hat.

TRAVELLERS' FARE
If you're not travelling first class, head for the Concession Car in the middle of the train for bean & cheese burritos and egg muffins.

OVERHEARD
'Is this the *Chatanooga Choo Choo*?'

SIDINGS

Durango has a railroad museum and an historic downtown, but its most celebrated attraction is the Mesa Verde, the rocky remnants of the vanished Anasazi civilisation, designated a World Heritage Site. Little has changed since AD 600, when Ancestral Puebloans thrived in this mysterious collection of cliff dwellings. You can explore everything from simple, one-room berths to villages of more than 200 adobe buildings. The ceremonial houses, or 'kivas,' reveal thousands of well-preserved artefacts. Along with ancient petroglyphs, the *kivas* help tell the story of the Anasazi people. Full- or half-day tours are available.

Around Silverton, the Old Hundred Gold Mine Tour gives an insight into the lives of the miners who filled the trains of the DRG. With a four-wheel drive, you can take the Alpine Loop connecting Silverton, Lake City and Ouray through ghost towns and old mining claims. Animas Forks, one of the best-preserved ghost towns in the state of Colorado, is only 12 miles away. There are numerous hiking and mountain-biking trails in the Uncompahgre and Weminuche Wilderness areas, with an abundance of alpine lakes, waterfalls and fields of wildflowers.

As the railway winds and climbs the canyon, the scale of the landscape is daunting. The train twists round every bluff of the V-shaped valley, with nothing but the river and track at the foot of the sparsely wooded slopes. With glimpses of distant, snow-crowned mountains, it seems incredible that the pioneers kept this service going through the winter. Explosive black powder and steam-powered ditch-digging machines were used to break up the snow drifts.

Suddenly, the valley ends and the train bursts into open country at the confluence of several valleys, having climbed 900 metres since Durango. After a mile, and passing the 'Y' where locomotives turn, the train rolls into Silverton – one of Colorado's most extraordinary towns.

When the railway opened in 1882, banjo-toting miners, Civil War veterans, Ute Indians and a handful of tourists would have disgorged on to Silverton's crude wooden platform. Today, the town lives off the railway and the lure its chequered past. Silverton's fortunes have fluctuated from more than just the price of its minerals; in 1918, some ten per cent of the population died in six weeks during the devastating Spanish flu epidemic, and it became something of a ghost town after daily trainloads of silver ore stopped coming, replaced by sporadic boxcars of lead and zinc ores.

The layover at Silverton allows time for a walk around the town's streets of Victorian buildings, designated a National Historic District. They include a hotel with a tin-stamped ceiling – even the catalogue from which the ceiling was ordered is still here – and a bullet lodged in a saloon wall, plus an old town jail and the historic Mayflower gold mill. It's like stuff of an old Western, topped off by a museum and Mining Heritage Centre. Few heritage railways can boast such a rewarding destination.

TRAVEL INFORMATION

Durango Station (www.durangotrain.com). Trains run daily from May until October, and on selected days during winter. Journey time is three-and-a-half hours each way, and train departures are generally between 8am and 9.45am. If you don't want to do the return journey on the train, there's also an historic bus. The train's Presidential Class features a large, exclusive, open-air viewing platform.

Start
WHITBY
Finish
PICKERING
Via
GOATHLAND
Journey time
90 MINUTES

Restoration drama

Opened in 1836, and recently revived, the North Yorkshire Moors Railway is an epic British journey. By **Anthony Lambert**

Children cluster excitedly round the green locomotive as its safety valves lift and a plume of steam shoots skyward, announcing that it's ready for the off, like a racehorse in the gate. Moments later, with the wave of a green flag and a blast on a pea whistle, the guard starts the journey from the Yorkshire seaside resort of Whitby to the historic market town of Pickering. In the end, however, the green locomotive will prove to be no racehorse, taking 90 minutes to cover the 24 miles. But that's no matter, because there's so much to see along the way.

They must have been proud men, the burghers of Whitby. They weren't having any old engineer building their railway, thank you very much. If a railway was to be built, they would have the best railway-builder that brass could buy, and in 1832 (just two years after the opening of the first 'proper' railway, the Liverpool & Manchester) that was the father of railways himself, George Stephenson.

Actually, the burghers of Whitby were also desperate: the town's traditional industries of shipbuilding, whaling and alum production were in decline, so a fillip to trade was needed. These

Larpool Viaduct over the River Esk in Yorkshire

days, pints are still pulled in the Angel Inn, where locals first met to discuss the iron road to Pickering. Stephenson was asked to report on the prospects for a horse-drawn railway; he opined that the investment would be 'amply rewarded'. But his construction estimates were wrong; the money required to build the 24 miles turned out to be double Stephenson's figure.

The full railway opened with due pomp and circumstance in 1836, when not even London and Birmingham were yet linked by rail. It remained an isolated curiosity until 1845, when it was connected at the Pickering end to the burgeoning national network.

A touch of class: Pullman dining carriages are brought out for special dinner journeys, left; Northdale Scar, above

In due course, the railway became part of the North Eastern Railway (NER), and settled into a lopsided existence: lucrative holiday trains balanced by meagre takings from locals in winter.

It wasn't enough, and in 1965 the axe fell on the route, despite fierce local opposition to closure. This sentiment found expression in the formation of the North Yorkshire Moors Preservation Society, which team up with North Yorkshire County Council to buy the line: both realised the potential of railway access to the North York Moors National Park. The NYMR reopened in stages between 1973 and 1975 and has gone from strength to strength, today carrying over 300,000 passengers a year – more than any other heritage railway in Britain – with a turnover of £5 million. It couldn't survive without its hundreds of volunteers, and the guard now seeing off the train at Whitby is one of them.

A Heartbeat away

Whitby's elegant railway station, with its Romanesque five-arched portico, is situated in a lively area by the picturesque harbour – a scenic starting point. Easing out of the station along the north bank of the Esk, past innumerable colourful boats, the train is soon dwarfed by the imposing red-brick bulk of the 13-arch Larpool Viaduct, which used to carry trains along the coast, but is now part of the National Cycle Network.

The river is crossed nine times as the railway climbs through Ruswarp and Sleights to the junction at Grosmont, where the NYMR leaves the tracks it shares with 'normal' trains bound for Middlesbrough. Standing on the tranquil platform at Grosmont in verdant surroundings, you will find it hard to believe that 150 years ago, the air would have been filled with the sounds of industry from the furnaces of a nearby ironworks.

Pulling out of the station, the train enters a short tunnel. Beside it, the parallel smaller tunnel with crenellated portal was the original tunnel through which horses plodded. Today, a different

kind of animal strolls through: it is now a footpath to the railway's locomotive shed and works, and thus a favourite of trainspotter types.

The area of Beck Holes was once mined for ironstone and whinstone, and today's picturesque stone cottages were built for the miners. To the west, the course of the original railway led to the foot of an inclined plane, now a scenic walk that leads up to Goathland, a village in the Esk Valley.

The course of the new line provides stirring sights and sounds from the locomotives, rising as it does at an almost continuous 1 in 49 gradient, aggravated by sharp curves. It would be a dull soul who wasn't impressed by the stentorian barking that rings through the woods – and echoes off the retaining walls – as the locomotive makes a Herculean effort to heave the train into the platform at Goathland. There is invariably a cluster of people at the north end of the station, watching the drama of the train as it completes its last half-mile of climbing.

BELLS & WHISTLES

BEST BIT
Beautiful restoration of train interiors and period atmosphere at stations along the route.

TOP TIP
Arrive at Grosmont by train from Middlesbrough – itself a stunning journey.

PHOTO OP
A picnic on a sunny day on the bank above Darnholm.

PACK THIS
Goggles if you want to lean out of the window.

ANORAK INFO
Gala weekends for enthusiasts, held throughout the year with visiting locomotives.

USEFUL PHRASE
'Do you have Black Sheep on tap?'

SOUVENIR
Hand-crafted firing shovel from the shop at Grosmont or online.

TRAVELLERS' FARE
The NYMR runs frequent lunch and dining trains, and there are cream teas at Pickering Station.

DESIGN DETAIL
The goods shed at Goathland is the most imaginative café on a heritage railway in the UK.

OVERHEARD
'They don't make them like this any more.'

Speaking of drama, this is *Heartbeat* country, and many come to see the setting for the television series in which the railway has played a major role. Goathland station is a perfectly restored Victorian period piece that also featured in *Harry Potter and the Philosopher's Stone*. The 1865 building is the youngest on the line, and has the crow-stepped gables commonly seen on NER stations. Behind it is a coal staithe (or depot), once a common feature, and at the south end is the goods shed, now a café. It has been brilliantly adapted: the seating areas are inside open wagons, with cut-down barrels as seats.

Goathland marks a transition from deciduous woods and fields to the open bracken- and heather-covered moorland of Newton Dale. This deep channel was gouged out by glacial meltwater in the last ice age and provides the perfect trench for the railway as it climbs to the summit of the line, two miles after leaving Goathland. The coniferous plantations date back to a government campaign in the 1920s to reduce reliance on imported timber.

Just after the summit, passengers are unwittingly supported by sheaves of heather bound in sheepskin, felled trees and fence posts. They form a kind of raft on the bog, to spread and absorb the weight of the train. This was the only way the track could be floated across Fen Bog, 12 metres deep. The area is now a nature reserve, known for dragonflies and birdlife.

Curving beneath the flank of Northdale Scar, the line skirts Cropton Forest to reach Newton Dale Halt, opened in 1981 to provide access to woodland walks. High above the line are the ruins of Skelton Tower, built as a shooting lodge in 1850 by the Rev. Robert Skelton, who used it to write sermons or enjoy a quiet drink, depending on whom you believe. Past remote Levisham Station, the line is straight for two miles, before wending through more woods and past a trout farm to arrive at Pickering's attractive station.

TRAVEL INFORMATION

Trains run daily from Whitby to Pickering from late March to the end of October (www.nymr.co.uk). In winter, there are often weekend trips, and special services at Christmas and February half-term (note: between Grosmont and Pickering only). Ask about special dining trips in a Pullman carriage. Grosmont and Whitby are both on the national railway network (www.northernrail.org).

Trip planner

PLAN AHEAD

● Most national rail networks publish online timetables; some allow online reservations and ticket sales, so if your rail journey is key to your holiday, book it before you leave.

● If you can't make a booking before you leave, reservations can usually be made upon arrival at your destination, provided you arrange them a couple of days in advance and don't intend to travel on a public holiday. In some locations (ie the UK and the USA), you may also save money by booking early.

● If you are travelling with a tour operator, such logistics should be taken care of and be included in the price. If you are planning this yourself, you should consider whether you intend to break the journey at any of the stations en route.

ON THE TRAIN

● Different classes of travel may offer vastly different amenities, including better toilet facilities, which can be primitive in some trains – always carry tissues. In many cases, travelling first class is worth the extra outlay; it may also mean that you will be travelling with people who have a better grasp of English, too.

● The availability of food and drink varies widely from train to train, so be prepared. In many trains, food may not offered from conventional sources, ie the restaurant car, but will be sold from platforms and from vendors walking through the train. Bring a blanket for long journeys, as some trains can get cold at night.

● If you are going to spend a lot of time leaning out of windows, for photographic purposes, it can be a good idea to wear some kind of protection for your eyes, particularly on steam- and diesel-hauled trains.

● Many of the new generation of European trains now have power sockets by the seats and on-board WiFi internet for those who are prepared to pay for it.

WATCH OUT FOR

● For extra security on long-distance journeys, carry a lock to secure your luggage to your berth.

● Beware of trains that split apart. A double destination on the departure board may mean that only half of the train is going where you're going, so make sure you're in the right section.

● In some European countries, such as Germany and France, you will be required to validate your ticket at machines on the stations, which will stamp it with the date and time. You may be fined if you travel with a ticket that hasn't been validated.

● Many stations in Europe have a train composition board on the platform. These illustrate where your allocated carriage will come to rest alongside the platform – this is useful if you are boarding at a mid-way point in a train's journey, and have lots of luggage.

TRAVEL ADVICE

Safety and visas

For British travellers, the Foreign and Commonwealth Office website (www.fco.gov. uk) has information on political situations, health dangers and crime issues worldwide.

For American travellers, the State Department website (www.travel.state.gov) does much the same job.

Both of the above websites also stipulate which destinations require visas, and whether these need to be obtained in advance, or at the border station, and their respective costs.

Passports

Some countries require a specific number of months' validity on your passport when you travel, and some also require a minimum number of blank pages.

Note that on some train border crossings, ie Turkey to Syria, border police will require foreign visitors to hand over their passports to be examined at leisure. This may be alarming, but it is standard practice.

Travel insurance
Buy adequate travel insurance; annual schemes often work out to be the best value. Many tour operators insist on insurance, if just to try to get you to purchase theirs. Don't invest in both your own and a tour operators' insurance – it just complicates matters!

Immunisations
Check with your GP that your immunisations are up to date. A few destinations recommend their visitors have specific vaccinations (yellow fever for Peru, for example), and in general it is a good idea to have a look at the websites of the World Health Organisation (www.who.int) and the Centre for Disease Control (www. cdc.gov/travel).

Money
Make sure you have the right currency for your destination before you set off, particularly if you are crossing a border and arriving somewhere at night, when banks are closed. Check that your credit card is

valid in your country of travel. If your trip has been organised through a tour operator, check which costs are covered in your original fee – and ask how much cash you need to carry.

TOUR OPERATORS

For a truly simple train holiday, let a tour operator do all the planning for you.

Specialist railway tour operators

Classic Train Journeys does nostalgic and scenic trips in North American. (www. classictrainjourneys.com).

Explore The small group specialist has just launched a dedicated rail journeys programme, with a selection of adventurous worldwide itineraries (www.explore.co.uk).

Ffestiniog Travel Escorted rail tours with an emphasis on scenic routes and nostalgia (www.festtravel.co.uk).

Fjord Tours Specialist in the scenic round route from Oslo to Bergen, via Flåm, and out onto Sognefjord (www.norway nutshell.com).

Great Railway Journeys European, worldwide and short breaks on trains, using both 'normal' (ie scheduled) and luxury trains. Trips are usually escorted by a group leader (www.greatrail.com).

GW Travel Train owner and tour operator, offering sightseeing train cruises in

countries such as Russia, China, India and South Africa (www.gwtravel.co.uk).

Orient Express Train owner and tour operator, with luxury trains in South America, Europe and South-east Asia (www. orient-express.com).

Rail Select A subsidiary of Great Railway Journeys, this company arranges tailor-made, unescorted, train-based holidays (www.railselect.com).

Rocky Mountaineer Vacations Tours of Canadian Rockies based on sightseeing by rail, but with accommodation in hotels, not trains (www.rocky mountaineer.com).

The Russia Experience Tour operator with packages based around the Trans-Siberian and Trans-Mongolian trains (www.trans-siberian.co.uk).

The Society of International Railway Travelers is a US-based tour operator which sells the 'world's top 25 trains' (www.irtsociety.com).

Treyn Escorted rail-based holidays in UK and Europe, with more of an accent on the destination than the journey (www.treynholidays.co.uk).

Luxury train operators

Blue Train Classic run between Cape Town and Pretoria (www.bluetrain.co.za).

Danube Express Assorted routes through eastern Europe (www.danube-express.com).

Desert Express, Namibia Luxury train from Windhoek to Swakopmund (www.desert express.com.na).

GW Travel Tour operator behind many of the world's luxury trains, with a speciality in Russia, China, India and South Africa (www.gwtravel.co.uk).

Rovos Rail Super luxury trips throughout southern Africa (www.rovos.co.za).

Luxury Train Club specialises in selling holidays with the world's top private trains (www.luxurytrainclub.com).

Orient Express Luxury trains in South America, Europe and South-east Asia (www.orient-express.com).

Transcantabrico Tour train through green Spain, from Santiago de Compostela to León (www.transcantabrico. feve.es).

Travel companies

In addition to the train specialists above, several mainstream tour operators also sell rail-based packages, usually on luxury private trains. They include **Bales Worldwide** (www.balesworldwide.com), **Cox and Kings** (www.cox andkings.co.uk), **1st Class Holidays** (www.1stclass holidays.com), **Noble Caledonia** (www.noble-caledonia.co.uk), **Voyages Jules Verne** (www.vjv.co.uk) and **Trans Indus** (www.trans indus.co.uk). In the US, Seattle-based **Mir Corporation** (www.

mircorp.com) specialises in journeys in Russia and Asia, many of them railway-based. In Canada, **Ride the Trains** (www.ridethetrains.com), part of Ellison Travel, has a wide selection of global journeys.

INFORMATION AND TICKETING WEBSITES

Eurail promotes and sells train travel within Europe, particularly to the American market. There is a useful selections of routes, organised by most scenic or by speed, and with on-board sleeper accommodation (www.eurail.com).

European rail is a ticketing agency that can organise most European destinations (www. europeanrail.com).

German Railways' website is a comprehensive information source about travel in Germany and beyond, particularly in eastern Europe (www.bahn.de).

The Man in Seat 61 is an enthusiast by the name of Mark Smith, whose thorough website (and now book of the same title) has sound advice and detailed information about rail travel in almost every quarter of the world (www.seat61.com).

National Rail has UK timetables, travel information and fares (www.national rail.co.uk)

Rail Europe sells the European high-speed network (www.rail europe.co.uk).

Railteam links all the European high-speed networks, with information on services, but doesn't sell tickets or make bookings (www.rail team.co.uk).

S D Enterprises is a UK-based specialist in Indian railway journeys, both on private luxury trains and the national network (www. indiarail.co.uk).

SNCF has comprehensive domestic timetables for France and journeys from there to other countries (www.voyages-sncf.com).

Spanish Rail is a UK-based agency that represents Spain's national network Renfe. It specialises in international journeys to and from Spain, as well as domestic travel (www.spanish-rail.co.uk).

Switzerland Travel Centre provides information and makes reservations all over the Swiss transport network, including buses, boats and trains (www.stc.co.uk).

Trenitalia has detail for journeys outside Italy as well as comprehensive domestic timetables (www.trenitalia.com).

Note: most of the European rail agencies will also sell multi-country InterRail passes, in varying durations, from five days to one month. Passes are available in both Youth (12-25) and Adult (26+) categories.

Best for...

Families

Hamburg's model railway, p58
The Eurostar, p62
iDTGV, Paris to Nice, p72
The Bernina Express, p90
Kalka to Shimla, p155
La Spezia to Genoa, p199
Barcelona to Puigcerda, p210
North York Moors Railway, p243

Luxury

The Orient Express, p26
The Canadian, p42
The Indian-Pacific, p48
The Ghan, p53
The Cassiopeia, p82
The Hiram Bingham, p187
Luxury train cruises, p227

Adventure

The Trans-Mongolian, p17
Sarajevo to Ploce, p108
Istanbul to Damascus, p118
Shanghai to Lhasa, p140
Hanoi to Ho Chi Minh, p134
Colombo to Badulla, p170

Meeting the locals

The Trans-Mongolian, p17
Sarajevo to Ploce, p108
Bucharest to Budapest, p112
Istanbul to Damascus, p118
Bangkok to Chiang Mai, p127
Hanoi to Ho Chi Minh, p134
New Delhi to Kalka, p149
The Trans-Karoo, p160
Cairo to Aswan, p166
Colombo to Badulla, p170
Barcelona to Puigcerda, p210

Bridges and tunnels

The Bernina Express,p90
Kalka to Shimla, p155
Lima to Huancayo, p175
Los Mochis to Chihuahua, p192
La Spezia to Genoa, p199

Sleeping on board

The Orient Express, p26
The Sunset Limited, p34
The Canadian, p42
The Indian Pacific, p48
The Cassiopeia, p82
Stockholm to Narvik, p214
Caledonian Sleeper, p220
Luxury train cruises, p227

Mountain scenery

The Canadian, p42
The Bernina Express, p90
Shanghai to Lhasa, p140
The Trans-Karoo, p160
Colombo to Badulla, p170
Settle to Carlisle, p182
Los Mochis to Chihuahua, p192
Nîmes to Clermont-Ferrand,
    p206
London to Fort William, p220
Durango to Silverton, p239

Sea views

iDTGV, Paris to Nice, p72
Hanoi to Ho Chi Minh, p134
La Spezia to Genoa p199

Lakes and rivers

The Trans-Mongolian, p17
The Sunset Limited, p34
The Canadian, p42

The Bernina Express, p90
Cairo to Aswan, p166
Los Mochis to Chihuahua, p192
Stockholm to Narvik, p214
Durango to Silverton, p239

Watching wildlife

The Canadian, p42
The Trans-Karoo, p166
Stockholm to Narvik, p214
Caledonian Sleeper, p220

Speed demons

Barcelona to Málaga, p68
iDTGV, Paris to Nice, p72
Munich to Frankfurt, p77
Bullet train, p87

Travellers' fare

Chinese dining car on the
    Trans-Mongolian, p17
The Orient Express, p26
Munich to Frankfurt, p77
The Cassiopeia, p82
Bangkok to Chiang Mai, p127
New Delhi to Kalka, p149
The Trans-Karoo, p160

History enthusiasts

The Orient Express, p26
Berlin to Budapest, p96
Görlitz to Zittau, p104
Sarajevo to Ploce, p108
Bucharest to Budapest, p112
Istanbul to Damascus, p118
Kalka to Shimla, p155
Harz Mountain Railway, p234
Durango to Silverton, p239
North York Moors Railway, p243

Index of places

World Map

See p256

TORONTO to VANCOUVER
on the Canadian, p42

DURANGO to SILVERTON, p239

NEW ORLEANS to LOS ANGELES
on the Sunset Limited, p34

LOS MOCHIS to CHIHUAHUA
on the Chepe, p192

LIMA to HUANCAYO, p175

CUSCO to MACHU PICCHU
on the Hiram Bingham, p187

- ● CROSSING CONTINENTS pp14-59
- ● STATE OF THE ART pp60-87
- ● BORDER BUSTERS pp88-123
- ● CULTURAL EXPERIENCES pp124-179
- ● SCENIC SPECTACULARS pp180-231
- ● HERITAGE RAILWAYS pp232-247

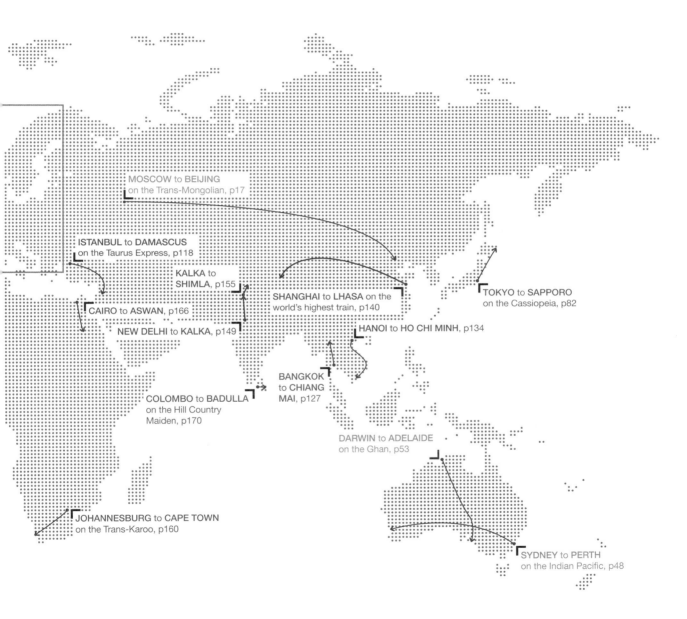

MOSCOW to BEIJING
on the Trans-Mongolian, p17

ISTANBUL to DAMASCUS
on the Taurus Express, p118

KALKA to
SHIMLA, p155

SHANGHAI to LHASA on the
world's highest train, p140

CAIRO to ASWAN, p166

TOKYO to SAPPORO
on the Cassiopeia, p82

HANOI to HO CHI MINH, p134

NEW DELHI to KALKA, p149

BANGKOK
to CHIANG
MAI, p127

COLOMBO to BADULLA
on the Hill Country
Maiden, p170

DARWIN to ADELAIDE
on the Ghan, p53

JOHANNESBURG to CAPE TOWN
on the Trans-Karoo, p160

SYDNEY to PERTH
on the Indian Pacific, p48

Europe Map

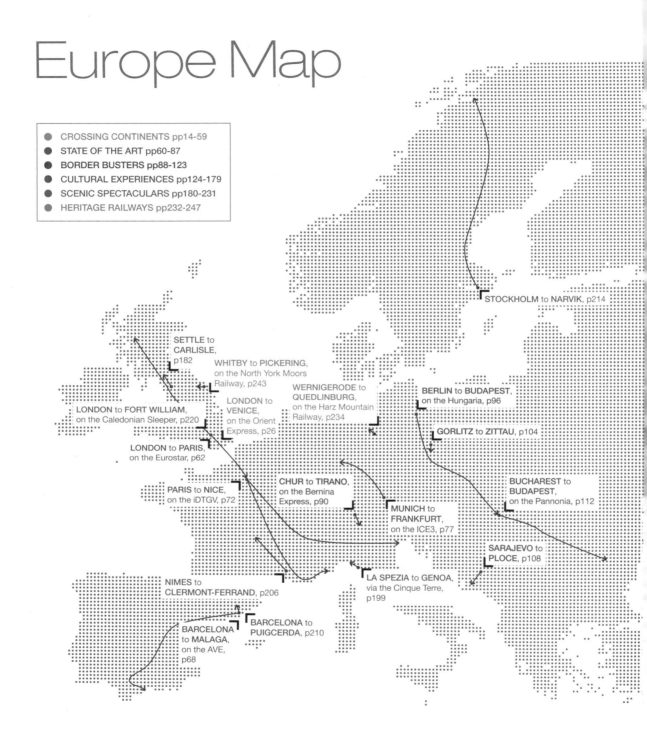

- CROSSING CONTINENTS pp14-59
- STATE OF THE ART pp60-87
- BORDER BUSTERS pp88-123
- CULTURAL EXPERIENCES pp124-179
- SCENIC SPECTACULARS pp180-231
- HERITAGE RAILWAYS pp232-247

STOCKHOLM to NARVIK, p214

SETTLE to CARLISLE, p182

WHITBY to PICKERING, on the North York Moors Railway, p243

WERNIGERODE to QUEDLINBURG, on the Harz Mountain Railway, p234

BERLIN to BUDAPEST, on the Hungaria, p96

GORLITZ to ZITTAU, p104

LONDON to FORT WILLIAM, on the Caledonian Sleeper, p220

LONDON to VENICE, on the Orient Express, p26

LONDON to PARIS, on the Eurostar, p62

CHUR to TIRANO, on the Bernina Express, p90

PARIS to NICE, on the iDTGV, p72

MUNICH to FRANKFURT, on the ICE3, p77

BUCHAREST to BUDAPEST, on the Pannonia, p112

SARAJEVO to PLOCE, p108

NIMES to CLERMONT-FERRAND, p206

LA SPEZIA to GENOA, via the Cinque Terre, p199

BARCELONA to PUIGCERDA, p210

BARCELONA to MALAGA, on the AVE, p68